Aristotelianism and Magic in Early Modern Europe

Bloomsbury Studies in the Aristotelian Tradition

General Editor:

Marco Sgarbi, Università Ca' Foscari, Italy

Editorial Board:

Klaus Corcilius *(University of California, Berkeley, USA)*; Daniel Garber *(Princeton University, USA)*; Oliver Leaman *(University of Kentucky, USA)*; Anna Marmodoro *(University of Oxford, UK)*; Craig Martin *(Oakland University, USA)*; Carlo Natali *(Università Ca' Foscari, Italy)*; Riccardo Pozzo *(Consiglio Nazionale delle Ricerche, Rome, Italy)*; Renée Raphael *(University of California, Irvine, USA)*; Victor M. Salas *(Sacred Heart Major Seminary, USA)*; Leen Spruit *(Radboud University Nijmegen, The Netherlands)*.

Aristotle's influence throughout the history of philosophical thought has been immense and in recent years the study of Aristotelian philosophy has enjoyed a revival. However, Aristotelianism remains an incredibly polysemous concept, encapsulating many, often conflicting, definitions. *Bloomsbury Studies in the Aristotelian Tradition* responds to this need to define Aristotelianism and give rise to a clear characterization.

Investigating the influence and reception of Aristotle's thought from classical antiquity to contemporary philosophy from a wide range of perspectives, this series aims to reconstruct how philosophers have become acquainted with the tradition. The books in this series go beyond simply ascertaining that there are Aristotelian doctrines within the works of various thinkers in the history of philosophy, but seek to understand how they have received and elaborated Aristotle's thought, developing concepts into ideas that have become independent of him.

Bloomsbury Studies in the Aristotelian Tradition promotes new approaches to Aristotelian philosophy and its history. Giving special attention to the use of interdisciplinary methods and insights, books in this series will appeal to scholars working in the fields of philosophy, history and cultural studies.

Available titles:
A Political Philosophy of Conservatism, by Ferenc Hörcher
Elijah Del Medigo and Paduan Aristotelianism, by Michael Engel
Early Modern Aristotelianism and the Making of Philosophical Disciplines, by Danilo Facca
Phantasia in Aristotle's Ethics, by Jacob Leth Fink
Pontano's Virtues, by Matthias Roick
The Aftermath of Syllogism, edited by Marco Sgarbi, Matteo Cosci
The Reception of Aristotle's Poetics in the Italian Renaissance and Beyond, by Bryan Brazeau
The Scientific Counter-Revolution, by Michael John Gorman
Virtue Ethics and Contemporary Aristotelianism, edited by Andrius Bielskis, Eleni Leontsini, Kelvin Knight
Aristotle's Syllogism and the Creation of Modern Logic, edited by Lukas M. Verburgt and Matteo Cosci
The Legacy of Aristotelian Enthymeme, edited by Fosca Mariani Zini

Aristotelianism and Magic in Early Modern Europe

Philosophers, Experimenters and Wonderworkers

Edited by
Donato Verardi

BLOOMSBURY ACADEMIC
LONDON • NEW YORK • OXFORD • NEW DELHI • SYDNEY

BLOOMSBURY ACADEMIC
Bloomsbury Publishing Plc
50 Bedford Square, London, WC1B 3DP, UK
1385 Broadway, New York, NY 10018, USA
29 Earlsfort Terrace, Dublin 2, Ireland

BLOOMSBURY, BLOOMSBURY ACADEMIC and the Diana logo are trademarks of Bloomsbury Publishing Plc

First published in Great Britain 2023
This paperback edition published 2025

Copyright © Donato Verardi and Contributors, 2023

Donato Verardi has asserted his right under the Copyright, Designs and Patents Act, 1988, to be identified as Editor of this work.

Cover image: Aristotle (1637), Jusepe de Ribera (© Archivart / Alamy Stock Photo)

All rights reserved. No part of this publication may be reproduced or transmitted in any form or by any means, electronic or mechanical, including photocopying, recording, or any information storage or retrieval system, without prior permission in writing from the publishers.

Bloomsbury Publishing Plc does not have any control over, or responsibility for, any third-party websites referred to or in this book. All internet addresses given in this book were correct at the time of going to press. The author and publisher regret any inconvenience caused if addresses have changed or sites have ceased to exist, but can accept no responsibility for any such changes.

A catalogue record for this book is available from the British Library.

A catalog record for this book is available from the Library of Congress.

ISBN: HB: 978-1-3503-5716-7
PB: 978-1-3503-5720-4
ePDF: 978-1-3503-5717-4
eBook: 978-1-3503-5718-1

Series: Bloomsbury Studies in the Aristotelian Tradition

Typeset by Deanta Global Publishing Services, Chennai, India

To find out more about our authors and books visit www.bloomsbury.com and sign up for our newsletters.

Contents

List of figures — viii
Notes on contributors — ix

Introduction *Donato Verardi* — 1

1 Aristotelian philosophy and illusionism in late medieval Europe
   Thibaut Rioult — 15
2 The roles of *experimentum* and the *vis imaginativa* in medieval and
   early modern magic *Peter G. Maxwell-Stuart* — 39
3 The image of Aristotle as a magus and the Aristotelian foundation
   of magic in early modern Italy *Donato Verardi* — 61
4 Making and unmaking marvels in early modern
   Europe *William Eamon* — 83
5 Aristotelianism, chymistry and mechanics in early seventeenth-
   century Europe: The techno-magical approach *Arianna Borrelli* — 105
6 Aristotelianism, magic and experiments in early modern English
   meteorology *Jennifer Mori* — 145
7 Natural magic, experimentalism and tarantism in a Dutch
   Aristotelian professor *Manuel De Carli* — 171
8 The domestication of spirit power in a German handbook on
   natural magic *Michael Pickering* — 193

Index — 217

Figures

1.1 P. Bruegel the Elder (designer), P. van der Heyden (engraver) and Hieronymus Cock (publisher), *The Fall of the Magician Hermogenes* — 22
1.2 The Children of the Moon, from *Mittelalterliches Hausbuch von Schloss Wolfegg* — 23
4.1 Dowsing for minerals, from Agricola, *De re metallica* — 85
4.2 The astronomical clock on the Strasbourg Cathedral — 93
4.3 Lowering the Vatican obelisk. Woodcut from Domenico Fontana, *Della trasportatione dell'Obelisco Vaticano* — 94
4.4 A crane for lifting heavy objects — 97
5.1 The *perpetuum mobile* presented by Cornelis Drebbel to King James I in 1607, drawing from the illustrated recollections of Hiesserle von Chodaw — 116
6.1 Folio advertisement for weather glasses — 146
6.2 Robert Fludd's household weather glass — 152
6.3 London Guildhall Library MS 06619 — 159

Contributors

Arianna Borrelli (PhD) is Fellow at the Käte Hamburger Kolleg 'Cultures of Research' (RWTH Aachen University) and teaches at the Technical University Berlin (Germany), where she habilitated in 2018. The overarching focus of her research is the relationship between scientific knowledge and the strategies employed to represent, communicate, store and transform it. Her fields of interest include medieval mathematical cosmology, early modern meteorology and mechanics, and quantum theories from their early days up to the present. Recent publications: 'The great yogurt project: Models and symmetry principles in early particle physics', in M. Friedman and K. Krauthausen (ed.), *Model and Mathematics* (2022), 221–54; 'Giovan Battista Della Porta's construction of pneumatic phenomena and his use of recipes as heuristic tools', *Centaurus* 62 (2020): 406–24.

Manuel De Carli (PhD) is a research associate at the CESR of the University of Tours (France). In 2019, he obtained his PhD at the Universities of Tours (France) and Roma Tre (Italy), defending a thesis on the Dutch Aristotelian philosopher Wolferd Senguerd (1646–1724). He has written several research papers and book chapters on tarantism and occult qualities in the fields of history of sciences and medicine. Recent publications on these subjects are 'L'occulte et le tarentisme en Hollande aux XVIIe et XVIIIe siècles: l'œuvre de Wolferd Senguerd (1646–1724)', *Revue d'Histoire des Sciences* 74, (2021/2): 381 405; 'Tracing Senguerd's Footprints: Sciences and Tarantism at Leiden University (1667–1715)', in Fabrizio Baldassarri and Fabio Zambieri (ed.), *Scientiae in the History of Medicine*, (Rome-Bristol: 'L'Erma' di Brethscneider, 2021), 289–311.

William Eamon (PhD) is Regents Professor of History Emeritus at New Mexico State University (USA). His research focuses on the history of science and medicine in early modern Europe. He has also published on the history of medieval technology and on magic, astrology and the occult sciences in early modern Europe. He is the author of *Science and the Secrets of Nature: Books of Secrets in Medieval and Early Modern Culture* (Princeton University Press 1994) and *The Professor of Secrets: Mystery, Magic, and Alchemy in Renaissance*

Italy (National Geographic 2010). He is currently writing a book, *Science and Everyday Life in Early Modern Europe*.

Peter G. Maxwell-Stuart (PhD) is Reader in History in St Andrews (UK). His field of interest and research encompasses the occult sciences – magic, astrology, alchemy and witchcraft – principally of the medieval and early modern periods, but he does venture further back and further forward as well. His last research publications are *The British Witch* (Amberley 2014) and an edition and translation of Martin Del Rio's *Disquisitionum Magicarum Libri Sex* which is appearing in six volumes (Brill 2022–3).

Jennifer Mori (PhD) is Professor of History at the University of Toronto (Canada). Her current research interests lie in early modern English book history, the history of science and popular culture. Recent publications on these subjects are 'Popular Science in Eighteenth-Century Almanacs: The Editorial Career of Henry Andrews of Royston, 1780–1820', *History of Science*, 54 (2016) and 'Prognostic Birds and Vulgar Errors. Popular Naturalism in Early Modern England, 1550–1800', in Richard Raiswell and James A. T. Lancaster (ed.), *Evidence in the Age of the New Sciences*, International Archives of the History of Ideas (Cham: Springer International Publishing, 2018). She is working on a monograph for Brepols entitled *Everyday Nature in English Popular Print, 1660–1800*.

Michael Pickering (PhD) heads-up Academic Programs at Trinity College, University of Melbourne (Australia). His research focus is the intersection between radical Pietism and magic, and his recent work focusses on the little-known physician Johann Nikolaus Martius. Michael's latest book, *Fear in the German-Speaking World, 1600–2000* (Bloomsbury 2020), co-edited with Thomas Kehoe, engages with the field of the history of emotions.

Thibaut Rioult (PhD) is a postdoctoral researcher and a member of the SciFair team at the University of Antwerp (Belgium) where he leads the project 'Objets chargés: mettre en scène l'âme des choses' (*Charged objects: performing the soul of things*). He is also a member of the THETA team (Théories et Histoire de l'Esthétique, du Technique et des Arts) at the Centre Jean Pépin (Paris, CNRS/ENS, UMR 8230). His doctoral thesis investigated the 'Illusion of Supernatural and Illusionists during the Renaissance Period' (Paris, ENS, 2018). He has written several research papers and book chapters on magic and illusionism in various fields (philosophy, history, performance studies, media studies and aesthetics).

Donato Verardi (PhD) is Fellow at the Warburg Institute, University of London (UK). He is the author of several books and articles on Renaissance thought and culture. His recent work has considered presentations of Aristotle as a magus in early modern contexts as well as the role of magic, technology, and material culture at the dawn of the modern world. He has lately co-edited, with Rebekah Compton, the volume *Magical Materials in Renaissance Philosophy, Literature, and Art* (Agorà & Co. 2022).

Introduction

Donato Verardi

This book provides a unique perspective on the early modern reception of Aristotle's authority on an unlikely subject: magic.[1] Indeed, while the connection between Platonism and magic is assumed in scholarship on the early modern period, the Aristotelian side tends to be overlooked, when it actually represented one of the pivotal points of these discussions.[2] Aristotle's natural philosophy and logic both found a place within debates on magic in early modern Europe,[3] and magic, along with Aristotelianism, offered a significant contribution to the rise of early modern experimentalism.[4]

When it comes to Aristotelians and Aristotelianism, it is necessary to clarify the meaning of the expression 'thinking in an Aristotelian fashion', which can differ in certain places and at certain times, depending on which texts are attributed to Aristotle and which, among them, are the specific objects of the discussion.[5] The same clarification is desirable when using the term 'magic', an equivocal, complex and liminal term, often attached, in the early modern period, to other tricky terms, such as 'natural', 'mathematical' and 'theurgic'. In its deleterious meaning, magic was also connected to the notion of *goëtia*, that is, the false theurgy practised with the help of evil demons.[6] The fact itself that several apocryphal books on topics related to the vast and elusive plan of magic were attributed to Aristotle well explains the need to delineate more precisely the role of the Philosopher's authority in these discussions.

Scholars such as Charles B. Schmitt, Jill Kraye and Charles Burnett, among others, have made an enormous contribution to the understanding of the many complex paths that led, from the Middle Ages to the Renaissance, to the formation of the image of Aristotle as a magus.[7] Indeed, the concept of Aristotle that was current in the fifteenth and sixteenth centuries is somewhat different from ours; this is precisely because, although there was no lack of doubts about the Aristotelian authorship of certain spurious works, many of them were accepted as authentic during the Renaissance. For many protagonists of the cultural debate of the time, Aristotle had not only written the works that we now know to be authentic (such as the *Physics*, the *Metaphysics*, the *Organon* or the *De anima*) but also spurious works devoted to natural magic, to astrology and to physiognomy and alchemy.

It is well known that Aristotelianism has numerous variations, so much so that Schmitt has emphasized the existence of a multiplicity of them.[8] Throughout its history, the Aristotelian scholarship displayed a wide adaptability and transformative capacity, and, in early modern Europe, it also included thinkers particularly interested in magic. In this historical context, the attribution of magical works (in a broad sense) to the Philosopher went hand in hand with a precise argumentative strategy, aimed at accommodating Aristotelian philosophy to the needs of a scientific and cultural context that was experiencing profound changes. A problem that is anything but exclusively philological, the idea of an Aristotle as an author of magic texts and as an expert in the occult sciences, therefore, involved consideration of his authority in these disciplines which were so popular at that time and of their eventual contribution to the production of new knowledge.[9]

Despite the presence of authoritative literature on the impact of this peculiar image of Aristotle and his contributions to the historical and conceptual developments of some occult disciplines such as physiognomics, chiromancy and alchemy, the history and influence of what, in early modern Europe, was configured as a real magical current of the Aristotelian tradition remain in large part to be reconstructed.[10] The chapters contained in this volume accept this fascinating hermeneutic challenge from an interdisciplinary and transnational perspective, with topics that draw upon both learned and popular forms of philosophy, opening up innovative research paths on various aspects that are currently seldom explored by both historians of Aristotelianism and of magic.

At the centre of the volume are several significant questions: How important was the idea of an Aristotle as a magus in the philosophical and social justification of magic on the part of his followers in the early modern period? What role did Aristotle's authority as magus play in the transformation of magic into an experimental science and in strategically defending its integrity? Regarding Aristotelian philosophers, experimenters and wonderworkers interested in the occult, how did the image of Aristotle as a magus interact with Aristotle's other sides – that is, that of the logician, the metaphysician or, starting from the Renaissance, the expert in mathematical and mechanical disciplines? Did this interaction also impact the development of the so-called 'popular science', or the first attempts to found the series of experimental practices that would later take the name of technology?

In the seventeenth century, the need for an Aristotelian to attribute occult texts to Aristotle was no longer necessary in order to deal with issues relating to magic. Between the end of the sixteenth century and the first decades of the seventeenth century, in the field of physics, the study of magical objects and their occult qualities was largely favoured by the (mainly Jesuit) tradition of commentaries. In the seventeenth century, the close link between Aristotelianism and the Aristotelian corpus (which the genre of the commentary guaranteed) gradually but inexorably loosened, making the question of occult qualities a theme in its own right.[11]

This being the case, how does the reflection on the occult develop among the modern followers of Aristotle? And what happened among those who, on the threshold of the eighteenth century, continued to write programmatically about natural magic?

From its very beginning, Aristotelianism was confronted with the philosophical problem of illusion. In the opening chapter of this volume, Thibaut Rioult addresses the relationship between thoughts about Aristotle by his followers and 'illusionism' (the art of illusion as practised by the medieval 'wonderworkers' or 'jugglers') throughout the thirteenth and fifteenth centuries. During the thirteenth century, the encounter between magic and Aristotelianism induced 'a new way of thinking about magic and illusionism, transforming a performance art into an intellectual tool for critical thinking'. Rioult's historical reflection is centred around the proposal of William of Auvergne (†1249), who was the first to insert 'the archetypal figure of medieval jugglers' into scholarly discussions. At that time, the ecclesiastical need to fight the Cathar heresy and to limit the powers of magic and demons led William to theorize the concept of 'natural magic' and to consider that illusionism was part of the same milieu. Aristotelian natural philosophy was the breeding ground for this reflection. As Rioult shows, illusionism engaged in a dialogue with Aristotelian rationalization, causal analysis, motion theory, dialectic and perceptual systems. About two centuries later, the *Malleus Maleficarum* (1486) inherited William's categorization and, thanks to its subversion of Aristotelico-Thomist categories, built an ontology of illusion that expanded the powers of the devil and bypassed scholastic 'limiting demonology'.[12]

In texts like the *Secretum philosophorum* (probably written at end of the thirteenth century by an English follower of Roger Bacon), juggling tricks were not viewed as mere entertainment but, Rioult writes, as 'the means of experimental research on perceptions'.[13] The paper by Peter G. Maxwell-Stuart deals in depth with the theme of the experiment in the *Secretum philosophorum* and in other texts related to the genre of 'experiments books' or 'books of secrets'. Between the Middle Ages and the early modern period – Maxwell-Stuart writes – the books of secrets or *experimenta* 'formed an important resource for those who wanted to explore the hidden sides of Nature, and no one, perhaps, was more significant than Aristotle, who had a good many books foisted upon him during the Middle Ages, of which the *Secretum Secretorum* was one'.[14] Doubts were raised very early about the Aristotelian attribution of the *Secretum*, already a 'bestseller' in the Middle Ages.[15] Although it was never included in the university *curriculum*, numerous professors referred to it in their commentaries on other Aristotelian works up to the late Renaissance.[16] The *Secretum secretorum* introduced a peculiar feature within the 'Aristotelian' *corpus*: the knowledge that Aristotle presented there had an essentially 'operational' nature, linked to the dimension of experience and *experimentum*. It is precisely this interpretation of Aristotle's natural science that the *Secretum* has transmitted over the centuries,[17] intersecting the operative needs of magic with the theoretical framework of natural philosophy.

The word *experimentum* contains its own ambiguities, which were exploited by medieval and early modern writers dealing with magic. The word implied something that one had already experienced, an experience that one was using to repeat or test something, something which would demonstrate the truth of a past experience or of a set of experiences and also, more concretely, a magical device for conveying a specific experience to other people. Integral to these processes was the *vis imaginativa*, the power exerted by images in one's head, either images that one had already created or images that had been introduced into one's brain from the outside and were stored in the 'imagination' for later use or reference. According to the Renaissance magus, Heinrich Cornelius Agrippa (1486–1535), the imagination was an active agent, not a passive one, and played a crucial role in any operation of magic. For Agrippa, the intensity of the *vis imaginativa* could also be acting on external objects and even upon the outcome of an *experimentum*.[18] As Maxwell-Stuart points out, the tradition of *experimenta* and the role of the *vis imaginativa* proved to be 'key factors in preparing the mind of later inquisitors into Nature for an intense personal experience of Nature itself by immersing them in the details of her intricate working'.[19] What *experimenta* and the *vis imaginativa* have in common is 'an assumption that Nature not only can, but ought to be investigated and that the rewards of such investigation will be beneficial both to the investigator and to humanity as a whole'.[20]

In his study devoted to Francesco Storella (about 1529–75), a professor of logic in Naples and one of the first teachers of the magus Giordano Bruno

(1548–1600), Donato Verardi investigates the peculiar contribution of the image of Aristotle as a magus promoted by Storella to the theoretical development of early modern natural magic. Starting from the important annotated edition of the *Secretum secretorum* (1555) produced by Storella, Verardi reconstructs the relationships between Storella's attribution of the *Secretum* and other magical works to Aristotle and his own peculiar conception of logic, considered as an instrument capable of guaranteeing a syllogistic science of 'singulars', that is, of those empirical data, even of those unusual and irregular ones, that were the subject of the investigations of alchemist and natural magicians. Verardi contextualizes Storella's work in the internal debates of the Neapolitan Aristotelian world of the time, also highlighting the contrary voices, one above all that of the logician Girolamo Balduino, to the idea that syllogism could be considered a cognitive tool of the singular in nature. In addition, he investigates the argumentative strategies implemented by Storella in his justification, in an Aristotelian key, of the seemingly more execrable aspects of magic, such as those inherent in *veneficia*, and namely of those poisonings erroneously attributed to the diabolical practices of so-called witches that could be explained, according to Storella, through the doctrines on the occult virtues of poisons offered by peripatetic natural philosophy. On the social level, this philosophical justification of the *veneficium* leads Storella to refute the belief in witchcraft, which was considered extraneous to the most authentic lesson of the Aristotelian tradition. In this heated struggle in favour of the alleged witches, which saw Storella side by side with natural magicians such as Giambattista Della Porta (1535–1615) and Bruno, the removal of Aristotle's authority from the field of demonology, and its inclusion in the ranks of the magi, was strategic.

The essay by William Eamon takes another look at the central place of natural magic in the formulation of early modern experimental science. As Eamon argues, the concept of natural magic emerged in the fifteenth century alongside (and in radical opposition to) the criminalization, by both the Church and the state, of common ritual magic that people traditionally used to enlist the help of occult powers in order to produce results that would be helpful in everyday life. The centrepiece of the essay is the Neapolitan scholar and magus Della Porta and his struggle to 'unmake' the marvels attributed to demons and to replace demonic magic with an experimental natural magic that made all marvels natural. The project was deeply personal for Della Porta: he had been harassed by the Inquisition after publishing his enthusiastic first book, *Magia naturalis* (1558), which proclaimed that marvels could be created naturally by deploying occult qualities that were empirically knowable. In unmaking demonic marvels,

Della Porta revealed a strategy for disabling the harsh reality of the persecutions of witches and their devastating impact on the people. As Eamon shows, Della Porta's main contribution to early modern experimental science was precisely to show that nature could be made to bend to human will and understanding by deploying supranormal (preternatural), but not supernatural, forces.

Della Porta's experience confirms the coexistence of various kinds of Aristotelianism in early modern Italy. His proposal, in fact, although contrary to the stereotypical Aristotelianism of the inquisitors and demonologists (an element that united him with a long Aristotelian tradition which, from Pietro Pomponazzi reached Storella), was openly inserted within the *philosophia naturalis*, or rather of an eclectic, inclusive and vital peripatetic framework, within which Della Porta continued to place and 'justify' many of the experimental results of his natural magic.[21] Della Porta's experiments, Eamon writes, 'were also demonstrations – not of the theoretical principles of natural magic but of the awesome power of occult forces and the magus's ingenuity and skill in manipulating them'.[22] This open and elastic interpretation of the *philosophia naturalis*, which he interpreted as a kind of provisional theoretical background for his experimental research, allowed Della Porta to erode the field of the occult in nature without completely abandoning the framework provided by the physics of qualities.[23] On the other hand, as Della Porta himself sometimes did, between the sixteenth and seventeenth centuries various investigators of nature continued to follow the traditional Aristotelian philosophy on many points even though they declared that they wanted to provide alternative explanations (as sometimes actually did) to those of the Philosopher.[24]

An example of the vitality and multiplicity of Aristotelianism that characterized the scientific debate at Della Porta's time is the role of *Mechanica* (a treatise on the mathematical principles of mechanics attributed at that time to Aristotle) in the erosion of the space granted to the occult in nature. As Anthony Grafton pointed out, in the Renaissance period, the rediscovery of the Aristotelian *Mechanica* suggested to its readers that 'there was nothing very magical about great machines'.[25] According to Eamon, when the infallibility of mathematics was added to engineering – in some measure, 'through the influence of ps.-Aristotle's *Mechanica*' – it became easier 'to separate the magical from the mechanical'.[26] On the other hand, Della Porta himself was able to benefit from this important acquisition in his project for the reform of artificial magic.[27] As Eamon shows, 'machines enabled people to visualize another kind of power: not of spells but of pullies, levers, and other simple machines made comprehensible by mathematics'.[28] Harnessing the forces of nature to produce wonders 'that ease the burden of human labor and increase society's material wealth and well-being was the technological dream of the Renaissance engineers. It was also the dream of the Renaissance magus'.[29] It is in this joint effort to erode the field of the superstition in favour of the useful and the marvellous that the dream of natural magic met that of engineering in early modern Europe.

In her essay, Arianna Borrelli further develops the theme of the relationship between engineering and natural magic, turning her attention to the construction of technical artefacts and to the 'magical' conceptual horizon within which these instruments were conceived in early modern Europe. During the Renaissance, some practitioners of natural magic became interested in newly developed technical devices, building upon them a variety of speculations on the workings of nature. Using the perpetual motion machine built by the Dutch engineer and natural philosopher Cornelis Drebbel as an example, Borrelli argues that, in some cases, the natural magical framework could be particularly fitting not only to prompt but also to productively guide investigations of nature. Natural magic allowed its practitioners to approach the creation and use of technical artefacts as a means to explore natural phenomena and tentatively conceptualize them in innovative ways by loosely combining elements from different natural philosophical views, such as those derived from Aristotelian, mechanical or chemical philosophy. Borrelli suggests referring to this particular branch of Renaissance natural magic as 'the techno-magical approach', of which both Della Porta and Drebbel were contemporary representatives. According to Borrelli, techno-magical practices 'represented a fertile ground for the development of new methods of natural philosophy precisely thanks to their open, exploratory character, which allowed to search for new ordering principles in nature by creating, transforming, combining, or rejecting both experiences and philosophical frameworks'. This context, Borrelli continues, promoted 'the emergence of both mechanical and chemical philosophies, as well as the revision and transformation of the Aristotelian framework' throughout the seventeenth century.[30]

Magic was not only an object of reflection for philosophers and natural magicians but also a real part of pre-modern daily life. This is particularly evident for the weather, a natural element that had strong supernatural associations throughout the fifteenth, sixteenth and seventeenth centuries. Since classical antiquity, meteorology was regarded as a sort of 'natural divination'. Although founded upon the careful observation of plant and animal behaviours, its logic was correlative – that is, based on correlations of signs. This made it simultaneously magical and empirical. English meteorology, which is at the heart of Jennifer

Mori's essay, was characterized by this correlative logic of signs until the 1800s, and meteorology continued to contain subjective and objective elements. The traditional lore of shepherds was famous for these auguries, and during the seventeenth-century weather prediction was based on a near-universal belief in the sublunary interdependencies of what educated men, accustomed to the lexicon of the peripatetic tradition, called the Aristotelian elements. This was the framework into which seventeenth-century Englishmen placed the 'new' instruments of science: the thermometer and barometer. In an essay centring on popular rather than elite science, Mori analyses different epistemologies: the magical, the mechanical and the syncretic, which were used by authors and amateur instrument-makers in their attempts to understand and prognosticate the weather. Mori traces a history of meteorology that runs through vernacular print and manuscript, illustrating how books and human networks 'intersected to create a culture of innovation and testing' in seventeenth-century England. She concludes that the instruments were assimilated into general English usage via older *mentalités*, as opposed to the acceptance of much 'new' science. Indeed, Mori writes, what the history of weather instrument making in England demonstrates

> is that vernacular epistemology, like early modern popular culture in general, is additive rather than substitutive. Insofar as the change took place in English thinking about the weather, this did not involve a significant paradigm-shift in perceptions of, and attitudes to, nature. The disenchantment of the world began, practically speaking, with a slow shift along an ancient continuum away from the supernatural towards – and eventually beyond – existing conventions of 'natural' logic within the Aristotelian framework.[31]

In his study, Manuel De Carli brings the theme of natural magic and the tools of the 'new' science into the classrooms and laboratory of the professor of peripatetic philosophy at the University of Leiden, Wolferd Senguerd (1646–1724). Starting from Senguerd's reflection on the tarantula (a small spider to which tradition attributed the extraordinary power to afflict the soul of the person who was bitten by it), the essay illustrates 'the *modus operandi* of an Aristotelian professor of the seventeenth century in explaining the occult causes of the marvellous effects handed down by the tradition of natural magic'.[32] The issue was at the centre of the Senguerd's thought since his academic training. In the *Disputatio philosophica inauguralis de tarantula* (1667) and in the *Tractatus physicus de tarantula* (1668), tarantism, or the melancholy disease caused by the bite of the tarantula, is presented as a phenomenon consisting of many aspects traditionally explained through occult qualities. Senguerd wanted to demonstrate that these aspects could be equally explained without recourse to occult qualities. Senguerd's position regarding the occult underwent a redefinition in his later *Disquisitio de tarantula* (1715). The work is printed together with the *Rationis atque experientiae connubium*, a manual aimed at offering, to an audience of specialists, an account of his private courses on pneumatics, together with instructions for the experimental use of the air pump. Within this work, the study of the many hidden aspects of tarantism is developed in a renewed experimental framework, also because of the clearer influences of English experimental philosophy and Senguerd's increasing work as an experimenter in the *Theatrum physicum*. Thus, approaching the problem from a hypothetical-deductive perspective in the *Disquisitio de tarantula*, Senguerd re-examined the magical object of the tarantula in a light that reflected both the acquisitions on the occult elaborated in his works on canine rabies and the new acknowledgements on elasticity obtained thanks to the use of the air pump.

Michael Pickering's paper discusses the subject of natural magic as addressed by an eighteenth-century German physician, relating it to debates on occult qualities and the notion of *technologia*. In his treatise on natural magic, the (today little-known) Braunschweig physician Johann Nikolaus Martius presented a theory of matter in which the wondrous, hidden properties of nature could be drawn forth by the skilled *medicus* to provide remedies to a variety of ailments. Citing authors of the medieval scholastic tradition, such as Albertus Magnus, Thomas Aquinas and Roger Bacon, as well as drawing on the authorities of Aristotle and Agrippa, Martius affirmed the legality and legitimacy of natural magic. As part of his theoretical discussion on the occult operations of magic, Martius drew a distinction between artificial magic – hand-crafted mechanical devices that operate on mathematical principles and 'without nature's powers' – and natural magic. The latter, according to Martius, depends upon an activation of the inner virtues of natural bodies via sympathetic means. In the case of artificial magic, words do not activate the physical forces required to make the devices operate; however, in natural magic, Martius argues that words – whether in the form of verbal utterances such as spells or curses, or written characters – had some capacity to activate the occult properties of nature. Words also served to codify the otherwise subjective experiences involved in such an invocation of natural powers, and it is in this way that Martius – as Pickering shows – provides something of a 'technological manual' of how to understand operations at a distance through the example of transplantation (and all the sub-categories that he delineates).

Martius' emphasis on visualizing the occult properties of nature is one of the most interesting elements of his proposal. As Pickering shows, in the context of early eighteenth-century German metaphysics, there was a growing awareness that the distinction between manifest and occult properties was a false one, and that 'no properties could ever be considered truly manifest'. Thus, 'one can understand Martius' visualization of sub-visible particles and their operations as, in part, a refutation of Scholastic *scientia* with its emphasis on the visible and manifest; and his reluctance to give up occult properties in toto as evidence of the obvious fact that his investigation deals precisely with those properties of nature that are, by definition, known only through their effects'.[33] In other words, in Martius, the 'occult' (a sort of philosophical 'regulatory idea' of the empirical research of the magus) still remains an essential point so that natural magic, consecrated to the understanding of what is mysterious is in nature, is conceivable.

The chapters in this volume touch on different linguistic fields (Arabic, Latin and the various vernacular languages) and cross a large diachronic space, from the fourteenth century to the first half of the eighteenth century, broadening the boundaries of the debate to include the whole of the European landscape. From late medieval and Renaissance discussions on the attribution of magical works to Aristotle, this collection moves onto the attempts of some Aristotelians (attempts that were at times concealed, and at other times more explicit) to justify magic philosophically and socially. Magic, in turn, is considered the 'mother science' of the nascent operative natural philosophy that was developing in early modern Europe. In this very complex picture, different and sometimes even antithetical visions of what was believed to be 'Aristotelianism' meet and clash. It is a debate that shows all the adaptability and openness of Aristotelianism to the new philosophies, including magic, with its emphasis on the operative and 'wondrous' character of knowledge. As emerges from the chapters contained here, in early modern Europe there were many – and not only among Aristotelian philosophers in the strict sense – who were aware that it was Aristotle himself who taught, among the first, that philosophy, and with it every form of true knowledge, 'begins in wonder'.[34]

Notes

1 On the problem of Aristotle's authority in Early Modern Period, see Eva Del Soldato, *Early Modern Aristotle. On the Making and Unmaking of Authority* (Philadelphia: University of Pennsylvania Press, 2020).

2 Daniel Pickering Walker, *Spiritual and Demonic Magic: From Ficino to Campanella* (London: The Warburg Institute, 1958); Frances A. Yates, *The Occult Philosophy in the Elizabethan Age* (London: Routledge, 1979), 37–71; Paola Zambelli, *White Magic, Black Magic in the European Renaissance* (Leiden: Brill, 2007); Brian P. Copenhaver, *Magic in Western Culture. From Antiquity to the Enlightenment* (New York: Cambridge University Press, 2015).

3 See Donato Verardi, *Logica e magia. Giovan Battista Della Porta e i segreti della natura* (Lugano: Agorà & Co., 2017).

4 John Henry, *Knowledge Is Power, How Magic, the Government and an Apocalyptic Vision Inspired Francis Bacon to Create Modern Science* (Cambridge: Icon Books, 2002); John Henry, 'The Fragmentation of Renaissance Occultism and the Decline of Magic', *History of Science* 46 (2008): 1–48; John Henry, *Religion, Magic, and the Origins of Science in Early Modern England* (London: Routledge, 2012); On the relationship between magic and science in the early modern period, see also the recent work by Mark A. Waddell, *Magic, Science, and Religion in Early Modern Europe* (Cambridge: Cambridge University Press, 2021).

5 Charles Schmitt, *Aristotle and the Renaissance* (Cambridge and London: Harvard University Press, 1983); Luca Bianchi, *Studi sull'aristotelismo rinascimentale* (Padua: Il Poligrafo, 2003); Del Soldato, *Early Modern Aristotle*; Hellen Hattab, 'Renaissance Aristotelianism(s)', in *The Cambridge History of Philosophy of the Scientific Revolution*, eds David M. Miller and Dana Jalobeanu (Cambridge: Cambridge University Press, 2022), 58–74.

6 See Rebekah Compton and Donato Verardi eds, *Magical Materials in Renaissance Philosophy, Literature, and Art* (Lugano: Agorà & Co., 2022).

7 See Richard Sorabji ed., *Aristotle Transformed: The Ancient Commentators and Their Influence* (London: Bloomsbury, 2016). On the pseudo-Aristotle and on the place of the occult sciences in the pseudo-Aristotelian *corpus*, see Lynn Thorndike, 'The Latin pseudo-Aristotle and Medieval Occult Science', *The Journal of English and Germanic Philology*, 21 no. 2 (1922): 229–58; Charles B. Schmitt, 'Francesco Storella and the Last Printed Edition of the Latin *Secretum Secretorum* (1555)', in *Pseudo-Aristotle. The Secret of Secrets. Sources and Influences*, eds William F. Ryan and Charles B. Schmitt (London: The Warburg Institute, 1982), 124–31; Schmitt, *Aristotle and the Renaissance* (Cambridge-London: Harvard University Press, 1983); Schmitt, *Pseudo-Aristoteles Latinus. A Guide to Latin Works Falsely Attributed to Aristotle before 1500* (London: The Warburg Institute, 1985); Charles Burnett, 'Arabic, Greek and Latin Works on Astrological Magic attributed to Aristotle', in *Pseudo-Aristotle in the Middle Ages*, ed. Jill Kraye, William F. Ryan and Charles B. Schmitt (London: The Warburg Institute, 1986), 84–96; Burnett, 'Aristotle as an Authority on Judicial Astrology', in *Florilegium Mediaevale, Études offertes à Jacqueline Hamesse à l'occasion de son éméritat*, eds J. Meirinhos and O. Weijers

(Louvain-la-Neuve: Brepols, 2009), 41–62; Liana Saif, *The Arabic Influences on Early Modern Occult Philosophy* (London: Palgrave, 2015); See also Manfred Ullmann, *Die Natur-und Geheimwissenschaften im Islam*, Handbuch der Orientalistik, I, VI, 2 (Leiden: Brill, 1972), 76–7; 220; 406; 424–5; David Pingree, 'The Diffusion of Arabic Magical Texts in Western Europe', in *La diffusione delle scienze islamiche nel medio evo europeo* (Rome: Accademia Nazionale dei Lincei, 1987), 57–102; C. H. Lohr, 'The Sixteenth-Century Transformation of the Aristotelian Natural Philosophy', in *Aristotelismus und Renaissance. In memoriam Charles B. Schmitt*, eds E. Kessler, C. H. Lohr and W. Sparn (Wiesbaden: O. Harrassowitz, 1988), 89–99; Steven J. Williams, 'Defining the *corpus aristotelicum*: Scholastic Awareness of Aristotelian Spuria in the High Middle Ages', *Journal of the Warburg and Courtauld Institutes* 58 (1995): 29–51; D. Verardi, 'Francesco Storella e l'Aristotele negromante', *Bruniana & Campanelliana* 25 no. 2 (2019), 541–9.

8   Schmitt, *Aristotle and the Renaissance*, 10–33. See also Edward Grant, 'Ways to Interpret the Terms "Aristotelian" and "Aristotelianism" in Medieval and Renaissance Natural Philosophy', *History of Science* 25 (1987): 335–58; J. M. M. Hans Thijssen, 'Some Reflections on Continuity and Transformation of Aristotelianism in Medieval (and Renaissance) Natural Philosophy', *Documenti e studi sulla tradizione filosofica medievale* 2 (1991): 503–28.

9   Between the sixteenth and seventeenth centuries, at the dawn of the so-called scientific revolution, a heated debate on impiety or, on the contrary, on the adaptability of Aristotle's philosophy to the principles of the Christian faith contributed to further complicate this picture. See Craig Martin, *Subverting Aristotle: Religion, History, and Philosophy in Early Modern Science* (Baltimore: John Hopkins University Press, 2014).

10 On the authorship of the *Physiognomonica* attributed to Aristotle, see Aristotle, *Physiognomonica*, ed. Sabine Vogt, in *Aristoteles Werke in deutscher Übersetzung*, gen. ed. Christof Rapp, vol. 18.6 (Berlin: Walter de Gruyter, 1999), 43ff. On the impact of this work on physiognomy in the early modern age, see Paola Zambelli, '*Aut diabolus aut Achillinus*. Fisiognomica, astrologia e demonologia nel metodo di un aristotelico', *Rinascimento* 18 (1978): 58–86; Cecilia Muratori, 'From Animal Bodies to Human Souls: (Pseudo-)Aristotelian Animals in Della Porta's Physiognomics', *Early Science and Medicine* 22, no. 1 (2017): 1–23. On *chiromantia*, see R. Ambrose Pack, 'A pseudo-Aristotelian Chiromancy', *Archives d'Histoire Doctrinale et Littéraire du Moyen Age* 36 (1969): 189–241; Charles B. Burnett, 'The Earliest Chiromancy in the West', *JWCI* 50 (1987): 189–95; Burnett, *Magic and Divination in the Middle Ages: Texts and Techniques in the Islamic and Christian Worlds* (Aldershot, Great Britain, Brookfield: Variorum, 1996); Laetitia Marcucci, 'Révéler les secrets del la nature à la lecture des signes du corps à la Renaissance', *Arcana naturae* 1 (2020): 97–118. See also Jean-Patrice Boudet, *Entre science et*

nigromancie. Astrologie, divination et magie dans l'Occident médiéval (XII̊-XV̊ siècle) (Paris: Publications de la Sorbonne 2006), 100–1. On alchemy, see *L'alchimie et ses racines philosophiques. La tradition grecque et la tradition arabe*, ed. Cristina Viano (Paris: Vrin, 2005); Sylvain Matton, *Philosophie et Alchimie à la Renaissance et à l'Âge classique. Scolastique et alchimie (XVI-XVII siècles)* (Paris, Milan: s.é.h.a-Arché, 2009).

11 This is understandable also in light of the fact that new manuals appeared in both Jesuit and non-Jesuit circles. In the seventeenth century these manuals were a response to significant changes in the pedagogical field and they addressed the public of philosophy students who could also aspire to be students of the faculty of theology, law and medicine. These manuals, which progressively replaced the didactic use of the classic commentary, contained a condensation of the philosophy of the Stagirite, presented in an easy-to-read form and as compatible with the Christian, Catholic or Protestant faith. See Schmitt, *Aristotle and the Renaissance*, 97–8 and 104–6; Charles Lohr, *Latin Aristotle Commentaries, II: Renaissance Authors* (Florence: Olschki, 1988); Lohr, *Latin Aristotle Commentaries: V. Bibliography of Secondary Literature* (Florence: Sismel, Edizioni del Galluzzo, 2005). See also Roger Ariew, 'Aristotelianism in the 17th Century', in *Routledge Encyclopedia of Philosophy*, Vol. 1, ed. Edward Craig (London: Routledge, 1998), 386–93; *Descartes: Principia Philosophiae (1644–1994)*, eds Jean Robert Armogathe and Giulia Belgioioso (Naples: Vivarium, 1996); C. Martin, *Subverting Aristotle*, passim; Mark A. Waddell, *Jesuit Science and the End of Nature's Secrets* (Surrey and London: Hasgate/Routledge, 2015), 53–85; Michael John Gorman, *The Scientific Counter-Revolution. The Jesuits and the Invention of Modern Science* (London: Bloomsbury, 2020).

12 Infra, 17.
13 Infra, 25.
14 Infra, 40.
15 See Lynn Thorndike, *A History of Magic and Experimental Science*, vol. 2 (New York and London: Columbia University Press, 1964), 246–78.
16 Steven Williams, *Secret of Secrets. The Scholarly Career of a pseudo-Aristotelian Text in the Latin Middle Ages* (Ann Arbor: University of Michigan Press, 2003), 183–343.
17 Chiara Crisciani, 'Il *Secretum secretorum* in Occidente: tre casi', in *Appropriation, Interpretation and Criticism: Philosophical and Theological Exchanges between the Arabic, Hebrew and Latin Intellectual Traditions*, eds Alexander Fidora and Nicola Polloni (Barcelona, Rome: Fédération Internationale des Instituts d'Études Médiévales, 2017), 231–60: 234; Elly Truitt, 'Knowledge and Power: Courtly Science and Political Utility in the Work of Roger Bacon', *Revista Española de Filosofía Medieval* 28, no. 1 (2021): 99–123.
18 See infra, 53.

19 Infra, 54-55.
20 Infra, 55.
21 See Donato Verardi, *La scienza e i segreti della natura a Napoli nel Rinascimento. La magia naturale di Giovan Battista Della Porta* (Florence: Firenze University Press, 2018).
22 Infra, 90.
23 See Donato Verardi 'L'aristotelismo di G.B. Della Porta e il dibattito sulla conoscenza del singolare a Napoli nel Rinascimento', *Giornale critico della filosofia italiana* 95, no. 2/3 (2016): 313-23; Verardi, *La scienza e i segreti della natura a Napoli nel Rinascimento*.
24 See Craig Martin, *Renaissance Meteorology. Pomponazzi to Descartes* (Baltimore: The Johns Hopkins University Press, 2011), 82.
25 Anthony Grafton, *Magic and Technology in Early Modern Europe* (Washington: Smithsonian Institution Libraries, 2005), 44.
26 Infra, 100.
27 See Donato Verardi, 'Art and Magic of Animated Statues. The Secret Virtues of Albertus Magnus' Talking Head in Giambattista Della Porta's *Natural Magick*', in *Magical Materials in Renaissance Philosophy, Literature, and Art*, Compton and Verardi eds, 83-106.
28 Infra, 100.
29 Infra, 99.
30 See infra, 111.
31 Infra, 163.
32 Infra, 172.
33 Infra, 201.
34 Aristotle, *Metaphysics*, A, 2, 982 b 13-16.

1

Aristotelian philosophy and illusionism in late medieval Europe

Thibaut Rioult

1.1 A questioning coincidence

Departing from his master Plato, Aristotle valued the study of nature and the phenomena per se. The first sentence of *Metaphysics* emphasizes the human 'love' of the senses (*aisthḗseōn agápēseis*) and the pivotal role of visual perception.[1] Thus, this philosophy has always had to struggle with illusion, always coming back to haunt its 'perceptual realism'.[2]

This prospective and experimental study aims to underline some of the connections between Aristotelian philosophy and illusionism in the thirteenth to fifteenth centuries. By 'illusionism', I primarily refer to the art of illusion practised by the medieval 'juggler' (meaning 'conjurer', 'prestidigitator', 'cups and balls performer' or *bateleur* in French). Despite some recent and interesting works,[3] illusionism still lacks in-depth academic research.

One particular fact, which has gone unnoticed, deserves special attention and prompted an investigation: from a theoretical point of view, the first appearance of an intellectual use of illusionism was grounded in thirteenth-century Aristotelian environment, raising of natural philosophy and fight against heresies. Indeed, to our knowledge, the bishop of Paris[4] William of Auvergne (c. 1180–1249)[5] was the first to use the notion of 'sleight of hand' in the process of coining the pivotal concept of 'natural magic'. For the first time, the archetypal figure of medieval jugglers was enrolled in scholar discussions. This was a turning point. Before him, this figure was used by theologians in context of moral condemnation of vain entertainment or knowledge (cf. John of Salisbury,[6] Thomas of Chobham[7]). After him, important scholars trained at the University of Paris – as his contemporary Roger Bacon (†1294) or later Nicole

Oresme (†1382) – reused this discipline as a source of technical knowledge or as a critical tool to question magic.[8]

As we will see at the end of this study, William's theoretical conceptions were also hijacked by the *Malleus Maleficarum* (1486), where they provided a framework for demonic actions and supported an illusionistic ontology, subverting the Aristotelico-Thomism.

How did a technical paradigm, inherited from marginal jugglers, become a pivotal concept of medieval thought? Its ability to enter in synergy with medieval Aristotelian epistemology could be one of the answers.

1.2 Philosophical and theological stakes of thirteenth Aristotelianism

From the last half of twelfth century onwards, the progressive introduction of Graeco-Arabic knowledge brought both a new Aristotelian corpus (consisting of *libri naturales* and Arabic commentaries) and magic and Hermetic literature,[9] which arouse great interest among scholars and serious concerns among theological authorities. The picture was complicated by the presence of some 'magical' texts attributed to Aristotle himself. This confusing element fuelled a heated debate throughout the Middle Ages up to the Renaissance, providing the backdrop to the long-standing controversy about the rational status of magic.

Several ecclesiastical condemnations and prohibitions marked the beginning of the thirteenth century (1210, 1215 and 1231). For instance, in 1210, several bishops led by Peter of Corbeil, archbishop of Sens and Peter of Nemour, bishop of Paris, explicitly condemned the study of the '*libri Aristotelis de naturali philosophia*' and their Arabic commentaries, on pain of excommunication.[10] However, despite the attacks, Aristotelianism quickly gained acceptance into the University, becoming a major reference for new generations of scholars. William of Auvergne fully belonged to the generation of thinkers, which structured the University of Paris.[11] He was one of the main driving forces behind the emergence of scholastic thought.[12]

Even if he cannot be considered strictly as a pure Aristotelian,[13] according to Roland J. Teske, William of Auvergne 'was the first of the thirteenth-century theologians to appreciate the value of the Aristotelian philosophy'.[14] Despite the condemnations, he knew and quoted most of Aristotle's works (*Ethics,*

Metaphysics, Physics, On Soul, On Sleep and Dreams, On the Heavens, etc.) and engaged complex discussions with his thought.[15]

Globally, with Aristotle, came a new model of knowledge or *scientia*, based on logical and rational demonstration (minimizing the intervention of God in nature). According to S. P. Marrone, 'the idea of *science* and the desire to be *scientific* shaped the scholasticism of the thirteenth century and signalled it as something new in the medieval West'.[16] More precisely, Aristotelianism provided an effective paradigm for an expectation already present in scholars of the twelfth century, as Adelard of Bath (†c. 1152) or William of Conches (†c. 1150).[17] The latter explicitly claimed the possibility to investigate the unknown natural powers and search the reasons in all things.[18] Research of natural causes has become a common aspiration of scholars. Supported by Aristotelianism, natural philosophy became the main prism for understanding the world.[19] Breaking from the role of divine illumination as stated by traditional Augustinism, leveraging Aristotle's naturalistic epistemology, William of Auvergne emphasized the purely human and natural dimension of understanding.[20]

From a politico-religious perspective, it is worth noticing that William of Auvergne's works took place during the Cathar Crusade (1209–29) and the ensuing repression. The Church mobilized her intellectual resources to refute Cathar philosophy. Consequently, the challenge for William of Auvergne was to come up with a coherent world view that could prevent people from falling into error, and a fortiori into idolatry and heresy. Mainly in his *De universo*, he attacked a simplified version of Manichees (assimilated to Cathars) dualism[21] and 'used Aristotle against the Cathars'.[22] Philosophy was an argumentative tool to refute the existence of an evil principle, subordinating to God.

William's theorization of both a specific 'limiting' demonology[23] and of the concept of 'natural' magic (consequently 'limited') was also part of this attempt to restrain the powers and the scope of the non-divine supernatural. It called for illusionism theoretical support.

1.3 Was another ontological foundation possible?

In order to situate properly the choices made by the Latin West, an *excursus* through comparative philosophy seems necessary. Indeed, at the same time, in the Islamic world and mainly in Persia, medieval philosophers led the Greek heritage in other directions. In contrast, their Neoplatonist Aristotelianism, pushed to the extreme, helps to understand Latin Aristotelianism. Avicenna (†1037) and

Suhrawardī (†1191), under the influence of the *Theology* of the pseudo-Aristotle (actually the last three *Enneads* of Plotinus), proposed an alternative ontology.

Avicenna emphasized the role of Intelligences and assimilated them to angels. He increased their number, their role (more active) and their ontological status, breaking with 'the idea (common to Islam and Christianity) of the Angel as servant of the supreme God and messenger'.[24] On this basis, Avicenna provides a complex theory of individuation, which rejects Aristotelian hylomorphism and builds a personal link between the human soul and its own Angel.[25] The multiplication of celestial beings (angels-Intelligences) is consubstantial of Avicenna's emanationism. However, this thesis contradicted the standard creationist view of monotheism, assuming a free and omnipotent God, not tied to a complex hierarchy of autonomous celestial beings. As Corbin stated: William of Auvergne was one of 'the most significant opponent'[26] of this doctrine in his *De universo*. For the bishop of Paris, 'the great danger is to hold that the Angels can intervene in the course of human events'.[27] Indeed, for most Western theologians, 'theology would combat all emanationism, claim the creative act as a prerogative of God alone, end the human soul's soliloquy with the Angel Active Intelligence'.[28]

The main consequence of Avicennian cosmo-angelology, theorized and amplified by Suhrawardī (trained as an Aristotelian but converted to Platonism), was the assumption of an independent intermediary world, where a contact would be possible between material and spiritual. 'The world of the Imaginal is the world where visions [. . .] take place, and the events of the soul, which are as real as those of the sensible world but which take place at *another level of being*.'[29] It was called *'ālam al-mithāl* (litt. world of images) by Islamic philosophers (or *mundus imaginalis* by Corbin).[30] This is 'a world, a mode of being and a mode of knowledge [. . .] but which, far from being *unreal*, are perfectly real in their own right, of a *sui generis* reality'.[31] Thus, the human soul could travel in this interworld and could be elevated to 'archangelic lights' or fall in 'demonic forms'.[32] Turning its back on this Neoplatonist conception, Western theology deprived angels and devils of their own ontological space[33] and condemned them to haunt the reality level of humans. It also condemned itself to discuss demons with the categories of natural philosophy.

1.4 Undermining demonic powers with natural magic and juggling

William of Auvergne's *On the Universe* (*De universo*, 1230–40)[34] is one attempt to provide a systematic view of material and immaterial world, on a rational basis. Of course, this work could not avoid the question of the supernatural. Dealing with the nature of wonders and supernatural phenomena, he proposed a conception of demonology and magic aligned with the religious and metaphysical background briefly presented as *supra*. Indeed, to fight against the dualist trends (as Catharism), which considered Good-God and Evil-Devil as two ontologically equal principles, William of Auvergne built a *limiting demonology*. This concept was partially inherited from the Early Middle Ages and more particularly from the *Canon Episcopi*, which stated the belief in witches was a heretical superstition.[35] William also searched to prevent all possibility of (idolatrous) contact between humans and demons. The demons were physically limited (they have no body), limited in number (creation of new ones is impossible), limited in terms of space or dignity (they live in hell, wastelands or toilets).[36]

The main contact zone between humans and devils was magic. Indeed, most of magic treatises of the twelfth and thirteenth centuries belonged to the category of 'addressative magic', which directly asked spiritual entities (demons, angels or spirits) for their interventions[37] and risked of turning quickly into idolatrous worship. However, William of Auvergne (who was aware of these books and their philosophy)[38] broke with the traditional moral condemnation of magic of his predecessors. For instance, Hugh of St Victor declared in his *Didascalion* (c. 1135) that 'magic is not a part of philosophy but rather stands outside it, making false claims'.[39] William opted for a very different and fascinating strategy. Rather than engaging himself in a frontal opposition with magic, he tried to siphoning off its powers (a few years later, this position has been clearly personified by Roger Bacon).[40]

For the first time in the West, William of Auvergne used the concept of 'natural magic' in three of his works (and not two, as scholars usually stated), the *De legibus* (c. 1230), the *De virtutibus* (c. 1228) and the *De universo* (c. 1230–40). Of course, the concept did not arise *ex nihilo* – the ground was prepared in the studies of a few scholars of the twelfth century (mainly John of Seville, Domingo Gundisalvi and Daniel of Morley).[41]

William revealed its important theological issues in his *De legibus*:

> [the science of] this kind of work is natural magic (*magica naturalis*), which philosophers call nigromancy according to physics (*nigromanciam secundum phisicam*), most licit in itself, and the eleventh part of all natural science (*scientie naturalis*). Thus those people ignorant of this kind of science believe that demons produce these wonders, which nature works through virtues imputed in them

by the creator, and for that reason alone attribute to demons not only a great power and wonder but even omnipotence, and in this doubles the injury to the creator.[42]

William positioned 'natural magic' as an intellectual device to break the normally accepted link between magic and demons and challenge the actual efficiency of their powers. The introduction of natural science widened the field of causal research and led to a major epistemological shift of paradigm. Although William developed his discourse in a theological and demonological context, he proposed a very interesting 'technicalization' of magic.

In his *De universo*, William of Auvergne specified the meaning of what he called 'natural magic',[43] describing the three generic types of magic, based on their *technical means*:

> This brings me to these works, which are called magical works (*opera magica*) and illusions (*ludificationes*), of humans or demons. In the first place, I say that they are of three kinds. The first is made by agility and skill of the hands, such as the [secret] storing (*repositiones*) and exchanging (*transpositiones*) of certain things, which are commonly called sleight of hand (*traiectationes*), and these are great marvels to men, until they know how they are done.
>
> The second type is that of those [magical works] which contain nothing true except appearance; they are made by the subtraction or application of certain things.[44]

In his *De virtutibus*, William also alluded to the use of 'marvellous things' (*rebus mirabilibus*) by natural magic (or rather, the use of the marvellous *virtues* of things).[45]

William did not precisely name the different categories, creating uncertainty around the definition of the notion of 'natural magic'. Consequently, it appeared as a blend between two fields that were part of the natural production of wonder: sleight of hands and use of natural and secret properties of things. This blurring between prestidigitation and spectacular science continues to underpin illusionism even now.

The third magic type was not clearly defined but seems to refer to '*praestigium*', meaning an illusion produced by direct constrictive action on sight, as Isidore of Seville (†636) defined it.[46] For William, *praestigium* occurred without, or sometimes with the help from demons, thus not totally excluding them from the field of magic and straddling both demonic and natural magic traditions.

1.5 'By agility and skills', the local (secret) motions

If, far from considering it as anecdotal, one takes seriously the fundamental position of illusionism in this threefold characterization of magical techniques, it appears that the first (and most simple) way to produce magical wonders is to use manipulations. Using the unusual term *'traiectationes'* (meaning 'manipulations by rapid movement of hands'), which was the emblem of the juggler operations, and the semantic field of locomotion of things (*trans-positiones, re-positiones*), William implicitly (or unconsciously) mobilized the key Aristotelian concept of *local motion*.

Sleight of hands provided an efficient framework to conceptualize both human first level of 'magic' and demons' all in one. Once blended together, the 'magical' feats of the juggler and the demon and their means of action can also be transposed.

The necessity of a transposition from human to demon (key for the building of limiting demonology) could explain why William of Auvergne restricted human illusionism to sleight of hand. In opposition to Roger Bacon, he excluded the role of secret instruments, probably because they were useless regarding his main theological issues. On his side, Bacon emphasized the operations done *'per instrumenta subtilia'*,[47] which were more interesting from his 'experimental' point of view.

William's theoretical framework of illusionism, based on the archetype of the cups and balls player, can be seen as an attempt to give a concrete and robust foundation to the Augustine (†430) evocation of demon transformations:

> I believe they were not made through the metamorphosis of men, but were slyly substituted (*subpositas*) for them on their removal, just as the hind was for Iphigenia, the daughter of king Agamemnon. For juggleries [or simply: illusions] (*praestigiae*) of this kind could not be difficult for the demons if permitted by the judgment of God.[48]

The most beautiful illustration of these demons-jugglers was provided by Bruegel in his *Fall of the Magician Hermogenes* (1565) (Figure 1.1), visually synthetizing the long-lasting tradition of illusionistic demonology, depicting demons performing at least ten classical tricks from the Renaissance repertoire (which were probably also known in medieval times). Bruegel was exemplary in illustrating limiting demonology and did not hesitate to make fun of demons.

However, in Aristotle's philosophy, the 'motion' (*kínēsis*) cannot be reduced to 'locomotion' but covers more generally all 'changes' and 'generations'[49] (including emotions, imaginations etc.). This conceptual network has been largely reused by

Figure 1.1 P. Bruegel the Elder (designer), P. van der Heyden (engraver) and Hieronymus Cock (publisher), *The Fall of the Magician Hermogenes*, 1565, engraving, 29.2 cm × 22.4 cm. Public Domain Source: The Met Open Access. Harris Brisbane Dick Fund, 1928.

demonologists (particularly in the *Malleus Maleficarum*)[50] as a way to 'rationalize' the means of demonic operations. Very interestingly, all these characteristics are associated with the juggler through the important iconographic corpus of The Children of the Moon (fifteenth century).[51] Linking moon, cups and balls performer, pilgrim, trapper (manipulating appearance to catch birds) and water-related activities (fisher, miller, swimmer), these illustrations provided a visual representation of the symbolic network of change (generation, manipulation, metamorphosis, transformation, imagination, travel, fluidity etc.) (Figure 1.2).

1.6 'How to distinguish true from false': illusionism as critical tool

As is obvious through his threefold categorization, for William, magic relied on *visible* marvels, breaking with natural rules. Pushed over to the side of illusion,

Figure 1.2 The Children of the Moon, from *Mittelalterliches Hausbuch von Schloss Wolfegg* [*c.* 1480], f°17r. Public Domain Source: Wikimedia Commons.

magical effects mainly became an issue of perception. Among other texts (e.g. Ibn al-Haytham's *Optics*), the translations of Aristotle's *De anima* brought to the West pivotal concepts for the study of perception and psychology.[52] In the intellectual context of this (re)discovery of perceptual questions and structuration of medieval *perspectiva* (meaning 'science of phenomena'), it was not entirely surprising to find a reference to magicians in William's reflection on the process of sensory perception.[53]

> For sight is not free to judge that something white is other than white [...] For the modification that is impressed upon the sense by the sensed object in general is like a witness from the sensed object testifying as to what sort it is [...] It is possible to find the same thing in the other senses when they are not impeded by illness or another cause. We say this on account of the tricks [or sight constrictions, illusions][54] of magicians (*prestigias magorum*) and the illusions of demons.[55]

Indeed, even if the senses were in good shape, magicians could deceive them. This raised an important problem because primary perceptions imposed themselves and were not submitted to any critical judgement.

This awareness could explain the desire of scholars like Peter Peregrinus of Maricourt, Roger Bacon or the anonymous author of the *Secretum philosophorum*, to discover the tricks of magicians and jugglers. Written probably at the end of the thirteenth century by an English follower of Bacon, the *Secretum philosophorum*[56] (*The Secret of Philosophers*) is a turning point in the history of illusionism. Its *incipit* explains that it contains 'certain secrets which, by vulgar opinion, are impossible, but which philosophers [consider to be] necessary and secret'.[57] However, the intention of this very complex text has still not been clarified. Indeed, it has led to multiple unconventional approaches to deal with the *trivium*. The 'grammar' section provided ink recipes (incl. invisible inks) and cyphers, the 'rhetoric' section told riddles and the 'dialectic' section revealed conjuring tricks. This treatise could be a clever parody of scholastic works, considered from an amusing perspective. It served perhaps as a basis for pedagogical and entertaining teaching of clerics.

The introduction of the dialectic part, which dealt with illusionism, not only explicitly cited Aristotle on truth but also seemed to mobilize also implicitly his perceptual theory:

> Dialectic teaches how to distinguish true from false, or from the apparently true. For God made in man a rational soul and gave it five senses, which are taste, smell, sound, vision and touch, so that with them, along with intelligence, man could distinguish good from bad, true from false, or true from apparently true. But since by these senses, man distinguishes true from false, or true from

apparently true (which is the same), and since the sense is often deceived with respect to its proper object (as will be shown below), let us first see how sense is deceived. And once this is known, immediately it will also be known how to distinguish true from false, because, according to Aristotle, when one opposite is known, so is the other [*Topica* I.14 (105b33)].[58]

The reference to the 'proper object of senses' (*idia aisthēta* in Aristotelian terms) could lead us to consider this illusionistic reflection as a pragmatic critic of some of Aristotle's propositions derived from *De anima* II, 6 (418a11), which stated that particular senses could not be wrong (*non contingit errare*) about their proper object.[59] Medieval scholars frequently used this proposition to question illusion.[60]

Even if, as Goulding remarked, 'despite the promises of liberal learning in its preface, the *Secretum philosophorum* is most closely related to the genre of "experiments books" or "books of secrets"',[61] the anonymous author seemed to implicitly tackle this perceptual issue. Taking the opposite view, he repeatedly insisted on the fact that senses are 'deceived with respect to [their] proper object (*decipitur circa proprium obiectum*)'.[62] Thus, we can reasonably hypothesize that the *Secretum philosophorum* – through illusionism – engaged precisely a discussion with the common Aristotelian conception of 'particular senses'. It did not comment theoretically on the proposition of the *De anima*, but pragmatically refuted it, providing at least one *experimentum* deceiving each sense: gustation (No. 1 & 2), olfaction (No. 3 & 4), hearing (No. 5), vision (No. 6–29) and tactile perception (No. 30 & 31). The juggling tricks explained were not mere entertainment but the means of experimental research on perceptions. Following the *scientia experimentalis* promoted by R. Bacon, the anonymous author made a critical use of the corpus of secrets and *experimenta* to challenge the theoretical proposition of natural philosophy.

Nevertheless, during the Middle Age, the discussion about illusion went far beyond natural philosophy. As we have already seen with William of Auvergne, it was closely connected to other domains, more particularly demonology.

1.7 Radical illusion: From sleight of hand to ontological manipulations

The history of the theory of witchcraft is long and complex. Alain Boureau identified that the 'demonological turn' occurred at the end of the thirteenth century, with the writing of *De malo* (c. 1272) of Thomas Aquinas.[63] Following the seminal work of Trevor-Roper, a few scholars have underlined the role of Aristotelian paradigm in the theorization of witchcraft (as opposed to the Neoplatonist paradigm, which corroborates the analysis of the 'oriental' ontology presented in *supra*).[64]

The most famous treatise of witchcraft, the *Malleus Maleficarum*[65] (*The Hammer of Witches*) was published in 1486 or 1487. This bestseller of the Renaissance period written by two Dominicans, Heinrich Institoris and Jacob Sprenger, mainly tried to demonstrate the reality of witchcraft and the witches' conspiracy, from a social, physical, theological and philosophical point of view. They achieved this goal by whatever means possible, paradoxically not hesitating to use illusion as proof of reality.

To support this point, the treatise reused the threefold magical categorization of William of Auvergne and spread widely the illusionistic demonology. Indeed, even if the *Malleus Maleficarum* didn't explicitly cite William in this case, the fact that it made some references to him (esp. to *De universo*)[66] and especially used the uncommon expression '*traiectionibus*' seems sufficient philological evidence to make this connection.

Contrary to the theories of William of Auvergne, illusions were not a way to limit the power of demons but a means to demonstrate their abilities. As a result of a profound theoretical reversal, juggler's feats became 'proofs of concept' of demonic activities. Obviously, if a human knows how to do this through tricks, a demon must know even better! They also provide the entry point for the inventory of demonic means of action.

> Hence, speaking in general terms about the art of illusion on the part of humans (*humana prestigiosa arte*), let us say that this can happen in three ways. One is without demons, and this is better termed 'illusion' (*delusio*), because it happens artfully (*artificialiter*) through manipulation (*agitatione*) on the part of people who show or hide certain objects, as happens in the sleight of hand performed by jugglers and mimes (*traiectionibus per ioculatores vel per mimos*). Another way also takes place without the virtue of demons, inasmuch as it takes place naturally through the virtue of natural bodies, particularly minerals. Those who possess these things are able, in accordance with a certain virtue inherent to these things, to show an object or make it appear different from the way that it in fact is. [. . .] The third sort of deception (*delusionis*) is the one that happens through demons, though with God's permission. As has been explained, by nature demons have a certain power over lower objects (*res inferiores*) that they can exercise over them when God allows, so that at that time things appear

other than the way that they are. In connection with this, it should be noted, third, that there are five ways in which a demon can use an illusion (*illudere*) on someone so that he judges an object to be other than the way that it is. The first way is with an artful sleight of hand (*artificiali traiectione*), as has been said. For whatever a human knows how to do by art, a demon can know better. The second way is the natural use of some object (*naturali applicatione*), in the manner already stated. He interposes (*interpositionem*) some body so that another body is concealed [. . .]. The third way is when in an assumed body he shows himself to be something which he is not. [. . .] The fourth way is when [. . .] he disturbs the organ of vision [. . .] The fifth way is to work on the faculty of imagination [. . .] The Devil can impose an illusion upon a man's senses (*illudere sensus*) through the art of illusion (*prestigiosa arte*), and hence there is no difficulty to keep him from hiding the male member through the art of illusion (*prestigiosa arte*).[67]

Indeed, with more than forty occurrences of terms derived from *praestigi-(um)*, the *Malleus Maleficarum* strongly emphasized the illusory dimension of demonic actions, as a paradoxical way to both show and prove their reality. Eventually, I would like to argue that the *Malleus Maleficarum* built actual illusionistic ontology, leveraging the Aristotelian couple of substance and accident (gr. *ousía/ sumbebēkós*, lat. *substantia/accidens*).

Written in the beginning of the tenth century, the *Canon Episcopi* declared the belief in witches to be heretical and their transformations impossible. Included in the authoritative *Decretum Gratiani* (twelfth century), it prevented the ecclesiastical reflection on witches for centuries. During the fifteenth century, it became the 'stumbling block of all witchcraft theoreticians'.[68] The *Malleus Maleficarum* was a war machine directed against the canon, which devoted all its efforts to undermining it in many ways.

Trying to subvert the *Canon Episcopi*, the two Dominicans explained 'there are two kinds of change: substantial and accidental [. . .] It is the first sort that the *Canon* speaks of'.[69] This statement was only made possible by the new Aquinian ontology. But, far from being a product of his demonology, it was the illegitimate son of his Eucharistic theology, which involuntarily provided the ideal conceptual scheme for supporting the maximal extension of diabolic illusory powers.

The real presence of Christ in the Eucharist is one of the fundamental mysteries of Christianity. During the Mass, when the priest – repeating the words of the Last Supper – declares, '*Hoc est corpus meum*. This is my body', an invisible change occurs. The nature of this 'change' (symbolic, real etc.)

fuelled the debate for centuries. During the twelfth century, realists (Lanfranc) overcame the symbolists (Berengar of Tours) after a long controversy.[70] The Fourth Lateran Council (1215) acknowledged this victory, by defining that which occurred during consecration as *transubstantiation* (without providing a clear definition). Thomas Aquinas radicalized the position of Lanfranc[71] and tried to clarify philosophically this theological pivotal question. If the bread becomes the body of Christ, how can it maintain the appearance of bread? Or, in Aristotelian terms, how can the accidents of bread be present without its substance? In order to rationally ground transubstantiation, Thomas needed to bypass the traditional couple of matter and form. He replaced it with the couple of substance and accident, inherited (or rather 'uprooted')[72] from Aristotle's categories. This substitution was necessary to make an *ontological disconnection*, which was impossible under the hylemorphic paradigm, thanks to the 'separability of accidents'.[73] Indeed, 'matter is much weaker than accident: it has no being of its own, whereas accident has a being of its own'.[74] Contrary to Aristotle, the Aquinian accident could be maintained without the support of a substance. Supported by this twisted Aristotelianism, Thomas cut off the link between what is perceived and what it actually is.

Thomas tried to clearly differentiate the transubstantiation of the Eucharist and the illusions of magicians (*magorum præstigiis*), to prevent a potential assimilation between them.[75] However, he did not succeed in preventing the capture of this two-level ontological structure by demonology. Indeed, the ontological disconnection provided the perfect couple to theorize divine transubstantiation, which modified the substance without altering its accidents, but as a counterpoint, it also opened an unlimited field abandoned to the demons. Great illusionist and master of local motion, the Devil could seize the 'accidental' world while leaving – very orthodoxly – its substance unchanged.

Playing with the appearances of orthodox concepts and doctrines, in their own way, theologians and demonologists practised philosophical illusionism!

1.8 Towards a cultural and philosophic illusiography

During the thirteenth century, the encounter between magic and Aristotelianism – through William of Auvergne – induced a new way of thinking about magic *with* illusionism, transforming a performance art into an intellectual tool for critical thinking. Since then, interest in this popular art form has increased among medieval and Renaissance thinkers (R. Bacon, Oresme, Pacioli, Rabelais, Cardano, Della Porta, F. Bacon, Campanella etc.). The current confusion between magic and illusionism is still part of the centuries-old heritage of William's theories.

Illusionism was considered in the light of both its methods (sleight of hand, secret devices, natural property of things) and its effects (simulated magic). This double approach helped to set up a 'limiting demonology', leveraging the concepts of local motion and of illusion or *praestigium*. Illusion was first analysed in terms of Aristotelian perceptual theory. But, with the double (Aquinian and demonologic) subversion of the couple of substance and accident, illusion became one of the principal means of action used by the Devil.

A few years later, protestant thinkers (such as Calvin) would make use of the problems raised by the divided ontological structure to attack the reality of Eucharist, comparing priest to both a juggler and a sorcerer.[76] This polemic used would lead to the major refutation of witchcraft by illusionism operated by the Calvinist Reginald Scot in *The Discoverie of Witchcraft* (London, 1584), which set forth clearly, for the first time, the sleight-of-hand *principles* of the art of juggling,[77] still in use today.

Nowadays considered as mere entertainment for children, illusionism has nevertheless a long and complex history, linked – as we have seen – to the intellectual adventure of the Latin West. Since the Platonic *thaumatopoios* (wonderworkers, shadow puppeteers or jugglers) of the cave,[78] illusionism is both a mystifying and a critical tool that has been challenging philosophy, which in turn marginalized it. By its capacity to challenge the false evidence of the sensitive appearances and of the supernatural, illusionism has always maintained a deeply subversive power. Aristotelianism and illusionism face each other, on either side of (super)natural phenomena. From the construction to the deconstruction of perceptual reality, they question it each in their own way, complementarily.

Notes

1. Cf. Aristotle, *Metaphysics*, A 1, 980a21, trans. Joe Sachs (Santa Fe: Green Lion Press, 1999), 1.
2. Cf. Sarah Broadie, 'Aristotle's Perceptual Realism', *The Southern Journal of Philosophy* 31, no. S1 (1993): 137–59.

3   Rob Iliffe, 'Lying Wonders and Juggling Tricks: Nature and Imposture in Early Modern England', in *Everything Connects: In Conference with Richard H. Popkin*, eds James Force and David S. Katz (Leiden: Brill, 1998), 183–210; Philip Butterorth, *Magic on the Early English Stage* (Cambridge: Cambridge University Press, 2005); Michael Mangan, *Performing Dark Arts: A Cultural History of Conjuring* (Chicago: Intellect Books & The University of Chicago Press, 2007); Giuseppe Crimi, *Illusionismo e magia naturale nel cinquecento* (Rome: Aracne, 2011); Patrizia Castelli, 'I prestigiatori del male', *Accademia* 16 (2014): 27–47; Thibaut Maus de Rolley, 'Le diable à la foire: Jongleurs, bateleurs et prestigiateurs dans le discours démonologique à la Renaissance', in *Die Kunst der Täuschung*, ed. Kristin Dickhaut (Wiesbaden: Harrassowitz, 2016): 173–95; Thibaut Rioult, 'Illusion du surnaturel et illusionnistes à la Renaissance' (PhD diss., École Normale Supérieure, Paris, 2018); Robert Goulding, 'Illusion', in *The Routledge History of Medieval Magic*, eds S. Paige and C. Rider (London: Routledge, 2019): 312–30; Christa Agnes Tuczay, 'Medieval Magicians as Entertainers: Magic as Demonic Illusion or Stagecraft', in *Pleasure and Leisure in the Middle Ages and Early Modern Age*, ed. Albrecht Classen (Berlin: De Gruyter, 2019), 161–87; Thibaut Rioult, 'L'illusionnisme renaissant entre secrets et merveilles', *Arcana Naturae* 1 (2020): 51–69; Christophe Poncet, 'Le *Bateleur* du Tarot de Marseille à la lumière des écrits de Marsile Ficin', *Arcana Naturae* 1 (2020): 71–95.

4   From a social point of view, this theorization was also rooted in the crowded Paris, the biggest city of Europe, very attractive for entertainers of all kinds, including jugglers.

5   Cf. Noël Valois, *Guillaume d'Auvergne, évêque de Paris (1228–49): sa vie et ses ouvrages* (Paris: Alphonse Picard, 1880); Lynn Thorndike, *A History of Magic and Experimental Science*, vol. 2 (New York: Columbia University Press, 1923); Amato Masnovo, *Da Guglielmo d'Auvergne a S. Tommaso d'Aquino. Volume primo: Guglielmo d'Auvergne e l'ascesa verso Dio* (Milan: Vita e Pensiero, 1945); Steven P. Marrone, *William of Auvergne and Robert Grosseteste. New Ideas of Truth in the Early Thirteenth Century* (Princeton: Princeton University Press, 1983); Roger French and Andrew Cunningham, *Before Science: The Invention of the Friars' Natural Philosophy* (London and New York: Routledge, 1996): 160–8; Franco Morenzoni and Jean-Yves Tilliette ed., *Autour de Guillaume d'Auvergne († 1249)* (Turnhout: Brepols, 2005); Steven P. Marrone, *A History of Science, Magic & Belief* (London: Palgrave Macmillan, 2015); and the numerous studies and translations of R. J. Teske.

6   John of Salibury, *Policraticus*, I, 8 (Turnhout: Brepols, 1993); Antonella Sannino, 'La dottrina della causalità nell'universo di Guglielmo d'Alvernia', *Studi Filosofici* 27 (2004): 31–68; Antonella Sannino, '*Nigromantia secundum physicam, nigromantia imaginum*: arte e immagine in Guglielmo d'Alvernia', in *La magia naturale tra Medioevo e prima età moderna*, ed. Lorenzo Bianchi and Antonella

Sannino (Florence: Sismel, Edizioni del Galluzzo, 2018), 81–130; Antonella Sannino, *Reading William of Auvergne* (Florence: Sismel, Edizioni del Galluzzo, 2022).

7   Thomas of Chobham, *Summa Confessorum* (c. 1216), art. 6, dist. 4, q. II, ed. F. Broomfield (Louvain: Nauwalaerts, 1968), 292.

8   For a study on illusionism in the works of William of Auvergne, R. Bacon and N. Oresme, cf. T. Rioult, 'Penser l'illusionnisme au Moyen Âge: magie naturelle, bateleurs et savants (XIIe-XIVe siècles)', *Arcana Naturae* 2 (2021): 5–55. See also the elements provided by Béatrice Delaurenti, *La puissance des mots* virtus verborum*: Débats doctrinaux sur le pouvoir des incantations au Moyen Âge* (Paris: Les Editions du Cerf, 2007).

9   Cf. David Pingree, 'The Diffusion of Arabic Magical Texts in Western Europe', in *La diffusione delle scienze islamiche nel medio evo europeo* (Rome: Accademia Nazionale dei Lincei, 1987), 57–102. On magical texts attributed to Aristotle: Charles Burnett, 'Arabic, Greek and Latin Works on Astrological Magic attributed to Aristotle', in *Pseudo-Aristotle in the Middle Ages*, eds Jill Kraye, W. F. Ryan and Charles B. Schmitt (London: The Warburg Institute, 1986), 84–96; Donato Verardi, 'Francesco Storella e l'Aristotele negromante', *Bruniana & Campanelliana* 25, no. 2 (2019): 541–9.

10 *Chartularium Universitatis Parisiensis*, ed. Heinrich Denifle (Paris: Delalain, 1889, t. I), 70; Catherine König-Pralong, *Avènement de l'aristotélisme en terre chrétienne. L'essence et la matière: entre Thomas d'Aquin et Guillaume d'Ockham* (Paris: Vrin, 2005), 135.

11 Jacques Verger, 'Conclusion', in Morenzoni and Tilliette, *Autour de Guillaume . . .*, 372.

12 Marrone, *William of Auvergne*, 38.

13 Masnovo, *Da Guglielmo d'Auvergne*, 16 sq.

14 Roland J. Teske, 'William of Auvergne and the Manichees', *Traditio* 48 (1993): 63–75, especially 63.

15 French and Cunningham, *Before Science*, 166.

16 Marrone, *William of Auvergne*, 9.

17 Marie-Dominique Chenu, *La théologie au douzième au siècle* (Paris: Vrin, 1966), 19 sq.

18 William of Conches, *Philosophia mundi*, I, 23 (*Patrologia Latina*, vol. 172, col. 56): 'Quoniam ipsi nesciunt vires naturae, ut ignorantiae suae omnes socios habeant, nolunt eos aliquid inquirere, sed ut rusticos nos credere nec rationem quaerere. . . Nos autem dicimus, in omnibus rationem esse quaerendam . . .' (own trans.); quoted by Chenu, *La théologie au douzième au siècle*, 26.

19 Stephen Gaukroger, *The Emergence of a Scientific Culture – Science and the Shaping of Modernity 1210–1685* (Oxford: Clarendon Press, 2007), 47 (cf. chp. 'Augustinian Synthesis to Aristotelian Amalgam', 47–86).

20 Marrone, *William of Auvergne*, 38.
21 Teske, 'William of Auvergne and the Manichees', 66: 'William's account of Manichaeism is also incomplete insofar as he makes no mention of the many elements of the Manichaean myth, or of Manichaean ethics, Christology, or liturgy. [...] The Manichaeism that William sets out to refute is essentially the doctrine that there are two first principles, the one good and the other evil'.
22 French and Cunningham, *Before Science*, 160.
23 Thomas B. de Mayo, 'The Demonology of William of Auvergne' (PhD diss., University of Arizona, 2006), particularly chp. 5, 'Demonic Intent, Nature and Powers', 161–215.
24 Henry Corbin, *Avicenna and the Visionary Recital*, trans. Willard R. Trask (Princeton: Princeton University Press, 1990), chp. 'Latin Avicennism and Iranian Avicennism', 55.
25 Corbin, *Avicenna*, 71–2: 'From this point of view, will its individuality still result from the only individuation of which Matter is the principle, and which constitutes only numerically different individuals within the same species [following Averroes and Aristotle]? Or is there not rather to be conceived for it an individuation in conformity with the angelic condition, which postulates not only a numerical individuation within the same species, but an individuality specific in itself [following Avicenna]?' See also Christian Jambet, 'Introduction', in Shihâboddîn Yaḥya Sohravardî, *Le livre de la sagesse orientale: Kitâb Hikmat al-Ishrâq*, trans. Henry Corbin (Paris: Gallimard, 2003), 7–74, especially 25.
26 Corbin, *Avicenna*, 106.
27 William of Auvergne, *De universo*, I, chp. 31, in *Opera omnia* (Paris: Muguet, 1674), t. I, 805b–806a, trans. Corbin, *Avicenna*, 108.
28 Corbin, *Avicenna*, 101. See also, French and Cunningham, *Before Science*, 167.
29 D. Shayegan, *Henry Corbin: Penseur de l'islam spirituel* (Paris: Albin Michel, 2011), 66 (own trans. and emphasis).
30 Henry Corbin, *Mundus Imaginalis, or The Imaginary and the Imaginal* (Ipswich: Golgonooza Press, 1976).
31 Henry Corbin, *L'Iran et la philosophie* (Paris: Fayard, 1990), 178 (own trans.).
32 Jambet, 'Introduction', 28; cf. also Henry Corbin, *Temps cyclique et gnose ismaélienne* (Paris: Berg International, 1982), 50 and 63 sq.
33 See also, on another level, William's refutation of the plurality of worlds (French and Cunningham, *Before Science*, 165–6).
34 William of Auvergne, *De universo* (*Opera omnia*, I, 593–1074). The *De universo* was 'drawn perhaps from early writings of the 1220s but put into final form in the 1230s, with finishing touches as late as 1240', Marrone, *A History.*, 85.
35 On medieval witchcraft regulations (incl. the *Canon Episcopi*), cf., among others, Edward Peters, 'The Medieval Church and State on Superstition, Magic and Witchcraft: from Augustine to the Sixteenth Century', in *Witchcraft and Magic in*

Europe: *The Middle Ages*, eds Catharina Raudvere, Edward Peters, and Karen Louise Jolly (London: The Athlone Press, 2002), 173–245.

36 Cf. Mayo, 'The Demonology of William of Auvergne', 154–6.

37 Cf. Nicolas Weill-Parot, 'Astral Magic and Intellectual Changes (Twelfth-Fifteenth Centuries). "Astrological Images" and the Concept of "Addressative" Magic', in *The Metamorphosis of Magic From Late Antiquity to Early Modern Period*, eds Jan Bremmer and Jan R. Veenstra (Louvain: Peeters, 2002), 167–87; Nicolas Weill-Parot, *Les 'images astrologiques' au Moyen Âge et à la Renaissance. Spéculations intelectuelles et pratiques magiques (XIIe-XVe siècle)* (Paris: Honoré Champion, 2002), 37; Jean-Patrice Boudet, *Entre science et* nigromance: *Astrologie, divination et magie dans l'Occident médiéval (XIIe-XVe siècle)* (Paris: Éditions de la Sorbonne, 2006), 138.

38 Antonella Sannino, 'Guillaume d'Auvergne e i *libri experimentorum*', in *Expertus sum. L'expérience par les sens dans la philosophie naturelle médiévale*, eds Thomas Bénatouïl and Isabelle Draelants (Florence: Sismel, Edizioni del Galluzzo, 2011), 67–88; Sannino, 'Ermete mago e alchimista nelle biblioteche di Guglielmo d'Alvernia e Ruggero Bacone', *Studi medievali* 41, no. 1 (2000): 151–209.

39 Hugh of St Victor, *Didascalicon*, VI, 15, ed. Charles H. Buttimer (Washington: Catholic University Press, 1939), 132: 'Magica in philosophiam non recipitur, sed est extrinsecus falsa professione, omnis iniquitatis et malitie magistra, de vero mentiens, et veraciter ledens animos, seducit a religione divina, culturam demonum suadet, morum corruptionem ingerit, et ad omne scelus ac nefas mentes sequacium impellit'. (trans. Marrone, *A History*, 23). Hugh (ibid., 133) provide also a glimpse on the role of illusion: 'Prestigia sunt, quando, per phantasticas illusiones circa rerum immutationem, sensibus humanis arte demonia illuditur [. . .] Praestigia Mercurius dicitur primus invenisse'. On Hugh, see also Boudet, *Entre science et nigromance*, 210–12.

40 Cf. Amanda Power, *Roger Bacon and the Defence of Christendom* (Cambridge: Cambridge University Press, 2013), 112 sq.

41 On the theorization of magic during twelfth and thirteenth centuries, see Boudet, *Entre science et nigromance*, chap. III, 119–55. The evangelical link between *magus* and wise scholar could also be studied; see for eg. Alain de Lille (†c.1202), *Liber in distinctiones dictionum theologicalium* (in *Patrologia Latina*, vol. 210, col. 847): '*Magus* proprie, in arte magica peritus, ut magi magi Pharaonis. Dicitur aliquis sapiens magus, unde in Ævangelio: *Cum natus est Jesus*, etc., *ecce magi venerunt*. Sic dicuntur magi, non a magica arte, sed a majoritate scientiae'.

42 William of Auvergne, *De legibus*, chp. 24 (*Opera omnia*, I, 69b): 'Et de operibus huiusmodi est magia naturalis, quam necromantiam, seu philosophicam philosophi vocant, licet multum improprie, et est totius licentiae naturalis pars undecima. Haec igitur mirifica homines ignari scientiae istius, quae natura operabatur

virtutibus sibi a creatore inditis, credebant daemones operari, et propter hoc solum potentiam magnam, et mirificam eisdem attribuerunt: sed etiam omnipotentiam: et hoc in duplicem iniuriam creatoris'; J. P. Boudet (*Entre science et nigromance*, 128) corrected this text providing the reading of the oldest manuscript (Paris, BnF, lat. 15755, fol. 71vb, thirteenth century): 'Et de hujusmodi operibus est magica naturalis, quam nigromanciam secundum phisicam philosophi vocant, licet multum improprie, et est totius scientie naturalis pars undecimal'; trans. Mayo, 'The Demonology of William of Auvergne', 202, modified following Boudet's corrections.

43 Marrone, *A History*, 94–5.

44 William of Auvergne, *De universo*, II, pars III, chp. XXII (Paris, BnF, Latin 15756, 13th cent., fol. 222 rv°, and edited [*ed.*] version of the *Opera omnia*, I, 1059): '[*ed.*: Chp. XXII. De tribus generibus magicorum operum, & de mirificis virtutibus quarundam rerum.] Post haec veniam ad opera hujusmodi, quae opera magica, & ludificationes, vel hominum, vel daemonum nominantur [*ed.*: nuncupantur]. Dico igitur in primis, quia horum tria sunt genera: alia namque fiunt habilitate agilitateque [*ed.*: agilitate, habilitateque] manuum, sicut repositiones, & transpositiones quarundam rerum, & vocantur vulgariter traiectationes [*ed.*: tractationes uel trajectationes], & sunt magnae admirationis hominibus, donec innotescant modi quibus fiunt. Secundum genus est eorum, quae non habent, nisi apparentiam, & nichil [*ed.*: nihil] omninò veritatis, fiunt tamen subtractione, vel adhibitione quarumdam rerum'. (own trans.). I follow the oldest and trustworthy reading of the ms., which only presents '*traiectationes*' (see also the ms. Vatican, Biblioteca Apostolica Vaticana, Vaticanus latinus 848, fol. 344 r°). *Lectio difficilior potior*! The term '*tractationes*', of more recent use in *De universo* manuscripts, seems to be an alteration of oldest '*traiectationes*'. The couple '*tractationes uel trajectationes*', probably due to editor collation of two manuscript traditions, seemed to appear in the Venetian edition of Damian Zenaro (1591, 998).

45 William of Auvergne, *De virtutibus*, chp. 9 (*Opera omnia*, I, 118b–119a, collated with ms. Paris, BnF, latin 14531, fourteenth cent., fol. 15v°b) : 'Et in rebus mirabilibus, quibus magia [*ms.*: magica] naturalis utitur, invenies quasdam virtutes praecellere aliis, & longè eminentiores atque praestantiores esse virtutibus naturalibus, quae in eadem anima, vel eodem animali inveniuntur'; William of Auvergne, *On the Virtues, Part One of On the Virtues and Vices*, trans. Roland Teske (Milwaukee: Marquette University Press, 2009), 78: 'And in marvelous things, which natural magic uses, you will find certain powers surpass others and are far more eminent and excellent than the natural powers that are found in the same soul or in the same animal'.

46 Isidore of Seville, *Etymologiarum Libri XX*, lib. 8, chp. IX, ed. Fridericus V. Otto (B. G. Teubneri & F. Claudii, 1833): 'Praestigium vero Mercurius primus dicitur invenisse. Dictum autem praestigium, quod praestringat aciem oculorum'.

47 Cf. Roger Bacon, *Part of the Opus Tertium of Roger Bacon*, ed. Andrew G. Little (Aberdeen: University Press, 1912), 47–8: 'Et postquam opera demonum excludantur, tunc similiter oportet fraudes hominum excludi, quas magi faciunt infinitis modis, per velocitatem manualem, per instrumenta subtilia, per consensum, per tenebras, per figmenta varia, in carminibus, et caracteribus, et constellationibus quas fingunt, et quibus colorant sua dicta et facta. Et isti nichil faciunt secundum veritatem artis et nature, sed seducunt homines; et multotiens operantur demones propter peccata istorum magicorum, et aliorum qui credunt eis, licet isti magici, et illi qui eis adherent, nesciant quod demones operantur'.

48 Augustine, *De civitate Dei*, lib. XVIII, chp. 18, eds Bernhard Dombart and Alfons Kalb (Turnhout: Brepols, 1955): 'non mutatis hominibus factas, sed subtractis credo fuisse subpositas, sicut cerua pro Iphigenia, regis Agamemnonis filia. neque enim daemonibus iudicio dei permissis huiusmodi praestigiae difficiles esse potuerunt'; trans. Marcus Dods, *City of God*, vol. 2 (Edinburgh: Clark, 1871), 238.

49 Pierre Aubenque, *Le problème de l'être chez Aristote* (Paris: PUF, 1962), 420 sq.

50 I do not have the space to correctly establish this point (which would require a specific study), but – with more than thirty occurrences of '*motus localis*' and its declensions – 'local motion' is one of the main means of devil action in *Malleus Maleficarum*.

51 Cf. Anton Hauber, *Planetenkinderbilder und Sternbilder: zur Geschichte des menschlichen Glaubens und Irrens* (Strassburg: Heitz & Mündel, 1916); Dieter Blume, *Regenten des Himmels: Astrologische Bilder im Mittelalter und Renaissance* (Berlin: Akademie Verlag, 2000); Breanne Herrera, 'The Children of the Planets: Freedom Necessity, and the Impact of the Stars – The Iconographic Dimensions of a Pan-European Early Modern Discourse' (PhD diss., Central European University, Budapest, 2012).

52 Among others, cf. Leen Spruit, *Species Intelligibilis, from Perception to Knowledge. Volume one: Classical Roots and Medieval Discussions* (Leiden: Brill, 1994); Simo Knuuttila, 'Aristotle's Theory of Perception and Medieval Aristotelianism', in *Theories of Perception in Medieval and Early Modern Philosophy*, eds Simo Knuuttila and Pekka Kärkkäinen (Dordrecht: Springer, 2008), 1–22.

53 It is worth mentioning that William of Auvergne did not use the treatises of *perspectiva* and, more generally, that this matter was not teached in Paris during his time, as Roger Bacon testified in his *Opus tertium*, chp. XI, in *Opera quaedam hactenus inedita*, vol. 1, ed. John S. Brewer (London: Longman, 1859), 37: 'Haec scientia [=perspectiva] non est adhuc lecta Parisius, nec apud Latinos, nisi bis Oxoniae in Anglia'. On *perspectiva*, see David C. Lindberg, *Theories of Vision from Al-Kindi to Kepler* (Chicago and London: The University of Chicago Press, 1976) and Graziella Federici Vescovini, *Le teorie della luce e della visione ottica dal IX al*

XV secolo: studi sulla prospettiva medievale e altri saggi (Perugia: Morlacchi Editore, 2003).

54 The borders of the concept of *praestigium* were quite blurred during Middle Age, covering a large range of meanings from sleight of hand to demonic illusion. Without context, it's particularly difficult to attribute a precise meaning for this term. Isidore of Seville used it without reference to sleights of hand (cf. William E. Klingshirn, 'Isidore of Seville's Taxonomy of Magicians and Diviners', *Traditio* 58 (2003), 59–90), but some medieval Latin-Greek glossaries associated it with the '*psēphopaíktēs*', the Greek cups and balls (pebbles) performer; cf. Georg Goetz ed., *Hermeumata Pseudodositheana* (Leipzig: Teubner, 1892), 10, 84 and 172. On the question of ontological reality of illusions, see Maaike van der Lugt, 'Abominable mixtures: the "Liber Vaccae" in the medieval west, or the dangers and attractions of natural magic', *Traditio* 64 (2009): 229–77, especially 238. On the opposition between *praestigium* and juggler's illusion in Renaissance demonology, see Maus de Rolley, 'Le diable à la foire'.

55 William of Auvergne, *De virtutibus*, chp. 9 (*Opera omnia*, I, p. 120bF, collated with ms. Paris, BnF, latin 14531, fol. 17r°a): '[*ms.*: ℂ] idem est reperire [*ms.*: *om.* reperire] in omnibus aliis sensibus aegritudine, vel alia occasione [*ms.*: acc(asi)one] non impeditis. [*ms.*: ,] Quod dicimus propter prestigias [*ms.*: prestigia] magorum, & illusiones daemoniorum'; trans. *On the Virtues*, 84.

56 Edited by Robert Goulding, 'Deceiving the Senses in the Thirteenth Century: Trickery and Illusion in the *Secretum philosophorum*', in *Magic and the Classical Tradition*, eds Charles Burnett and William F. Ryan (London: Warburg Institute, 2006), 135–62.

57 *Secretum philosophorum*: 'intitulatur isto nomine quod in eo continentur quedam secreta que reputacione vulgari sunt impossibilia, apud philosophos secreta et necessaria'. Ed. and trans. Goulding, 135.

58 *Secretum philosophorum*: 'Dyalectica docet discernere verum a falso vel ab apparenci vero. Fecit enim deus in homine animam racionabilem et donavit eam quinque sensibus qui sunt gustus, et olfactus, auditus, visio, tactus, cum quibus una cum intelligencia posset homo discernere bonum a malo, verum a falso. Sed cum per istos sensus discernit homo verum a felso sive verum ab apparenci vero quod idem est, et cum multociens sensus decipitur circa proprium obiectum, ut patebit infra, ideo prius videamus qualiter sensus decipitur. Et hoc cognito statim cognoscetur qualiter possit discernere verum a falso, quod secundum Aristotelem cognito uno oppositorum cognoscitur et reliquum'. Ed. and trans. Goulding, 143 and 152, resp. (own underlining).

59 Aristotle, *De anima* II, 6 (418a11–15), trans. Guillelmus de Morbeka (*c.* 1267) (translatio 'noua' – Iacobi Venetici translationis recensio) [sec. Thomae *comm.*, lib. 2, chp. 13] (from *Aristoteles Latinus Database – online*, Brepols): 'Dico autem

proprium quidem quod non contingit altero sensu sentiri, et circa quod non contingit errare'. See also the slightly different Latin trans. in Averrois Cordubensis, *Commentarium Magnum in Aristotelis de Anima Libros*, ed. Francis S. Crawford (Cambridge: The Mediaeval Academy of America, 1953), 224. English trans. from the Greek by Robert D. Hicks (Cambridge: Cambridge University Press, 1907), 75: 'By a special object of a particular sense I mean that which cannot be perceived by any other sense and *in respect to which deception is impossible*'.

60 For example, Bonaventure (†1274), *In Secundum Librum Sententiarum*, dist. VIII, pars II, art. I, q. III, 'An daemones possint illudere sensus', contra 1: '*Sensus particularis non errat*, ut dicit Philosophus, *circa proprium obiectum*, ergo non percipit nisi quod verum est; sed delusio sensuum non potest esse sine errore et deception: ergo, etc.' In *Opera Omnia* (Quaracchi: Collegii Bonaventurae, 1885), t. II, 227 sq. See also Tiziana Suárez-Nani and Barabara Faes de Mottoni, 'I demoni e l'illusione dei sensi nel XIII secolo: Bonaventura e Tommaso d'Aquino', in *Jakobs Traum. Zur Bedeutung der Zwischenwelt in der Tradition des Platonismus*, ed. Hans – Jürgen Horn (St. Katharinen: Scripta Mercaturae Verlag, 2002), 77–94. See also: John Buridan, *Quaestiones super tres libros* De anima *Aristotelis*, lib. II, q. 11; Buridan, *Questions sur le traité* De l'âme *d'Aristote*, trans. Joel Biard (Paris: Vrin, 2019), 'Est-ce qu'un sens peut se tromper à propos de ce qui lui est propre?', 278 sq. For an example of fifteenth century reuse of this argument (supporting the *Canon Episcopi*), see also Joseph Hansen, *Quellen und Untersuchungen zur Gescichte des Hexenwahns* (Bonn: Carl Georgi, 1901), 112 sq. On Aristotle's conception of illusion, see. M. A. Johnstone, 'Aristotle and Alexander on Perceptual Error', *Phronesis* 60 (2015): 310–38.

61 Goulding, 'Deceiving the Senses in the Thirteenth Century', 136.

62 *Secretum philosophorum*, experimenta No. 1 and 3, 143–4, trans. 153–4.

63 Cf. Alain Boureau, *Satan hérétique: naissance de la démonologie dans l'Occident médiéval (1280-1330)* (Paris: Odile Jacob, 2004).

64 Cf. Hugh Trevor-Roper, 'The European Witch-Craze of the Sixteenth and Seventeenth Centuries' [1969], *The Crisis of the Seventeenth Century* (Indianapolis: Liberty Fund, 1999), 83–177, especially 121–2; Richard Kieckhefer, *European Witch Trials: Their Foundations in Popular and Learned Culture, 1300-1500* (London and Henley: Routledge & Kegan Paul, 1976, reprint London, New York: Routledge, 2011), 79–80; Stuart Clark, *Thinking with Demons: The Idea of Witchcraft in Early Modern Europe* (New York: Oxford University Press, 1997), 235. On the influence of the Aristotelico-Thomistic anthropology and demonology on the structuration of witchcraft concept, see also Alain Boureau, 'Le sabbat et la question scolastique de la personne', in *Le sabbat des sorciers (XVe-XVIIIe siècles)*, eds Nicole Jacques-Chaquin and Maxime Préaud (Grenoble: Jérôme Millon, 1993), 33–46; Christine Pigné, 'Du *De malo* au *Malleus Maleficarum*', *Cahiers de recherches médiévales* 13 (2006): 195–220.

65 I use the first Latin edition: Jacob Sprenger [and Heinrich Institoris], *Malleus Maleficarum*, [Speyer, Peter Drach, 1486 or 1487], incipit: 'Appologia auctoris in malleus maleficarum' (Paris, Bibliothèque Mazarine, inc. 1282); trans. Christopher S. Mackay, *The Hammer of Witches: a Complete Translation of the Malleus Maleficarum* (Cambridge: Cambridge University Press, 2009).
66 Cf. Sprenger and Institoris, *The Hammer of Witches*, 170 n. 530, 210 (citing *De universo*, 2.3.13), 294 and 463 etc.
67 Ibid., I, q. 9; Lat. fol. 29rv; Eng. pages 197–9, own underlining, trans. mod.
68 Martine Ostorero, *Le diable au sabbat. Littérature démonologique et sorcellerie (1440-1460)* (Florence: Sismel, Edizioni del Galluzzo, 2011), 567: 'Ce texte est la pierre d'achoppement de tous les théoriciens de la sorcellerie au XVe siècle'. (Own trans.).
69 Ibid., II, q. 1, chp. 8; Lat. fol. 60r: 'Dicas quod est duplex transmutatio, substantialis et accidentalis. [. . .] de primis loquitur canon'; Eng. p. 331, transl. mod.
70 Pascaline Turpin, 'Querelle eucharistique et épaisseur du sensible: Bérenger et Lanfranc', *Revue des sciences philosophiques et théologiques* 95, no. 2 (2011): 303–22.
71 Ibid., 319.
72 König-Pralong, *Avènement de l'aristotélisme en terre chrétienne*, 127 (own trans.).
73 Cf. David Roderick McPike, 'Thomas Aquinas on the Separability of Accidents and Dietrich of Freiberg's Critique' (PhD diss., University of Ottawa, 2015).
74 König-Pralong, *Avènement de l'aristotélisme en terre chrétienne*, 146 (own trans.).
75 Thomas Aquinas, *Summa theologiae*, part. III, q. 76, art. 8: 'Nec hoc tamen pertinet ad aliquam deceptionem, sicut accidit in magorum præstigiis; quia talis species divinitùs formatur in oculo, ad aliquam veritatem figurandam, ad hoc scilicet quod manifestetur verè corpus Christi esse sub hoc sacramento, sicut etiam Christus absque deceptione apparuit discipulis euntibus in Emmaus'.
76 Cf. Rioult, *Illusion du surnaturel*, 241-4; AnnMarie M. Bridges, ''In the Flesh a Mirror of Spiritual Blessings': Calvin's Defence of the Lord's Supper as a Visual Accomodation', in *Quid est sacramentum? Visual Representation of Sacred Mysteries in Early Modern Europe, 1400-1700*, eds Walter Melion, Elizabeth C. Pastan, Lee P. Wandel (Leiden and Boston: Brill, 2019), 105–24, especially 110–12.
77 Cf. Rioult, *Illusion du surnaturel*, 318-28; Thibaut Rioult, 'Reginald Scot's *The Discoverie of Witchcraft* (1584)', in *Magic: A Companion*, ed. Katharina Rein (Oxford: Peter Lang Publishing, 2022), 33–44.
78 Plato, *Republic*, 514b.

2

The roles of *experimentum* and the *vis imaginativa* in medieval and early modern magic

Peter G. Maxwell-Stuart

2.1 Introduction

During the Middle Ages, theologians and natural philosophers developed a systematic way of looking at phenomena emanating from a series of interconnected physical and spiritual worlds which they and a host of non-human entities inhabited. This approach is well summarized by the Jesuit, Martin Del Rio (1551–1608), in his encyclopaedic *Disquisitiones Magicae*, first published in three volumes in 1599–1600 and subsequently revised and expanded until his death in 1608. Magic, he said, is 'a technique or method which, by means of natural, not supernatural, power effects a number of extraordinary and unusual things'.[1] This generality he further divided into three types which he called 'natural', 'instrumental' and 'diabolic' and subdivided these yet again to cover a wide range of operational intentions and practices from simple superstition to elaborate ritual attempts to achieve direct contact with God or evil spirits through what we might call out-of-body experiences or entry into states of elevated consciousness. Heinrich Cornelius Agrippa (1486–1535) began his *Three Books of Occult Philosophy* with a proposition, differently worded but similar in intention, which makes this clear. Agrippa writes:

> Since the world is threefold – elemental, celestial, and intellectual – and each inferior [part] is governed by one which is superior and receives [from it] an influx of its powers in such a way that the Archetype and supreme Creator Himself pours down His powers from them upon us via angels, the heavens, the elements, animals, plants, metals, and stones [. . .] magicians think, not

unreasonably, that it is possible for us to ascend, via those same steps, through each one of those worlds to the supreme Archetype Himself.[2]

Del Rio's 'Natural magic' related to the created universe and was regarded as potentially legitimate, in as much as it sought a greater understanding or appreciation of the mind of God by the endeavour to comprehend the workings of or reasons for natural phenomena. This endeavour, however, should not be misunderstood as stemming from any kind of proto-scientific frame of mind. According to Del Rio, created things, which included everything from invisible spirits and worlds to stones, trees and humankind itself, existed side by side and interrelated with spirit entities and states of being and could not be separated from them. A sixteenth-century physician, Abraham Yagel, once defined Nature as 'the divine will and judgment', which encapsulates the outlook well.[3] Investigation of the natural world therefore involved the investigator in that highly complex set of interrelationships which, in their turn, informed the aims of the investigation and were bound to affect its progress and, ultimately, its outcome. Consequently, *curiositas* or 'inquisitiveness' was not an unalloyed virtue, but as an activity to be regarded with a degree of suspicion since it could so easily be what St Augustine called 'a lust of the eyes' and 'the *disease* of curiosity' which wants to know simply for the sake of knowing.[4] Knowledge (*scientia*) was the result of someone's having skill or expertise in some activity or sphere and therefore a degree of understanding of it. Hence, the irrefragable relationship, for example, between astronomy, the study of the customary laws which govern the movements of the stars and their positions relative to each other and humankind upon the earth, and astrology, an explanation of those movements and relative positions as comprising a divine utterance. Both branches of inquiry appeal, etymologically and psychologically, to custom and precedent. Hence Isidore of Seville's definition of knowledge. 'To know (*scire*) gets its name from to learn (*discere*), because none of us knows unless he has learned.'[5]

From whom or from what did one learn? Books of 'secrets' were many and formed an important resource for those who wanted to explore the hidden sides of Nature, and no one, perhaps, was more significant than Aristotle who had a good many books foisted upon him during the Middle Ages, of which the *Secretum secretorum* was one. It is a compilation, addressed to Alexander the Great, of astrological, medical, gemmological, herbal and other practical observations on the hidden powers of natural objects, along with passages on alchemy, divination, poisons and magic, and there are more than 207 manuscript copies of it, and it was translated into several languages, including Persian,

Hebrew and Castilian, as well as Latin – an indication not only of its popularity but also of its potential influence. It was cited by such luminaries as Albertus Magnus and Roger Bacon, and Bacon appears to have been confirmed in many of his own pre-existing ideas after reading it. So, to that extent, if no more, it can be said to have encouraged his spirit of cautious inquiry into Nature. One notes, however, the importance of Aristotle's name which lent the compilation authority and apparent integrity.[6]

This appeal to established authority and to what has been established authoritatively informed, as is well known, the approach to all forms and branches of knowledge. So how did magic which, by definition and practice, sought to bring about change, fit into this intellectual schema? If it is reliant on past knowledge and practice, how can it investigate the world (whether there be one, three or more of them) with any expectation of finding or doing, let alone creating, anything new? It could be objected, therefore (as Maimonides, for example, appears to have done),[7] that magic does not subscribe to the laws of natural causality, but to the vagaries of chance, since magicians cannot compel their effects. Neither God nor His spiritual creations can be forced to comply with a human's spoken formulae or gestures or use of physical objects, and the compliance of angels and spirits with the magician's intentions depends entirely on their own willingness to co-operate or on their obedience to their superiors in the hierarchy of creation. Consequently Nature (i.e. the way created things are constituted and ordered, and the manner in which they behave consistently with and contingently upon their innate inclination and temperament) could not be regarded as subject to immutable laws, but rather to prescribed patterns (*regulae*) which might be modified or even radically changed by outside inclinations, tendencies or intentions.[8]

Magic, however, is not a body of knowledge in the same sense as, say, theology or astronomy is. Magic is an *ars*, a technique and a set of related techniques, in much the same way as carpentry is, or sculpting, or painting, although it differs from them in as much as the magician does not depend on innate talent (as well as practised skill) to achieve a successful outcome to his plied craft. Occasionally, however, the notion of an innate or God-given ability for or inclination to magic found expression. Aphorism 17 of the grimoire *Arbatel*, published in 1575, says that a person who is intended to be (*debet esse*) a genuine magician is guided (*producitur*) towards magic from his mother's womb and that anyone else who puts himself forward for this public duty (*officium*) is unsuccessful. This, it must be said, is little more than special pleading and implies that some people have a natural gift for or strong inclination towards magic in the same kind of way that a mathematician or a linguist or a musician has a particular talent which others who lack that gift will fail to emulate successfully. Everyone can pick out a simple tune on a piano, but few become concert pianists. Similarly, Giambattista Della Porta (1535–1615) says that there are some people who are so adept at these things (the skills necessary for successful practice of magic), because of a grace from Heaven (*coeli munere*), that they seem to have been fashioned by God. In other words, they have a highly developed talent and Della Porta emphasizes what he means by this in saying that a magician is 'by a gift of Nature, a workman (*artifex*) and good with his hands (*mechanicus*)'.[9] The idea that magicians are born, not made, however, is a minority view and not one supported by the Church, for example, which argued that human proclivity to sin offered a gateway to Satan whereby he could manipulate human weakness, such as curiosity, and subvert natural talent to fulfil his own pernicious ends. From the lofty ideal of seeking to understand the mind of God to the simple gesture and word of an individual who wanted to cure an illness, find buried treasure or harm his or her neighbour, magic, then, consisted of a set of techniques which depended on the co-operation of forces and powers beyond human to make it work, although that co-operation was unreliable and the dependence on it fraught with potential danger to the magician. This, of course, applies to all forms of magic: 'natural' (which will be the main focus of our discussion here), 'ritual' and 'diabolic'.[10]

2.2 Experimenta, secreta and scientia experimentalis

When we talk about medieval and early modern *experimenta*, we are discussing something different from modern understanding and usage of the words, 'experiment' and 'experimental'. *Experimentum* is derived from the verb *experior* which appears to imply that one is passing through a circumstance or set of circumstances and emerging from them.[11] Hence, *experimentum* essentially refers either to something – a circumstance or 'experience' – which has already happened and thus establishes a piece of knowledge based on that past event, thereby making that knowledge credible because the past is an authoritative source of dependable information. *Experimenta* are thus records of knowledge already gained and established, not attempts to establish knowledge by trial and error.[12]

Experimenta therefore relate more closely to *peritia* (practical knowledge or skill) than to *scientia*, which William Eamon calls 'demonstrable, causal knowledge', and refer, in the words of Michael McVaugh, 'not to an event planned to illustrate the rational order of Nature, but to an event lying outside that rational order'.[13] Hence, when Pliny said that physicians 'discunt periculis nostris et experimenta per mortes agunt', he did not mean that doctors conduct experiments upon their patients, but that 'they learn from the dangers they put us in and gain their experience through the deaths [they cause]' (*Naturalis Historia* 29.8.18). *Scientia* was thus a knowledge demonstrable by argument based on rational appeal to precedent, while *peritia*, of which *experientia* provided individual examples (*experimenta*), was knowledge derived from an accumulation of remembered observation.[14] In a sense, then, these two represent one of the differences between theoretical and practical knowledge, another being that *scientia* slowly came to belong to a realm of thought which, partly because of its reliance on formal precedent and authority, stood in danger of ossification, while *peritia* was and could be more fluid in its prescriptions. Its *experientia* was inevitably more individualistic since the observations upon which it rested were less easy to absorb into a pre-existing system of rational argument based upon long-established 'fact' (in the Latin sense of 'things having been done in the past' and therefore, by implication, now fixed and determined).

There is, however, an inherent ambiguity in *experientia*, partly because *experientia* expresses the personal and the immediate and partly because that immediacy can quickly pass into established past. Bernardus Silvestris (died 1178) illustrates this fluidity in his 'omne quod experitur sit experiendum', which may be translated, 'everything one experiences should be put to the test' (which is, or appears to be, more in accord with modern understanding of *experimentum* as 'experimentation'), or 'everything one puts to the test should be tried against experience', which is more likely to be what Bernardus intended.[15] Hence, *experimenta* are examples of knowledge whose validity and reliability are guaranteed by the personal experience of the individual recording them, or the records of such personal experience transmitted by those who have not necessarily observed or tried out their content for themselves. Either way, what is recorded is the particular case or instance rather than a generality, even if it is assumed, tacitly or otherwise, that the particular instance holds good in more than one case.[16] As Frank Klaassen points out, too, 'a text had to accord with [magical operators'] ideas about what magical and/or religious rites should look like, and if its rituals produced any subjectively convincing experiences, these too could affect how the text was understood or treated'.[17] It means, too, that *experimenta* were not undertaken to uncover new knowledge, but to confirm what was already known and well established.

The personal nature of the observation or experience, whether they were direct or not, also meant that these records were frequently known as *secreta* as well as *experimenta*. 'Secretum' means something separated or dissociated from other things and in consequence (via the notion of its being remote and solitary), private, hidden, rare and secret – and therefore possibly, too, something arising from or connected with magic. The word 'private' is important here. *Libri experimentorum* and *libri secretorum*, which abounded during the Middle Ages and early modern period, thus take their origin from the private papers of individuals putting certain of their personal experiences or observations on paper, or copying out those of others, which slowly accrued the authority of repetition and age. Thus, a *Secreta Secretorum* (attributed to Aristotle to give it greater authority) incorporates, among much that is not particularly secret since it merely summarizes the desiderata of a good ruler, the rules of physiognomy, instructions for the preservation of good health and a defence of the use of talismans, and provides a list of the 'secret' (i.e. hidden and magical) properties of certain herbs and stones. Likewise, the *Experimenta Alberti* [*Magni*], which can be dated to the late thirteenth or early fourteenth century, contains a mixture of the banal and the unusual, its secrets being those of the remarkable powers possessed by certain plants, stones and animal parts.[18] This is a pattern which is replicated by other and succeeding collections of *experimenta* or *secreta*. They had burgeoned during the twelfth century and Guillaume d'Auvergne (1190–1249), for example, was conversant with them. But he appears to differentiate between *libri experimentorum*, which he clearly associates with magic, and *libri naturalium narrationum*, 'books which give accounts of things in Nature' (*De universo* 2.3.22), a differentiation consistent with his view of natural magic as a whole which he sees as consisting of conjuring tricks and manufactured illusions, inexplicable phenomena arising from the secret properties inherent in Nature and natural objects, while diabolic magic depends on the actions of evil spirits exploiting those properties for nefarious purposes. It is therefore interesting to note that when talking about 'wonders' in India and the adjoining regions, he chooses to use the word *experimentores* to describe their practitioners (*De universo* 2.3.23).[19]

The link between magic and 'books which give accounts of things in Nature' was always strong. Scholars such as Michael Scot, court astrologer to the Holy Roman Emperor, Frederick II, translated works from both Arabic and Greek, thereby continuing the activities of earlier translators in Toledo, and while much of what Scot did involve works of astrology, it also included Aristotle's *Historia Animalium* and Avicenna on the same subject, and his position at the Imperial

Court, along with the patronage he enjoyed therefrom, meant that not only his versions of key texts of *secreta* but others, too, achieved increased circulation. Nor was it only the Imperial Court which served as a centre of transmission. The Papal Court, too, and the royal court of Alfonso X of Castile, ensured a similar success, as texts made their way thence to southern France, northern Italy, Brabant, and Central and Eastern Europe, mainly via the libraries of some of the larger monastic houses.[20] But the theoretical possibilities of contemplating the details of God's creation might easily slip from the realm of theory into that of practice, and it is clear that one questions – 'How does this work?' – could quickly become – 'How can I make this work to my advantage?' or, indeed, to someone else's disadvantage. This slippage can be seen in the *Sworn Book of Honorius* – not, to be sure, a *liber experimentorum* or *secretorum* so much as a grimoire – but, moving as it does from instructions on how to manufacture a seal which will enable the operator to obtain a vision of God, through other seals which grant a vision of angels, then enable him to constrain angels to his will, and finally to get a similar command of evil spirits, it illustrates well the potential glide from legitimate inquiry and practice to illegitimate.[21]

There is, however, a tacit acknowledgement in a number of these books that some marvels are no more than trickery. The *Secretum philosophorum*, for example, includes with its explanations of prestidigitation and illusion variants upon a pseudo-alchemical operation intended to make copper look like silver: 'certain kinds of tampering which are called entertainments'.[22] The 'secrecy' of these works was considered to be desirable for a mixture of reasons. Concealing the actual authorship under the adoption of a famous but long-dead scholar had the practical aim of protecting the author from possible prosecution, as well as clothing him, if anonymously, in the glamour of someone else's fame. On the other hand, the secrecy of the secrets was actually apparent rather than real, because the whole point of their disclosure of them was revelation, not concealment, one of its aims being to inform readers about the trickery often involved in many of the marvels so that they would not be tempted or misled into thinking that magic, rather than sleight of hand or illusion, was involved. Another important aim was to demonstrate the complexity of God's creation and so increase wonder at His omnipotence while, balanced somewhat uneasily between these two ends of the intentional spectrum, there were the motives of alchemists who hoped to equal or even improve on Nature, physicians who wished to make medicine more effective in combatting or curing disease, and magicians with grandiose notions about uniting Heaven and earth in a kind of re-creation of Eden before the Fall.[23]

By the time one reaches the sixteenth century, however, one notices some signs of change in the nature of *libri experimentorum* in some quarters. A *liber secretorum*, such as that of Catherine Tollemache, for example, is reminiscent of the pseudo-Aristotelian *Secreta*, in as much as it contains practical advice on gardening and lace making, alongside charms to get rid of warts or to make oneself invisible, while another from the mid-century (Folger manuscript V.b.26) is much more clearly a grimoire, its *experimenta* being instructions for the practice of ritual magic to achieve invisibility, to compel a thief to return stolen goods in person, to know everything past, present and future, to conjure a spirit, to enchant hazel rods so that they will indicate the spot where treasure is buried, to see whatever you wish in sleep, and so forth.[24] It is the use of the word 'experiment' to describe these, as opposed to all the other sets of instructions not so designated, that is interesting. The same apparent distinction can be found in the Antiphoner notebook whose first entry is labelled 'experimentum probatum', while the rest of the entries are either 'prayer' or 'charm' or 'for' (as in 'for fevers', 'for toothache' and so on).[25] John Dee's 'experimenta in speculo', unlike those of Leonardo da Vinci, were not wholly concerned with investigating optics and optical behaviour but were closely related to angelic magic and his scrying sessions with Barnabas Saul, Bartholomew Hickman, Arthur Dee and Edward Kelley.[26]

It is with this in mind, therefore, that we should read and interpret his remarks in his *Mathematical Preface to Euclid*. 'This Arte' (i.e. 'archemastrie', the pinnacle of the hierarchy of mathematical techniques which precede it)

> teacheth to bring to actuall experience sensible, all worthy conclusions by all the Artes Mathematicall purposed, & by true Naturall Philosophie concluded [. . .] And bycause it procedeth by *Experiences*, and searcheth forth the causes of Conclusions, by Experiences: and also putteth the Conclusions them selues in Experiences, it is named of some, *Scientia Experimentalis*.[27]

Now this has sometimes been taken as an indication that Dee was thinking in terms of testing hypotheses, which is how the phrase 'scientia experimentalis' might begin to suggest to a modern ear but, as György Szőnyi points out,[28] the 'sciences' outlined in the passage of the *Mathematical Preface* which leads to archemastrie are magical rather than 'experimental' or 'scientific' in any modern sense. Dee's *experimenta* were part of the record of his attempts to scale (like Faustus), the heights of Heaven with a view to achieving a greater understanding of God's marvels – the *virtutes*, *mirabilia* and *secreta* of the treatises attributed to Albertus Magnus, works which cannot, or should not, be taken as other than works treating of natural magic in the medieval sense.²⁹ Johannes Trithemius (1462–1516), abbot, first of Sponheim, then of the Schottenkloster in Würzburg and a voluminous writer on historical and devotional themes, but better known these days for his works on magic and cryptography, like Dee (in the words of Håkan Håkansson), 'viewed practical and subjective magic as two sides of the same coin', and it is that word 'subjective' which is particularly important to remember when faced by terms such as *experimentum* or *scientia experimentalis*.³⁰

Reliance upon personal observation could, of course, it was feared, lead to chaos or a blind alley if it was found to produce conflict between established *scientia* and the results of mere individual curiosity, with emphasis upon the superior validity of the latter over the former. Thomas Moffett (1553–1604), an English physician and natural philosopher, issued a pertinent admonition on this point. 'How foolishly and vainly man's wisdom doth many times vaunt itself [. . .] if not founded upon right Reason, the mistress of all Arts and Sciences.' Investigation of the natural world, he warned, could not always lead to greater understanding of it and, in the end, some of God's wonders could only be marvelled at and bear witness to the unbridgeable distance between His power and human limitation.³¹ Something of the blind alley can be seen from the notebooks of Clement Draper, arrested in 1581 and imprisoned for the next thirteen years. Deborah Harkness has described the way in which he used those notebooks to distil his voracious reading and record his own forays into alchemy and his thoughts about how practices and previous attempts to achieve a particular result might be improved in various ways. But she also issues a caveat that this was not the same as 'modern' experimentation. She writes: 'Draper's notebooks were designed, not to yield a specific output, but to perpetuate an ongoing study of Nature. His method of circulating and digesting experimental knowledge was therefore destined to serve only his interests and those of his community.'³² (Again, one has to beware of the word 'experimental' here. It means 'gained from or by experience, whether one's own or someone else's'.).

So how did the words *experimentum* and *experimentalis* come to metamorphose into their present accepted sense? The reservations expressed by the Church over too inquisitive a desire to plumb the depths of God's mind gradually lost their power to restrain *experimentores* and scholars alike from yielding to the allure of *curiositas*. The change was, in fact, inherent in the magic to which *experimenta* were closely allied, since magic not only dazzled with its picture of a creation teeming with wonders and secrets but constantly held out the possibility of human beings' finding out how to master the powers such wonders, and secrets held – the temptation of Faust throughout the ages.³³ Books containing details of those secrets and suggestions for their further exploration and exploitation were not only desirable; with the growth of printing, they became increasingly obtainable, and this had the effect, first of making their contents appear to be authoritative and approved, rather than simply records of individual and experience; second, of blurring the distinction between someone else's experience (direct or indirect) and the reader's own, because print suggested, in a way handwriting did not, that the information such books contained was universally true; and third, their publication also started to break down the separation between theory and practice – that is, between *scientia* and *peritia*, and hence between *scientia* and *ars*, an amalgamation which, in its turn, tacitly gave preference to the value of *ars/peritia* over *scientia* in its older sense.³⁴

This, it is worth noting, runs quite counter to what Francis Bacon (1561–1626) had in mind when he envisaged an exclusive role for the intellectual as opposed to the working practitioner. 'In the case of the very large number of *experimenta* carried out by manual workers [*mechanicorum*]', he wrote in his *Novum Organum*,

> the importance of those which [the workers] do most successfully and in which they take most pleasure, is revealed by their lack of importance. The uneducated manual worker is not bothered about investigating the truth at all and does not pay attention to or approve of anything except things which are of use to the task in hand. But there will be good ground for the hope of making further progress in the various branches of knowledge [*scientiarum*] when a good many *experimenta* are accepted and added to the investigation of Nature [*historiam naturalem*] – *experimenta* which are useless in themselves and merely serve to discover causes and make self-evident principles out of them. These [*experimenta*] I have been in the habit of calling 'shedders of light' [*luctifera*] to differentiate them from those which have practical outcomes [*fructifera*].³⁵

This clearly sounds very much like knowledge for the sake of knowledge, and although it cannot, in the light of the general thrust of Bacon's philosophy, be said that this is what he was proposing, it does show how far removed his ideas were from the majority of those who had discussed the relationship between theoretical and practical knowledge and had taken it for granted that their discussion would be firmly anchored in the deep waters of magic. Del Rio, whom we met earlier, makes this perfectly clear in his discussion of ancient and medieval automata. 'If one is told about some effect which goes beyond what natural causes are capable of doing', he says, 'one should class it as an unnatural event, *even though human ingenuity has been used to make the apparatus and cause it to move*.'[36]

2.3 The *Vis Imaginativa*

Del Rio also draws attention to an important aspect of magical working (i.e. the operation of magic by an individual or a group of individuals), namely, the power of the imagination to effect a change in a person or object at some kind of distance. 'It is quite likely', he says, 'that the imagination can, by chance, have an effect on a nearby object (provided they are very close together and the one is in physical contact with the other), if the imagination is strongly focussed upon it and the neighbouring object has a strong affinity with it'.[37] Agrippa generalizes that every human being has a powerful imagination which knows no bounds. 'This power', he says, 'exists in every human being from birth, but its strength and weakness differ in different people and is increased and diminished in accordance with how much it is exercised and used, and through [exercise and use] it is released from potentiality into action'.[38]

Here, again, however, it is important to be clear about what was understood by the words *imago* and *imaginatio*. An *imago* is an exact copy or likeness. When the word was used to refer to a picture, a bust or a statue, one has to remember that busts and statues were painted and therefore the 'image' was seen in colour. Therefore, when the word was used of a ghost or an apparition, the image was, again, seen in colour, not white, or grey or black, suggesting the vividness of a living person or object. Hence, an exact replica seen by the inner eye was seen in much the same way as an image seen by the eye of the body.[39] *Imaginatio* refers primarily to such a mental image and then to the faculty which produces, transmits and stores it. Pseudo-Augustine described it further as 'that power of the soul which perceives the physical form of physical objects which, however, are not present to it. Sensation perceives things in material form, imagination in immaterial form'. He then described its role in an intellectual process. 'When the sense [of sight] perceives something, the imagination turns it into a picture, deliberation [*cogitatio*] gives it shape, innate intelligence [*ingenium*] considers it carefully, judgement [*ratio*] comes to a conclusion, memory keeps this safe, discernment [*intellectus*] looks at each part of it separately and understanding [*intelligentia*] takes hold of it and draws it towards meditation or contemplation.'[40]

This 'imagination' had a seat in the brain, located, according to Avicenna, at the back of the front ventricle, and when an individual was awake, information was transmitted to the 'imagination' from the 'common sense' (*sensus communis*, i.e. the seat of cognition, sensation and voluntary motion, which receives data, processes them and then issues commands to the appropriate physical organs).[41] Hence, perhaps, the difference between *imaginatio* and the borrowed Greek *phantasia*, the former referring to the faculty in its active role, the latter to its passive or receptive function. In either case, however, there is a distinct emphasis on sight. Gómez Pereira (1500–67), a physician and natural philosopher, said that imagination was a faculty

> which has been entrusted with the task of putting together and separating, just as it pleases, things which have once been perceived sensorily, and of recognising them', and he adds, 'one can certainly not say [...] that [...] it is allowed to perceive a universal without looking at a mental image, since everyone understands this is a prerequisite.[42]

Exact copies of persons, objects or events belonging to the exterior world or having the appearance of so belonging thus entered a person's head as a result of his looking at them and/or remembering them, or because they had been put there by external forces such as evil spirits. Image-making and receiving was a crucial component, not only of magical thinking but of ancient, medieval and early modern understanding of the process of perception, which is why Del Rio explains the role of evil spirits' manipulation of the 'imagination' in terms of various kinds of visual trickery: (I) changing the way someone looks at an object, (II) changing the angle at which he or she looks at it, (III) fashioning an illusory object out of the elements, especially air, (IV) modifying the actual outward appearance of an object so that it looks like something else and (V) preventing someone from seeing the object (*Disquisitiones Magicae* Book 2, question 8).[43]

But was the imagination merely a passive recipient of visual impressions, whether these were genuine or not? The phenomenon of the evil eye (*fascinatio*) suggests otherwise. Symphorien Champier (1471–1539), a medical doctor, as was Gómez Pereira, was willing to provide an explanation of how it worked, although the explanation he offers is not his, but that of Marsilio Ficino. He writes:

> The eye opens, turns its attention upon someone, and hurls barbs contained in its rays into the eyes of the person opposite and, alongside the barbs, (which are the vehicles of its spirits), it introduces an exhalation to which we give the name 'sanguinary'. This violent barb slices open the eyes and, because it is being spurred on from the striker's heart, once it has struck [its target], it keeps on striking his midriff – the area which, so to speak, belongs to it.[44]

Nicole Oresme said something similar but drew attention to the imagination:

> If there is some elderly woman who, because of the wickedness which forms part of the way her brain is constituted, is jealous of a small child, or is disposed to make its very tender flesh shrivel up and waste away, it is possible she may create a [mental] image of the child in front of her and create a picture of what she wants so vividly and in such a distorted way without consciously knowing how she is doing it, that her own eyes will become infected because of this and produce some kind of maleficent property which will infect the child, (which has no resistance and is susceptible to an assault of this kind coming to it from outside), when she looks at it.[45]

Del Rio, too, preferred to explain the phenomenon in terms of contagious disease. Natural philosophers and theologians, he says, agree

> that alteration [in someone else] is effected by some poisonous property lodged in the decayed humours or the vicious temperament of the person who is doing the looking, and that this property is communicated by the vital spirits which are aroused by a rather passionate imagination and a somewhat strained concentration of the mind, and that once they have been roused they look for a way of reaching the eyes. As these [vital] spirits flow forth from the eyes – not just the sight, but the roused spirits bursting out along with the sight – they infect the air nearest to them with a damaging venom. This part of the air infects another, and in this way [the infection] arrives at the part of the air nearest the person who is to be infected. . . . . . This proximate air then insinuates itself into the eyes of the person to be harmed and from his or her eyes . . . it thrusts itself inside the body. (*Disquisitiones Magicae* Book 3, part 1, question 4, section 1)[46]

Temperamental and external factors, as well as health, however, might account for an active *vis imaginativa* which not only had the capacity to do harm but also to reach into the future via pictures presently in the imaginative faculty – a capacity known as 'second sight' or 'two sights' in Gaelic. An explanation of the ability is offered in ΔΕΥΤΕΡΟΣΚΟΠΙΑ by John Fraser, a Scottish minister, published in 1707:

> First, to enquire how much of this may come from a natural constitution and temperament, when confounded with a flatuous or Melancholick Distemper: and what influence an External Agent, namely an Angel, good or bad, may have upon the Organ of the Eye, and the fancy; and how far the *Medium* between the Organ of the Eye and an object visible may be disposed for their purpose, namely the Air and Light: And what Connection may be found betwixt the Representations made to the Eye or Fancy, and the future contingent Events, that

experience teaches do follow thereupon: as for example, A Man is seen Bleeding, or sew'd up in his winding sheets, who is shortly to be wounded, or assuredly to die.[47]

Al-Kindī (801–73) offered an explanation of how this *vis imaginativa* works. Everything in this elemental world, he said, emits elemental rays and these act upon other elemental rays which re-act, in their turn, upon the rays they receive, a reciprocity upon which any kind of magical action depends for its efficaciousness and the rays emitted by physical objects, after interacting with those emitted by the imagination, are affected, modified or changed in accordance with their nature and the circumambient circumstances and this, of course, is why the intention lying behind the use of words and gestures in magic affects the nature and performance of the rays and brings about alteration in the objects at which the intention is directed.[48] So, we can envisage the descent of power from the heavens as it begins with the planets and flows through the *vis imaginativa* which, in turn, comes down into images, words, music and physical objects. These then pour that power outward in ways which are psychological or physical, depending on what it is they influence, and thereby the power achieves its effects.[49] Paracelsus suggested that a man's seed was generated in his imagination and a woman's in her menstrual blood, and it was widely accepted that a pregnant woman's imagination might seize upon some object, an imprint of which would then become fixed in some fashion upon the unborn child, as Ambroise Paré (1510–90), a surgeon, explained. He writes: 'One frequently sees children who look like their father more than they do their mother because of the mother's great enthusiasm and imagination during the sex act – so much so that the child takes on the form and complexion of what she knows and imagines so strongly.' The intensity of the individual's feelings, therefore, whether deliberate or involuntary, plays an important role in modifying or changing the ability of the imagination to project its power outwards and direct it to a particular person or object. Johann van Helmont (1579–1644) also pointed to the role of the imagination in the creation and propagation of disease. It acts, he said, upon certain morbid seeds which are the actual carriers of disease and activates them by affecting a kind of diseased archetype (*idea morbosa*) inherent in the seeds themselves.[50]

The vehicle of transmission of the *vis* was the human *spiritus*, described by the physician Jean Fernel (1497–1538) as 'any corporeal or incorporeal thing that does not enter into the senses' and is therefore of mixed character, 'intermediate between the corporeal and the incorporeal. All immaterial substances that escape the senses exercise their influence on material bodies by means of spirit'.[51] A hundred years earlier, Nicholas of Cusa (1401–64) had proffered a not entirely dissimilar explanation:

> In the first part of the head, in a little chamber devoted to what things look like, there exists a *spiritus* which is much more rarefied and agile than the *spiritus* which is diffused via the arteries, and when the mind uses it as its instrument, it becomes more subtle so that, even when a material object is not in front of it, it can grasp what it looks like. This mental power is called 'imagination' because by its means the mind fashions a picture of the object for itself, despite the object's not being there. In this respect, [imagination] differs from sensation which grasps what a material object looks like only when the object is in front of it.[52]

Agrippa provides an explanation of the interaction between earthly objects and the heavens which combines to produce desired preternatural effects. He writes:

> We have to note that any kind of marvel effected by figures, when we draw them on pieces of paper or inscribe them on metal plates or statues is brought about only by the power they acquire from figures which exist in a higher place. [This comes] from a kind of passionate longing [*amore*] whereby a special natural quality or likeness joins them together, in as much as they are fashioned exactly like one another the same kind of way an echo picks up and repeats the sound from the opposite wall, and the sun's rays, collected together in a concave mirror, rebound and fall upon an object such as a piece of wood or something else which is combustible, and immediately burn it up; or like a harp which causes another harp to make a loud sound, simply because a form which looks like it and is shaped like it is placed in front of it [. . .] Likewise, the figures I mentioned become pregnant (so to speak) with the powers of the figures in the heavens, provided [the figures] have been properly imprinted on their objects or [the shapes] have been put together in accordance with the ritual proper to their ruling [figures].[53]

The imagination is thus an active, not a passive agent, literally an 'inflowing' from the heavens, and the intensity of feeling to which Paré refers and Agrippa implies by his use of *amor* in the foregoing passage, allied to the active imagination, plays an important role in any successful operation of magic. In the case of Agrippa, this intensity was not merely important, but crucial and he devotes several chapters of his *De Occulta Philosophia* to explaining how feelings (*passiones*) operate in magic. 'No one should be surprised', he says, 'that one person's soul and body can be affected [. . .] By someone else's feelings [*animus*], because the feelings [*animus*] are far more powerful, strong, and intense, and far more vigorous in their movement than gusts of air breathed out from the body'.⁵⁴ *Animus* is a word referring to breath, to the mind conscious of what it is doing and thinking, and to the feelings and passions. So, when Agrippa says that one person's *animus* can affect someone else, he means that someone labouring under a strong emotion and fully cognisant of what he or she wishes and intends to do is capable of projecting the power of that emotion and intention in such a way as to alter the other person's mind, feelings and even physical constitution.

While describing and explaining this process, he distinguishes between the exterior senses – sight, hearing, smell, taste and touch – and the interior (a definition he owes, as he says, to Averroes), these being, the common sense, the *vis imaginativa*, *phantasia* and memory. The task of the imagination, he says, is to retain the images sent to it from the exterior senses via the common sense which has collected them and supplied any deficiencies and corrected any faults they may have (*colligit atque perficit*). The imagination then passes them on to the *phantasia* which works out what they are images of and then hands them over, thus refined and defined, to the memory.⁵⁵ In this version, therefore, the imagination is essentially passive and the *phantasia* active, the opposite of the usual distinction (although it is true that, unless the writer is keen to preserve the difference, the two are frequently elided and used as though they were synonymous).⁵⁶ When the *passiones* – by which Agrippa means the feelings or emotional reactions generated by what he calls 'motions' or 'inclinations' stimulated by a person's perception of and interaction with something (*alicuius rei*) – are particularly strong, they not only have the ability to change the body to which they belong but can also pass beyond it in order to work upon a body which belongs to someone or something else, the result being that they produce a number of remarkable imprints both on the elements and on the external objects and can even remove or cause certain illnesses this way.⁵⁷ In the case of the individual himself's being affected by these strong emotions, the *vis imaginativa* even enables him to be transported from one place to another, the most obvious example, of course, being the transvection of a witch to a Sabbat, whether purely in imagination or in actual physical flight.⁵⁸

2.4 Conclusions

After long gestation and growth, and in spite of all reservations, doubts and occasional active opposition, the tradition of *experimenta* and the role of the *vis imaginativa* proved to be key factors in preparing the mind of later inquisitors into Nature for an intense personal experience of Nature itself by immersing them in the details of her intricate working, and actually the intensity of that experience may, as Agrippa thought, have an effect upon the outcome of an *experimentum* (in its modern sense), as modern *experimentores* are increasingly starting to realize.[59] What *experimenta* and the *vis imaginativa* have in common is an assumption that Nature not only can but ought to be investigated and that the rewards of such investigation will be beneficial both to the investigator and to humanity as a whole. *Experientia* as a vehicle for 'getting to know' offsets the potentially static character of *scientia*, practicality thus assisting theory to make its point by confirming it or, if needed, modifying or correcting it, or even expanding it, and the fact that books of *experimenta* or *secreta* were popular – even more so after the invention of printing made their acquisition cheaper and even more widespread – gradually laid the ground for a more willing acceptance of the notion that such investigation and practice was not as dangerous as *curiositas* tended to suggest but was actually desirable without necessarily being perilous to the soul.

Notes

1 Martin Del Rio, *Disquisitiones Magicae* (1608 edition), bk. 1, chp. 2. My translation. See Martin Del Rio, *Investigation into Magic*, ed. Peter G. Maxwell-Stuart (Manchester: Manchester University Press, 2009).
2 H. Cornelius Agrippa, *De Occulta Philosophia libri tres*, ed. Vittoria Perrone Compagni (Leiden and New York: Brill, 1992), bk 1, chp. 1, 85. My second translation.
3 D. B. Ruderman, *Kabbalah, Magic, and Science: The Cultural Universe of a Sixteenth-Century Jewish Physician* (Cambridge, MA: Harvard University Press, 1988), 161.
4 St Augustine, *Confessions*, 10. 35. 54 and 55.
5 Isidore of Seville, *Etymologiae* 1.1.1.
6 See further William F. Ryan and Charles B. Schmitt ed., *Pseudo-Aristotle: The Secret of Secrets, Sources and Influences* (London: The Warburg Institute, 1982); Lynn Thordike, 'The Latin Pseudo-Aristotle and Mediaeval Occult Science', *The Journal of English and Germanic Philology* 21 (April 1922): 229–58. Steven J. Williams, 'Roger Bacon and His Edition of the pseudo-Aristotelian Secretum Secretorum', *Speculum* 69 (1994): 57–73.
7 See Dov Schwartz, *Studies on Astral Magic in Mediaeval Jewish Thought* (Leiden and Boston: Brill, 2005), 38–9.

8   See further Lorraine Daston and Katharine Park, *Wonders and the Order of Nature, 1150-1750* (New York: Zone Books, 1998), 120–2.
9   *Arbatel*, ed. Joseph H. Peterson (Lake Worth: Ibis Press, 2009), 40. Della Porta, *Magia Naturalis* bk 1, chp. 3. I am grateful to Donato Verardi for his suggestions on this point. On Della Porta's natural magic see Donato Verardi, *Logica e Magia. Giovan Battista Della Porta e i segreti della natura* (Lugano: Agorà & Co, 2017).
10 Note that, while 'witchcraft' could be included in either natural or diabolic magic or both, depending on the intention of its practitioner, Paracelsus (1493–1541) thought that theologians should distinguish between 'magic' and 'witchcraft' on the grounds that magic is a repository of secret and desirable knowledge and therefore (by implication), witchcraft is not, Jolande Jacobi ed., *Paracelsus: Selected Writings* (Princeton: Princeton University Press, 1951), 137–8. See also Isabelle Draelants, 'The Notion of Properties: Tensions Between *scientia* and *ars* in Mediaeval Natural Philosophy and Magic', in *The Routledge History of Mediaeval Magic*, eds Sophie Page and Catherine Rider (London and New York: Routledge, 2019), 176–9.
11 'Imply' because the verb *perior* is unattested. But cf. Greek περάω, 'I traverse'.
12 Cf. the complexity of Aristotle's argument that ἐπιστήμη (understanding allied to skill) and τέχνη (practical skill or craft) appear to be very similar because both are linked to ἐμπειρία (experience) which comes from the memory of how and under what circumstances something has been done or has happened in the past, Aristotle, *Metaphysica* 1 (981a.2-3).
13 Quoted by William Eamon, *Science and the Secrets of Nature: Books of Secrets in Medieval and Early Modern Culture* (Princeton: Princeton University Press, 1994), 56.
14 As Robert Bartlett points out at the beginning of his discussion of Roger Bacon's 'scientia experimentalis', *The Natural and the Supernatural in the Middle Ages* (Cambridge: Cambridge University Press, 2008), 121.
15 Bernardus Silvestris, *Experimentarius*, regula II. Text in *Archives d'Histoire Doctrinale et Littéraire du Moyen Age* 77 (1977), 112.
16 My second translation of Bernardus also begins to suggest why Bernard of Clairvaux (*c.* 1090–153) placed a degree of emphasis on personal experience as a method of obtaining enlightenment, since personal observation is easily aligned with the discernment of spirits and that became increasingly important as medieval mysticism stretched and strained the boundaries of the individual's religious experience. See further Bernard McGinn, 'The Changing Shape of Medieval Mysticism', *Church History* 65 (1996): 197–219, especially 197.
17 Frank Klaassen, *The Transformations of Magic: Illicit Learned Magic in the Later Middle Ages and Renaissance* (University Park: The Pennsylvania State University Press, 2013), 4.

18 *The Book of Secrets of Albertus Magnus*, eds Frank H. Brightman and Michael R. Best (Oxford: Clarendon Press, 1973). As Owen Davies points out, this is not a grimoire, *Grimoires: A History of Magic Books* (Oxford: Oxford University Press 2009), 38-9. See further Sebastià Girait, 'El liber experimentorum, un llibre de màgia en occità falsament attribuit a Arnau de Vilanova', *Medioevo Romanzo* 41 (2017): 188-93, and Benedek Láng, *Unlocked Books: Manuscripts of Learned Magic in the Medieval Libraries of Central Europe* (University Park: The Pennsylvania State University Press, 2008), 51-61.

19 Paracelsus, on the other hand, uses *experimentator* as a term of abuse because he associates Baconian 'experimentation' as little more than lay-people's superficial and fragmentary knowledge, Charles Webster, *Paracelsus: Medicine, Magic, and Mission at the End of Time* (New Haven and London: Yale University Press, 2008), 154.

20 David Pingree, 'Learned Magic in the Time of Frederick II', *Le Scienze alla Corte di Federico II*, *Micrologus* (Turnhout: Brepols, 1994), 39-56. Charles Burnett, 'Michael Scot and the Transmission of Scientific Culture from Bologna via the Court of Frederick II Hohenstaufen', *Micrologus*, 101-26. Steven J. Williams, 'The Early Circulation of the pseudo-Aristotelian *Secret of Secrets* in the West: the Papal and Imperial Courts', *Micrologus*, 127-44. Klaassen, 2013, *Transformations*, 36.

21 See Steven P. Marrone, *A History of Science, Magic, and Belief from Medieval to Modern Europe* (Basingstoke: Palgrave Macmillan, 2015), 101-6.

22 *De sophisticationibus que vocantur iugulaciones*. Robert Goulding, 'Deceiving the Senses in the Thirteenth Century: Trickery and Illusion in the *Secretum Philosophorum*', in *Magic and the Classical Tradition*, eds Charles Burnett and William F. Ryan (London and Turin: The Warburg Institute, 2006), 147, 151, 161. 'Iugulacionibus' is surely an error for *ioculationibus*, since *iugulatio* means murdering someone by cutting his throat (*iugulum*).

23 Pamela Long, *Openness, Secrecy, Authorship: Technical Arts and the Culture of Knowledge from Antiquity to the Renaissance* (Baltimore and London: The John Hopkins Press, 2004), 171-5.

24 *The Tollemache Book of Secrets*, ed. Jeremy Griffiths (London: The Roxburghe Club, 2001); *The Book of Oberon*, eds Daniel Harms, James R. Clark, Joseph H. Peterson (Woodbury: Llewellyn Publications 2015), 107, 179, 351, 363, 399 (attributed to Roger Bacon), 416, 537.

25 Frank Klaassen ed., *Making Magic in Elizabethan England: Two Early Modern Vernacular Books on Magic* (University Park: The Pennsylvania State University Press 2019), 32.

26 John Dee (1527-1608/9). Urszula Szulakowska, *The Alchemy of Light: Geometry and Optics in Late Renaissance Alchemical Illustration* (Leiden, Boston and Köln: Brill, 2000), 37. Gabriela D. Horvath, *Theatre, Magic, and Philosophy: William*

Shakespeare, John Dee, and the Italian Legacy (London and New York: Routledge, 2017), 209.

27 Quoted by György E. Szőnyi, *John Dee's Occultism: Magical Exaltation Through Powerful Signs* (New York: State University of New York Press, 2004), 177.

28 Ibid., 178-9.

29 See further Jean-Patrice Boudet, *Entre Science et Nigromance: Astrologie, Divination, et Magie dans l'Occident Médiévale (XIIe-XVe siècle)* (Paris: Publications de la Sorbonne, 2006), 409-17.

30 Håkan Håkansson, *Seeing the Word: John Dee and Renaissance Occultism* (Lunds: Lunds Universitet, 2001). Cf. Arnau de Vilanova who was clear that the effects of the compound medicines he rated more highly than simples were made known to the physician by God via the physician's personal experience and observation, not by trial and error or 'experimentation' on the physician's part, *Antidotarium*, chp. 1. That is, *experimentum* is always done *sub specie aeternitatis*.

31 Quoted in Deborah Harkness, *The Jewel House: Elizabethan London and the Scientific Revolution* (New Haven and London: Yales University Press, 2007), 42-3. Moffett's 'sciences' refers, of course, to its Latin sense of 'branches of knowledge', without any of the implications of the modern understanding of the word.

32 Ibid., 209. But see also the whole of her chp. 5.

33 Cf. A. G. Molland's remarks on forbidden books (i.e. books of magic) and Roger Bacon's uneasy relationship with them. 'Bacon both fulsomely condemns such books and also asserts that many of them contain portions of genuine wisdom. The implication is clearly that, although they are in general to be eschewed, the pioneer investigator is under an obligation to examine them and extract those things that are licit', Andrew George Molland, 'Roger Bacon as Magician', *Traditio* 30 (1974): 445-60, especially 460.

34 Allison Kavey draws attention to the subsequent displacement of books of *experimenta* and secrets by even cheaper almanacs and books of prophecy with which they should not be confused, *Books of Secrets: Natural Philosophy in England, 1550-1600* (Urbana and Chicago: University of Illinois Press, 2007), 157.

35 Francis Bacon, *Novum Organum* (Oxonii: E Typographeo Clarendoniano, 1813), 1.99, 77-8.

36 Del Rio, *Disquisitiones Magicae* bk. 1, chp. 4, my translation and italics.

37 Del Rio, *Disquisitiones Magicae* bk. 1, chp. 3, quaestio 3. My translation.

38 Agrippa, *De Occulta Philosophia* bk 3, chp. 43, 539. My translation.

39 It is worth bearing in mind that the cosmetics used in the ancient, medieval and early modern worlds had a highly restricted palette and, as one can see from official portraits, for example, were intended to suggest such physical attributes as a fair skin, youthful cheeks, and so on. Their limitations therefore made those who used them resemble the painted marble of statues more than enhanced physical traits of

human beings, and so the vivid naturalism suggested by the theory of *imaginatio* is not the same as a modern sensibility, accustomed to sophisticated cosmetics and colour photography, would envisage it.

40   St Augustine, *De Spiritu et Anima*. Both quotations come from chp. 11.
41   See further Simon Kemp and Garth J. O. Fletcher, 'The Medieval Theory of the Inner Senses', *The American Journal of Psychology* 106 (1993): 559–76, especially 563, 564.
42   *Antoniana Margarita*, ed. José Manuel García Valverde, trans. Peter Maxwell-Stuart (Leiden and Boston: Brill, 2019), 2 vols, vol. 1., 399 and 415.
43   Agrippa also notes the more banal possible effects of eye-drops in producing illusory images, *De Occulta Philosophia* bk. 1, chp. 45, 169–70.
44   My translation. See Brian P. Copenhaver, *Symphorien Champier and the Reception of the Occultist Tradition in Renaissance France* (The Hague, Paris and New York: Mouton Publishers, 1978), 182. 'Spirits' here refers to a kind of rarefied or subtle matter produced, according to Galen, by interaction between the air and the blood. See further James J. Bono, 'Medical Spirits and the Medieval Language of Life', *Traditio* 40 (1984): 91–130. The *praecordia* ('midriff') literally refers to a muscle in front of the heart – hence the name – and thus expands to include the physical area of the body containing the heart, and so to the heart itself.
45   My translation. The extract is quoted by Michelle Karnes, 'Marvels in the Medieval Imagination', *Speculum* 90 (2015): 327–65, especially 362. In his *De Incantationibus*, first published in 1520, Pietro Pomponazzi (1462–1525) discusses the role of the imagination in relation to its being the cause of physical effects and changes, raising and answering doubts on the subject. See also John O'Brien, 'Reasoning with the Senses: the Humanist Imagination', *South Central Review* 10 (1993): 3–19.
46   Paracelsus, indeed, was strongly inclined to blame the *vis imaginativa* for human illness in general. See Webster, *Paracelsus: Medicine, Magic, and Mission at the End of Time*, 165.
47   Quoted in *The Occult Laboratory: Magic, Science and Second Sight in Late 17th-Century Scotland*, ed Michael Hunter (Woodbridge: The Boydell Press, 2001), 197.
48   Pinella Travaglia, *Magic, Causality, and Intentionality. The Doctrine of Rays in Al-Kindi* (Florence: Sismel, Edizioni del Galluzzo, 1999), 20–4, 46–8. See also Karnes, 'Marvels in the Medieval Imagination', 351–2.
49   D. P. Walker provides a clear diagram of the entire process in *Spiritual and Demonic Magic from Ficino to Campanella* (University Park: The Pennsylvania State University Press, 2000) (first published 1958), 77.
50   Paracelsus, *Liber de Generatione* in Karl Sudhoff, *Theophrast von Hohenheim, Sämtliche Werke*, (München and Berlin: Druck und Verlag R. Oldenbourg, 1933), Vol. 14., 314. Ambroise Paré, quoted by Marie-Hélène Huet, *Monstrous Imagination*

(Cambridge and London: Harvard University Press, 1993, 15). On Van Helmont, see Heinz Schott, 'Paracelsus and Van Helmont on Imagination', in, *Paracelsian Moments: Science, Medicine, and Astrology in Early Modern Europe*, eds Gerhild Scholz Williams and Charles D. Gunnoe (Kirksville: Truman State University Press, 2002), 142–5.

51 Jean Fernel, *On the Hidden Causes of Things: Forms, Souls, and Occult Diseases in Renaissance Medicine*, edition and translation of *De Abditis Rerum Causis*, J. M. Forrester (Leiden and Boston: Brill, 2005), 2.7.
52 My translation. Nicholas of Cusa, *Idiota de Mente*, chp. 8 (114–15).
53 Agrippa, *De Occulta Philosophia* bk. 2, chp. 23, 320.
54 Agrippa, *De Occulta Philosophia* bk. 1, chp. 65, 226.
55 Agrippa, *De Occulta Philosophia*, bk. 1, chp. 61, 216–19.
56 Ficino, however, did try to distinguish between them, even though he was not always consistent. See Horvath, *Theatre, Magic, and Philosophy*, 152.
57 Agrippa, *De Occulta Philosophia* bk. 1, chp. 65, 225–7.
58 Agrippa, *De Occulta Philosophia* bk. 1, chp. 64, 222–5.
59 See, for example, Robert Rosenthal, 'Biasing Effects of Experimenters', *ETC: A Review of General Semantics* 34 (1977): 253–64.

3

The image of Aristotle as a magus and the Aristotelian foundation of magic in early modern Italy

Donato Verardi

3.1 Introduction

The capacity for transformation and adaptation of Renaissance Aristotelianism are elements on which scholars working in this field of research have largely insisted.[1] Less evoked by specialists, however, is the fact that, in the Renaissance, Aristotelianism was also able to adapt to themes of magic. With the glaring exception of Pietro Pomponazzi (1462–1525) and his attempt to insert into an Aristotelian framework, the themes of natural magic generally traced back to the diabolical plane, this field of research still remains largely unexplored.[2] This is particularly true especially with regard to the complex universe of Italian Aristotelianism of the sixteenth century and its connections, little known to date, with those scientific environments in which, at the same historical juncture, a purely experimental reform of natural magic was being attempted. This chapter is consecrated to the Aristotelian foundation of magical knowledge as promoted in the work of Francesco Storella (1529–75), a professor of logic in Naples and Salerno and one of the first teachers of the famous magus Giordano Bruno (1548–1600).[3]

In his commentary on the *Secretum secretorum* – a work that he attributes to Aristotle and of which he provides the latest Latin edition, published in Naples and Venice in 1555 – Storella defines the magus as the wise man.[4] Storella links his commentary on *Secretum* to the lessons of authors such as Marsilio Ficino and Giovanni Pico della Mirandola, by constructing an image of Aristotle as a magus: an expert not only in logic, physics and metaphysics but also – as the *Secretum* helps to show – in the so-called occult sciences.[5]

The purpose of this chapter is to demonstrate how Storella's peculiar image of Aristotle as a magus suggests that Aristotelian philosophy can also be used to justify venefical magic, namely, that part of natural magic, capable of producing poisons, erroneously traced back to the diabolical practices of the so-called witches. The justification of venefical magic on an epistemological level, which stems from ideas implicit in Storella's works on the knowledge of the 'singular' and the marvellous in nature, leads in turn to refuting the belief in witchcraft practices, considered – even from an ethical point of view – extraneous to the most authentic lessons of Aristotelianism and to true magic.

In this scientific and ethical mission of Storella's proposal, Aristotle's reasons intersect with those of natural magicians of the time. Storella's intellectual story thus gives us a picture of the relationships that Aristotelianism and magic entertained in early modern Italy and of their common reform mission.

3.2 Francesco Storella. A logic to the occult

Storella's primary purpose was to guarantee a logic to the occult, looking at the 'singular' and irregular phenomena, which were the prerogative of natural magic, with the eyes of Aristotle himself.

Storella was born in Alessano, a small town in the region of Otranto, around 1529 and he died of apoplexy in Naples on 18 December 1575.[6] He was introduced to philosophical studies by his father Giovanni, who was a disciple of Pomponazzi. In Padua, Storella listened to the lectures of Bernardino Tomitano, Panfilo Monti and Marcantonio de' Passeri (known as Genua); he studied under excellent teachers and was a peer of other important figures, including Gabriele Falloppia, the surgeon from Modena. In 1548, at twenty-four years of age, he was elected by the students as Rector of the University of the Arts. In 1549, at the end of his year as Rector, he received the academic degree *Doctor Artium* and earned the title of 'public lector' after his discussion of the 150 *Conclusiones*. In 1550, Storella moved to Naples, where he became friends with Simone Porzio and Giovan Bernardino Longo. He dedicated his work *Logicalium Capitum Decas Prima* to the latter. In Naples he wrote *De Definitione Logices*, his *Explanatio in digressione undecimi commenti Averrois*, and *De inventore Logices*.[7]

In 1557, Storella taught at the *Studium* in Salerno and published the *Lybellus an singulare syllogismus ingredi*.[8] The following year, in 1558, he returned to Naples. This is a significant date, since in that same year the first edition of the *Magia naturalis sive de miraculis rerum naturalium* by Giambattista Della

Porta (1535–1615) appeared in Naples, at Matthias Cancer;[9] *Magia naturalis* became a fundamental work for those sections of naturalistic research which were committed to the study of *secreta naturae*.[10] 1558 is also the year in which Storella held a series of lectures in Naples, which were published as *De utilitate logices* in 1561.[11] Using an Aristotelian framework, *De utilitate logices* allowed Storella to make a further, decisive contribution to the scientific legitimation of the investigation into singulars (i.e. the rare or unusual empirical data which are the objects of the natural magician's investigation). In these lectures, Storella emphasizes how Aristotelian logic could be considered a cognitive tool of the natural *admirandum*. This is a position already supported by Storella in the *Libellus quo ad peripateticas aures singulare verum syllogismum ingredi*, a work devoted to the refutation of the theories of Girolamo Balduino.[12]

A former professor of logic in Salerno, Balduino claimed that the inductive method, when it starts from the singular, always leads to an apparent syllogism: not a true one. A singular proposition can only lead to a singular conclusion, betraying the universal character required of a syllogism if it is to be considered scientific. If, as Balduino suggests, science requires a development that is realized only at the level of the universal, the *sensatum* can only remain confined to particular cases, falling within the sphere of the *apprehensio simplicium*. For Balduino, the proposition which indicates something already known and which is apparent to our senses cannot, therefore, enter into the constitution of the syllogism.[13] This is a point shared also by Pietro Pomponazzi (1462–1525), who, despite a general approach aimed at providing a 'not impossible' explanation for rare and unusual events, was convinced of an individual disposition, insofar as it is irreducible to the Aristotelian *ut in pluribus*, 'non est syllogizabile'.[14] According to Storella, however, even if we admit that all singulars are known to our senses, their attributes could still be unknown – therefore, not known in its entirety. The example used by Storella to defend this thinking is the same that even Bruno, in his works on magic, would have indicated as the phenomenon of natural magic par excellence, namely magnetic attraction – an 'occult' phenomenon, as it is not entirely known, but still natural. For Storella, it is the occult character of the phenomenon that allows for that progressive and gradual process of knowledge which can be reached through the application of the customary rules of logical discourse.[15]

In *De utilitate logices*, Storella further specifies to what extent logic can assist natural magic in the study of the occult and singular phenomena of nature. Here, the author first insists on the logical foundation of natural magic and astrology, underlining how logic – if also understood in its nature as an 'instrument' –

can be useful both for the foundation of an astrology based on mathematical logic (as Ptolemy teaches in the *Centiloquy* and in the *Quadripartite*) and to the constitution of a natural magic in turn based on astrology, which is considered a cognitive tool of the natural *admirandum* opposed to diabolical deceptions.[16] In support of this, Storella recounts an episode that took place in Salerno while he was teaching there. At the home of a noble, he saw a manuscript of the *Picatrix*. Disgusted, he immediately looked away from the manuscript, but not before reading that the foundation of magic is in astrology, without which no experiment can be carried out.[17]

For Storella, who reinterprets a passage from the strictly forbidden *Picatrix* in the light of his own conception of natural magic, astrology (in its Ptolemaic meaning) guarantees the validity of the experiments promoted by this discipline – hence, also, its central role in natural magic. The rational structure of astrology, guaranteed by its logical and geometric-mathematical status, would thus theoretically base natural magic, transforming an otherwise solely empirical art into a philosophically based *ars*.

3.3 To attribute in order to prove. The *Secretum secretorum* and the Aristotelian foundation of the 'occult sciences'

The close link between Aristotelianism and astrology promoted by Storella is not in itself an unusual element in the cultural landscape of early modern Italy. Astrology was taught in universities, and, at that time, it was considered to be the 'mother science' of all the so-called occult sciences. In fact, by virtue of its geometric-mathematical status, it had the potential to situate disciplines thought to be outside the realm of science into the rational basis which defined the canons of scientificity at the time. Throughout the sixteenth century, the study of astrology in universities became less and less linked to the possible divinatory character of this discipline; in its natural meaning astrology maintained strong links with medical knowledge taught in schools. In the Italian context, texts such as Ptolemy's *Almagest* or the *Centiloquium* were included in arts, astrology and medical *curricula*, alongside many other medical-astrological texts.[18]

Before Storella, Pomponazzi, the greatest of the Renaissance Aristotelians, had previously resorted to making astrology an essential tool in his project of rational understanding of those occult phenomena otherwise outside Aristotelian science.[19] Storella, however, seems to go beyond Pomponazzi himself. For him, astrology is not simply an auxiliary tool for the Aristotelian philosopher in the act of justifying extraordinary phenomena which are otherwise the prerogative of demonological explanations. Astrology and with-it natural magic are themselves an integral part of Aristotelianism, since, as the *Secretum secretorum* shows, they are disciplines practised by Aristotle himself. Therefore, Aristotle being a magus and an astrologer means, according to Storella, that these disciplines must necessarily be consistent with the Aristotle's conception of logic, which ultimately justifies them as key components of philosophy. By bringing magic and astrology back into the sphere of Aristotelianism, Storella suggests the plausibility that a work such as the *Secretum secretorum* could conceivably be attributed to Aristotle.

Since its reception in the Islamic Middle Ages, the *Sirr al-asrār* (*Secretum secretorum*), along with the Pseudo-Aristotelian *Hermetica* and the so-called *Theology of Aristotle* (an Arabic paraphrase of Plotinus's *Enneads* IV–VI along with Porphyry's edition), helped establish Aristotle's image as a philosopher, sage and magus with consummate knowledge of occult properties and astral influences.[20] The first Latin version of the *Secretum secretorum* is attributed to Philip of Tripoli (of uncertain dating, before 1237 or between 1262 and 1271) and contained some chapters, such as the one on onomancy, which were later condemned as necromantic by the ecclesiastical authorities.[21] Very early doubts were raised about the Aristotelian attribution of the *Secretum*, which was already a 'bestseller' in the Middle Ages. The fact is that, although it has never been included in the university *curriculum*, numerous professors, from the Middle Ages to the Renaissance, referred to it in their comments on other Aristotelian works. Storella was among those who, in the sixteenth century, supported attributing the work to Aristotle.

Circumventing the problem of the controversies that have arisen in this regard, in the Preface to the *Secretum secretorum*, he points out that the *Secretum* is worthy of study regardless of the identification of its author. This is a statement that takes on greater significance when one notes the list of topics that Storella deems worthy of learning from the *Secretum*; in addition to the doctrine of good governance and war, he mentions the study of aspects of the planets and the partition of the time, the admirable virtues of plants and stones, physiognomics and alchemy.[22] Storella recalls how the attribution is denied by Giovanni Pico della Mirandola in the *Disputationes adversus astrologiam divinatricem* and Gianfrancesco Pico in his *De rerum praenotione* but is supported by other equally authoritative authors, such as, among others, Albertus Magnus,[23] Peter of Abano, Bartolomeo Moles, Bartolomeo Cocles, Agostino Nifo, Cristoforo Marcello and Alessandro Achillini, the author of the 1501 edition of the *Secretum secretorum*, published in his collection of pseudo-Aristotelian works entitled *Opus septisegmentatum*.[24] In support of this attribution, Storella also recalls the *auctoritas* of John Mesue's *De aegritudinibus oculorum* and that of Abenragel Alí's *De secretis secretorum*.[25]

In the *Secretum secretorum*, the astrological element is central, especially in regard to the medical theme of human complexions, which the author places in relation to the 'natures' of the planets. It is a cosmological and anthropological conception which, strongly characterized by astrology, was already rooted in a certain medical tradition in the Middle Ages (think of Peter of Abano, whom Storella quotes extensively in his commentary on the *Secretum secretorum*) and continued to appear in works by some Renaissance peripatetic philosophers such as Achillini, his pupil Bartolomeo Cocles Della Rocca and then Storella himself.[26] According to the doctrine of Aristotle and Averroes, the heavens are eternal and endowed with divine perfection.[27] This last feature of theirs would be connected with the *quinta essentia*, on which, according to the Hermetic tradition, their magical virtue would depend. According to a certain medico-astrological tradition, of which Storella himself is a part, the stars do not act by virtue of their substantial form, that is by *formaliter*, but by *effective*, that is, by virtue of their effects – even though Aristotle stated that celestial bodies like planets are perpetual, as well as endowed with an immutable essence. This doctrine of the 'complexions of the planets', which also finds support in the theses expounded in the *Secretum secretorum*, shows how the planets must be considered in relation to their effects, for which they are provided with the same combinations of elementary physical qualities as in the sublunary world: cold, hot, wet and dry. As in human temperaments, the complexions derive from the combination of their qualities and their proportions, so the *complexio stellarum* is ordered in the manner of human nature. In fact, the *complexio stellarum* tends to hot or cold, dry or wet.[28] This same theory of complexions characterizes the physiognomics of Peter of Abano, who founded this discipline on astrology, according to a *subalternatio* of sciences theorized in his *Lucidator*.[29] This approach is perpetuated in the fifteenth century, in Ferrara and Padua, by Michele Savonarola (1385–1468) in his *Speculum phisionomiae* and in the sixteenth century, among others, by Storella. This conception of the cosmos and of man underlies the *Secretum secretorum* and therefore allows Storella to justify the Aristotlean nature of some occult disciplines, the philosophical substance of which had often been questioned. Think of the emblematic case of chiromancy which, by virtue of its evidently divinatory character, presented itself, in the late Renaissance historical context in which Storella operated, as one of the most problematic. It is a theme around which, in the *Secretum*, Storella also had the opportunity to dwell and which involves the delicate relationship between physiognomics and chiromancy and between these two arts and astrology.[30]

Although, in the short section of the *Secretum* dedicated to physiognomics, the relationship of this discipline to astrology is only implicit, it is explained in the section dedicated to medicine, a discipline with which physiognomics has an inseparable link. In his sober annotation relating to physiognomics, Storella links this problem to the previous treatment by Achillini, continued by his pupil Cocles, author of a *Chyromantie ac physionomie Anastasis*. Reprinted several times during the sixteenth century, Cocles's work aimed to demonstrate how, according to the peripatetic philosophers-physiognomes (among which Albertus Magnus and Peter of Abano are counted), the passions of the soul always follow the bodily complexions, even if human prudence can always avoid fate. This approach is based on the medical theory of complexions, which in turn are related to the 'natures' of the planets. After reiterating the link of physiognomics with the medical tradition and with medieval peripateticism, in the third book Cocles delved into the role that the astrological element has in this discipline. In particular, he went back to the Ptolemaic lesson of the *Quadripartitum* and to the pseudo-Ptolemaic one of the *Centiloquium*, examining the natures of the planets and relating them to human natures, that is, to temperaments.[31] In the *Secretum*, Storella proves to know this controversy very well. Citing the condemnation of chiromancy by Gianfrancesco Pico della Mirandola, but supported by the doctrines of the *Secretum secretorum* and its Renaissance followers, Storella locates this discipline within an astrologico-medico-empirical approach that he recognizes to be characteristic of Aristotle's philosophy.[32]

This same approach, the result of a very precise conception of the cosmos and of man presented by the *Secretum*, also underlies the justification that Storella proposes for alchemy. Chiara Crisciani highlighted how the author of the *Secretum secretorum* refers several times to Hermes Trismegistus, thus configuring himself as a 'Hermetic Aristotle'.[33] Storella, in a chapter of the *Secretum* dedicated to alchemy, significantly refers to a 'very old' Neapolitan code of the Trismegistus, which he was able to view in Naples thanks to the diligence of his pupil, Aniello Torboli. Elsewhere, always in relation to alchemy as an Aristotelian discipline and citing the argument of Pietro Bono in *Pretiosa Margarita*, he notes how the condemnation of this art presented in the fourth book of the *Meteora* can be explained by means of an evolution of Aristotle's thought, who wrote the *Secretum* at a very advanced age, thus having the opportunity to ascertain over time the validity of this discipline.[34] It is interesting to note that Storella does not find it scandalous to refer, as an Aristotelian, to a Hermetic manuscript on alchemy. From Storella's point of view, this is largely consistent with the fact that Aristotle himself, in the *Secretum secretorum*, referred both to the teachings of Hermes and to alchemy as a legitimate discipline. Consistent with this position, in *De utilitate logices* Storella advocates for the logical foundation of alchemy, also referring, in the *Tractatulus quinquaginta contradictionum*, to the *Opusculo de alchimia* attributed to Albertus Magnus.[35]

Storella's interest in alchemy as a discipline that can be inscribed in an Aristotelian discourse is closely connected to his own idea of natural magic. As the *Secretum secretorum* teaches, a magus is one who is able to manipulate the natural occult qualities of plants and stones, producing – as Storella declares in *De utilitate logices* – 'marvellous effects'.[36] This is a conception of alchemy and magic that recalls the Albertine lesson set out in the *De mineralibus*, at the time also present in pseudo-epigraphic texts with a clear Albertist (and Hermetic) orientation. The pseudo-Albertine *Experimenta* or *Secreta Alberti* (also known as *Liber aggregationis*) opens emphatically with a reference to Aristotle. It is a work closely connected to the pseudo-Aristotelian *Secretum secretorum* which was part of what has been defined by Benedek Láng as the 'common tradition' of medieval natural magic.[37]

The pseudo-epigraphic works attributed to Albertus Magnus are texts in which, compared to Albertus's authentic works, the philosophical element is less evident, but still underlying. In these texts, which, in the Renaissance, would also have attracted the attention of natural magi such as Della Porta and Bruno, the marvellous character of the secret manifestations of nature is accentuated, to which the magus tries to provide a plausible explanation, between reason and experience.[38] In the chapter of the *Secretum secretorum* dedicated to the occult power of stones, Storella links this theme to Aristotle's *De lapidibus*.[39] He refers to what Albertus Magnus expounded in *De mineralibus* about a partial knowledge of this treatise.[40] Storella believes that the contents of both the *De plantis* and the *De lapidibus* by Aristotle correspond to the relative sections of the *Secretum secretorum*.[41] The reference to Albertus Magnus is important as it also helps us to understand Storella's ideas about magic (and alchemy) as well as the late Renaissance Neapolitan reception to Albertine theories about magic.

In his *De mineralibus*, Albertus Magnus distinguished natural science (based on hylomorphism) from magic, which he interpreted as a search for sufficient, astrological causes of occult qualities. The notion of occult quality is inextricably linked to that of celestial influence (*influxus*).[42] The magus does not seek the primary causes of occult things, as a metaphysician would do, but the sufficient ones: the planets and stars. Albertus traced the astrological approach of magi back to the lesson of Hermes Trismegistus.[43] In the Renaissance, some natural magicians strategically used the 'holy' authority of Albertus Magnus to legitimize natural magic, a prodigious but licit science capable of marvellous effects.[44] In the *Magia naturalis* of 1558, and then in the version expanded to twenty books in 1589, Della Porta based natural magic on the astrological doctrine of occult qualities, with an explicit reference to the authority of Albertus Magnus. From a cosmological point of view, this doctrine (which the anonymous translator of *Magia naturalis* into the Italian vernacular linked to the astrological tradition) was, thus, configured as the foundation of the magico-alchemical experimentalism promoted by *Magia naturalis*.[45]

A few years before the publication of first edition of the *Magia naturalis*, Storella comments on the sections of the *Secretum secretorum* that highlight the astrological origin of the occult virtues with references to the same doctrines of Albertus Magnus, of whom he expressly cites the *De mineralibus*.[46] Storella's commentary on the *Secretum secretorum* thus constitutes an interesting example of how, in Naples, at the same historical juncture, the Aristotelian world was moving in the same direction as natural magicians like Della Porta.[47]

3.4 To legitimize in order to deny. The image of Aristotle as a *veneficus* and the naturalization of the *veneficium*

We have seen how Storella's Aristotelian justification of magic is fundamental to attributing the *Secretum secretorum* to Aristotle. This attribution is confirmed by Storella in the *Catalogus ac cesura operum quae an Aristotelea sint est dubitatum*, a list drawn up by Storella relating to works to be considered authentically Aristotelian, which is currently preserved in a manuscript in the Ambrosiana Library in Milan.[48] As Charles B. Schmitt pointed out, the most significant thing about Storella's edition of *Secretum secretorum* lies 'in his attempt to present something approaching a complete and critical text'.[49] Storella's commitment as editor of the *Secretum secretorum* makes him exposed to a significant number of occult texts, some of which, also by virtue of their possible attribution to Aristotle,[50] are particularly inflammatory. In a phase immediately preceding the publication of the *Secretum secretorum*, of which the aforementioned *Catalogus* is a testimony, Storella states that necromantic texts such as the *Necromantia de regiminibus coelestibus* and the *Mors animae* are not attributable to Aristotle. However, he does not rule out that a *Liber Novem Judicum* (the Aristotelean attribution of which, he recalls, was defended by Guido Bonatti)[51] and a *De diebus infelicibus* (whose attribution is rejected by Giovanni and Gianfrancesco Pico della Mirandola) are to be attributed to Aristotle. Of the latter text, Storella claims to know that there is a copy in Lecce, while he reports that he also viewed a *De viginti octo mansionibus Lunae* attributable to Aristotle in Naples. All in all, these statements are coherent with Storella's discussion of the *Conclusiones*, orally presented when he was awarded his Paduan doctorate and published in 1549, wherein he first argued that natural magic – understood as a practice that excludes any relationship with diabolical entities, as well as being structured on solid astrological foundations – can be viewed through an Aristotelean lens.[52]

If, in the *Catalogus ac censura* of 1554, Storella fails to mention that Aristotle practised illicit magic, in the *Enumeratio librorum Aristotelis qui perierunt vel nondum in lucem venerunt*, also contained in the aforementioned Ambrosian manuscript and written outside Naples after 1558, he solidifies his conviction that Aristotle did, in fact, meddle in this kind of magic. If it is certain that Aristotle dealt with natural magic, alchemy and astrology even in writings that were later lost, then the *Liber de irradiationibus: necromantia, mors animae*, which Storella consulted during his stay in Naples, provides further evidence that he practised venefical magic (despite Achillini, Tiberio Bacilieri and Pomponazzi's insistence that Aristotle refuted belief in the existence of demons).[53]

In the Renaissance, the notion of *veneficium* can take on different meanings and it is, therefore, necessary to identify the meaning attributed to it by each author. Literally, as Heinrich Cornelius Agrippa of Nettesheim recalls in *De incertitudine et vanitate scientiarum*, venefical magic must be understood as a part of natural magic capable of producing poisons.[54] Even Girolamo Cardano (1501–76), who considered *veneficium* a practice worthy of severe reproach, in the *De subtilitate* emphasized its belonging to the sphere of natural magic, considering *veneficium* 'inter venena et praestigias'.[55] Since poisons were largely produced for harmful purposes, those opposed to it equated it with necromancy, as it was connected with all evidence to action evil of the devil (Jean Bodin does in *De la démonomanie des sorciers*).[56] On the other hand, Agrippa himself maintained a certain permeability between venefical magic and necromantic magic.[57] This permeability was absent in Della Porta's *Magia naturalis* (1558), where, in a neutral and agnostic vision of research, the Neapolitan magus inserted the discourse relating to poisons, and witchcraft, within the realm of nature.[58]

Storella clarifies the meaning attributed to the concept of *veneficium* in his *De utilitate logices*. In this work, Storella equates the *magus veneficus* with the necromancer, supporting the logical (Aristotelian) structure of venefical magic.

According to Storella, magic is *duplex*. The first form of magic is the natural one and consists of the practical part of the philosophy of nature; the second is the venefical magic of necromancers.[59] By using the expression 'practical part of philosophy', borrowed from Giovanni Pico della Mirandola,[60] Storella does not want to downgrade magic to the rank of simple practical art, but (as Bruno will later do[61]) seeks to show that it operates in direct contact with the natural world, while preserving its theoretical dignity. Since the devil, as the author writes, is a great logician, then venefical magic must be justified by a rigorous logical discourse. These are considerations that should also be read in close relation with his interest in the natural study of poisons, evidenced by the edition of the treatise on poisons by Averroes and by the attention paid to Peter of Abano, author of an important treatise about poisons which, in the *Enumeratio*, Storella strategically connects to Aristotle as venefical magus.[62] On the other hand, if the venefical magic of necromancers must be logically justified according to the dictates of Aristotle, then this justification cannot fail to include the natural study of the 'occult' properties of poisons (fulcrum of the *veneficium*) – objects of genuinely Aristotelian and, therefore, legitimate disciplines such as natural magic and alchemy.

In other words, Storella applies the same logical and physico-astrological rules that support natural magic (and alchemy) to the *veneficium* of necromancers, thus implicitly challenging, from the point of view of physics and logic, the distinction between, natural and necromantic magic. If there can be a distinction between the two forms of magic, it will be of a moral nature, venefical magic being reprehensible and harmful. In this sense, venefical magic is attributable to diabolical inspiration, while maintaining its natural dimension.[63]

In this 'rationalization' of venefical magic, Storella sides with natural magi in this opposition to the belief in witchcraft. As is well known, the problem of the *veneficium* is closely linked in the Renaissance to the evil actions of so-called witches. John Wier, one of the greatest Renaissance defenders of witches and a pupil of Agrippa, argued in his *De praestigiis daemonum et incantationibus ac veneficiis libri sex* that the *veneficia* are nothing more than detestable practices which, while natural, were also punishable. Wier's reference speaks particularly to the possibility for the *veneficae* (which are other than *lamiae*, old, ignorant and deluded women) to cause harm to people or animals by means of poisons. For authors like Bodin, on the other hand, the *veneficia* were practices which were always carried out because of an alliance with diabolical forces.[64] For his part, Della Porta would have declared in the *Magia naturalis* that in nature there is both good and bad, thus advocating a sort of naturalistic agnosticism that was completely incomprehensible to those who, like Bodin, saw nature as the theatre of good or evil spiritual forces which are allowed to act only by God.[65] Storella effectively excludes the possibility that the ignorant old women accused of witchcraft could practice that form of magic, thus participating in the composite sixteenth-century intellectual movement which, from Agrippa to Bruno, from Wier to Della Porta, would have refuted the beliefs in witchcraft by means of natural magic and medicine.

Storella contributes to the debate by proposing a kind of philosophical elitism of magic. As Wier had noted, in the practice of witchcraft it would be possible to recognize the active presence of the devil, the 'fraudulent master',[66] who, however, Wier specified, uses mentally ill old women. What Wier questioned was whether *veneficium* was the result of a pact with the devil. The diabolical pact was the backbone of the accusation of witchcraft carried out by the inquisitorial regime of the time. Without the recognition of the witch's active participation in this pact, this accusation had no juridical reason to exist and with it the possibility of condemning the alleged witch to death became void.[67]

In Storella's argument on the *veneficium*, the so-called witches are implicitly excluded from the possibility of practising it as they would been useless tools for the devil himself. The *magus veneficus* must have logical skills equal to those of the devil, skills completely absent, it goes without saying, in the so-called witches. On the other hand, as Storella recalled in his commentary on the *Secretum*, as the medical tradition that dates back to Galen and Averroes teaches, the so-called venefical practices have a philosophical and natural foundation and there is no need to resort to explanations such as that of the diabolical pact. Even the true magus, as Ficino, Giovanni Pico della Mirandola and the *Secretum secretorum* argue, has nothing to do with practices resulting from a diabolical pact, since, Storella precises, magic is a very noble art dedicated to wisdom. Although the *scientia* (and not a diabolical pact) could allow the magi to practice evil, the *sapientia* to which they nobly aspire, Storella declares mindful of the Aristotelian lesson would prevent them from taking such action. [68]

3.5 Conclusions

In light of these elements, which demonstrate that Storella engaged in the Aristotelian justification of the various forms of magic for numerous years, it is not surprising that, in the *Enumeratio*, written after the Neapolitan experience which ended at the end of 1558, Storella comes to attribute a 'necromantic' text such as the *Mors animae* to Aristotle. In the works dedicated to logic, published in Naples in the years 1557 and 1561, Storella arrives at the possibility of supporting the logical (Aristotelian) structure of magic, even a necromantic one, strategically brought back into the natural (though potentially evil) realm of the *veneficium*. The attribution to Aristotle of the venifico-necromantic book *Liber de irradiationibus: necromantia, mors animae* becomes a philological assumption which Storella employs strategically, banking on the fact that, as a professor of the time, the 'proof' of the truth of a doctrine is to be found in the text of Aristotle.

If, with Storella, it is possible to speak of an Aristotelian side of magic, which establishes its own foundations in Aristotle's logic, it is also possible to express oneself in terms of a Hermetic side of Aristotelianism. This peculiar Hermetic Aristotelianism (springing from the *Secretum secretorum*) is constantly intertwined with the Albertine and pseudo-Albertine tradition, from which it draws support in the process of legitimizing 'sister' disciplines such as natural magic and alchemy.

If the Albertine lesson, together with his own peculiar image of Aristotle as a magus, serves Storella to justify the tradition of magic from the point of view of science, the ethical lesson of Aristotle, for which the end of true wisdom can only be Good, is intertwined in Storella's texts with the lesson of Hermes, the wise man that not only the Renaissance magi but Aristotle himself in the *Secretum* had more or less explicitly followed in legitimizing magic.

According to Storella, the magus – and not the so-called witch – by virtue of his logical skills has all the tools to do evil through so-called *veneficium*. However, this is prevented by the ethical dimension of the true magic that the magus practices. The *veneficium* is thus traced back to nothing more than a scientific study, based on Aristotelian logic, of the natural properties of poisons – a study that the magus, like Aristotle, will never be able to bend to evil outcomes. Ethics, thus, intervenes to prevent science from turning into necromancy, while the latter, by virtue of its logical foundations, will resist being practised even by the so-called witches.

It is a path of both scientific and moral legitimation of magic which, in the Renaissance, was designed by those philosophers who, on the basis of ancient Neoplatonic and Hermetic wisdom, had defined themselves as magi and which Storella, through a philosophical and philological discourse that has its fulcrum in the *Secretum secretorum*, strategically locates in Aristotelianism. Aristotle's philosophy is thus torn from the paraphernalia of the inquisitor and the demonologist, and becomes the pivotal instrument of the scientific and ethical justification of the magus's investigation of the marvellous in nature.

Notes

1. Charles Schmitt, *Aristotle and the Renaissance* (Cambridge, MA, London: Harvard University Press, 1983); Luca Bianchi, *Studi sull'aristotelismo rinascimentale* (Padua: Il Poligrafo, 2003); Eva Del Soldato, *Early Modern Aristotle. On the Making and Unmaking of Authority* (Philadelphia: University of Pennsylvania Press, 2020); Hellen Hattab, 'Renaissance Aristotelianism(s)', in *The Cambridge History of Philosophy of the Scientific Revolution*, eds David M. Miller and Dana Jalobeanu (Cambridge: Cambridge University Press, 2022), 58–74.
2. Brian Copenhaver, *Magic in Western Culture. From Antiquity to the Enlightenment* (New York: Cambridge University Press, 2015), 272–84.
3. Vincenzo Spampanato, *Vita di Giordano Bruno, con documenti editi e inediti*, 2 vols (Messina: Giuseppe Principato, 1921), vol. 1, 217.
4. *Secretum secretorum* Aristotelis *ad Alexandrum Magnum* (Neapoli: Matthiam Cancer, Venietiis: s. e., 1555), f. 21v. See Charles B. Schmitt, 'Francesco Storella and the Last Printed Edition of the Latin *Secretum secretorum* (1555)', in *Pseudo-Aristotle. The Secret of Secrets. Sources and Influences*, eds William F. Ryan and Charles B. Schmitt (London: The Warburg Institute, 1982), 124–31. On the term *magus* see James Rives, '*Magus* and its Cognates in Classic Latin', in *Magical Practice in the Latin West: Papers from the International Conference held at the University of Zaragoza, 30 Sept–1 Oct 2005*, eds Richard L. Gordon and Francisco Marco Simón (Leiden: Brill, 2010), 53–77.
5. By 'occult sciences', I refer primarily to those disciplines, such as magic, alchemy and chiromancy which, in Storella's work, were based on astrology. Strictly speaking, astrology cannot be classified as an occult science, being rather, in Storella's thought, a discipline which, by virtue of its logical and geometric-mathematical status, guarantees a rational foundation for the 'occult' element present in them. On astrology as a geometric-mathematical science and its relationship with the occult sciences in the Renaissance, see Darrel H. Rutkin, *Sapientia Astrologica: Astrology, Magic and Natural Knowledge, ca. 1250–1800* (Cham: Springer International Publishing, 2019), XVII. On the place of astrology in the pseudo-Aristotelian *corpus*, see David Juste, 'Les textes astrologiques latins attribués à Aristote', in *The Medieval Legends of Philosophers and Scholars*, *Micrologus* XXI (Florence: Sismel, Edizioni del Galluzzo, 2013), 145–64. On the place of the occult sciences in the pseudo-Aristotelian *corpus*, see Lynn Thorndike, 'The Latin pseudo-Aristotle and Medieval Occult Science', *The Journal of English and Germanic Philology* 21, no. 2 (1922): 229–58; Charles Schmitt, *Pseudo-Aristoteles Latinus. A Guide to Latin Works Falsely Attributed to Aristotle before 1500* (London: The Warburg Institute, 1985); Charles Burnett, 'Arabic, Greek and Latin Works on Astrological Magic Attributed to Aristotle', in *Pseudo-Aristotle in*

the Middle Ages, eds Jill Kraye, William F. Ryan and Charles B. Schmitt (London: The Warburg Institute, 1986), 84–96; Burnett, 'Aristotle as an Authority on Judicial Astrology', in *Florilegium Mediaevale, Études offertes à Jacqueline Hamesse à l'occasion de son éméritat*, eds José Meirinhos and Olga Weijers (Louvain-la-Neuve: Brepols, 2009), 41–62; Liana Saif, *The Arabic Influences on Early Modern Occult Philosophy* (London: Palgrave, 2015); See also Manfred Ullmann, *Die Natur-und Geheimwissenschaften im Islam*, Handbuch der Orientalistik, I, VI, 2 (Leiden: Brill, 1972), 76–7, 220, 406, 424–5; David Pingree, 'The Diffusion of Arabic Magical Texts in Western Europe', in *La diffusione delle scienze islamiche nel medio evo europeo* (Rome: Accademia Nazionale dei Lincei, 1987), 57–102; Steven J. Williams, 'Defining the *Corpus Aristotelicum*: Scholastic Awareness of Aristotelian Spuria in the High Middle Ages', *Journal of the Warburg and Courtauld Institutes* 58 (1995): 29–51.

6 See Antonio Antonaci, *Francesco Storella filosofo salentino del Cinquecento* (Galatina: Editrice Salentina, 1966).

7 See Donato Verardi, 'Francesco Storella', in *Encyclopedia of Renaissance Philosophy*, ed. Marco Sgarbi (Cham: Springer, 2022), 3142–3.

8 Francesco Storella, *Libellus quo ad peripateticas aures singulare verum syllogismum ingredi adversus pseudologicos huius tempestatis luce clarus ostenditur* (Neapoli: Matthias Cancer, 1557).

9 Ioan. Baptistae Portae *Magiae naturalis sive de miraculis rerum naturalium libri IIII* (Neapoli: Matthias Cancer, 1558).

10 See Donato Verardi, *La scienza e i segreti della natura a Napoli nel Rinascimento. La magia naturale di Giovan Battista Della porta* (Florence: Firenze University Press, 2018).

11 Francesco Storella, *Libellus de utilitate logices* (Neapoli: Raymundus Amatus, 1561).

12 On Balduino, see Giovanni Papuli, *Girolamo Balduino. Ricerche sulla logica della scuola di Padova nel Rinascimento* (Manduria: Lacaida,1967).

13 *Quaesita logicalia* domini H. Balduini *De Monte Arduo philosophi celeberrimi omnibus per necessaria logicis videlicet . . . Eiusdem Balduini, ac Sarnensis Expositio super prohemium epitomatum logicalium Auerr. Cordubensis, Superadditae ipsis quesitis ponderationes, declarationes, et annotationes Vincentii Colle Sarnensis*, Neapoli 1561. See Giovanni Papuli, 'La teoria del *regressus* come metodo scientifico negli autori della scuola di Padova', in *Aristotelismo veneto e scienza moderna*, 2 vols, ed. Luigi Olivieri (Padua: Antenore 1983), vol. 1, 221–77.

14 See Vittoria Perrone Compagni, *Introduzione* a P. Pomponazzi, *De Incantationibus*, ed. Vittoria Perrone Compagni (Florence: Olschki, 2011), XXVIII.

15 Storella, *Libellus quo ad peripateticas aures singulare verum syllogismum ingredi*, c. 4v–5v. Giordano Bruno, '*De magia naturali*', in *Opere magiche*, eds Simonetta Bassi,

Elisabetta Scapparone and Nicoletta Tirinnanzi, dir. Michele Ciliberto (Milan: Adelphi, 2000), 162.
16 Storella, *Libellus de utilitate Logices*, c. 26v.
17 Ibid., c. 27r.
18 Donato Verardi, *Arti magiche e arti liberali nel Rinascimento. Da Ariosto a Della Porta* (Lugano: Agorà & Co., 2018). See also Graziella Federici Vescovini, 'L'astrologia all'Università di Ferrara nel Quattrocento', in *La rinascita del sapere*, ed. Patrizia Castelli (Venice: Marsilio, 1991), 293–306; G. Federici Vescovini, 'I programmi degli insegnamenti del Collegio di Medicina, Filosofia e Astrologia, dello Statuto dell'Università di Bologna del 1405', in *Roma magistra mundi. Itineraria culturae mediaevalis. Mélanges offerts au Père L. E. Boyle a l'occasion de son 75ᵉ anniversaire*, ed. Jaqueline Hamesse, t. I. (Louvain-la-Neuve: Brepols, 1998), 193–223; Luca Bianchi, 'I contenuti dell'insegnamento: arti liberali e filosofia nei secoli XIII-XVI', in *Storia delle Università in Italia*, 3 vols, eds Gian Paolo Brizzi, Piero del Negro and Andrea Romano (Messina: Sicania, 2007), vol. 2, 117–41; Marco Forlivesi, *La filosofia universitaria tra XV e XVII secolo* (Padua: Cleup, 2013).
19 Perrone Compagni, *Introduzione*, in Pietro Pomponazzi, *De Incantationibus*, XI-LXXI.
20 Liana Saif, 'A Preliminary Study of the Pseudo-Aristotelian *Hermetica*: Texts, Context, and Doctrines', *Al-ʿUṣūr al-Wusṭā* 29, no. 1 (2021): 20–80, especially 21–2. See also *Pseudo-Aristotle. The Secret of Secrets. Sources and Influences*; Burnett, 'Aristotle as an Authority on Judicial Astrology', 41–62.
21 Graziella Federici Vescovini, '*La scienza bizantina e latina: la nascita di una scienza europea. Lo pseudo-Aristotele e le tradizioni affini*', in *Storia della Scienza* (Rome: Istituto della Enciclopedia Italiana, 2001), 307–12.
22 A range of 'occult arts' with clear empirical implications were already considered legitimate both by Roger Bacon, who had written an important commentary on the *Secretum secretorum* in the Middle Ages, and by those who, like Bacon, had expressed themselves in favour of the authenticity of the work. As William Eamon pointed out, the 'Aristotelianism' of the *Secretum secretorum* enabled Bacon 'to make far more sweeping claims for "experimentation" than the authentic writings of Aristotle would ever have allowed him to make', William Eamon, *Science and the Secrets of Nature: Books of Secrets in Medieval and Early Modern Culture* (Princeton: Princeton University Press, Princeton, 1994), 51.
23 Storella correctly cites Albertus's *De animalibus*. See Albertus Magnus, *On Animals*, translated and annotated by K. F. Kitchell and I. M. Resnick (Baltimore and London: The John Hopkins University Press, 1999), vol. 1, Book VII, chp. 5, 647. It is necessary to highlight how, in the *Sententiarum*, Albertus Magnus attributed the *Secretum secretorum* to Hermes and not to Aristotle. See Albertus Magnus, *Sententiarum*, in *Opera*, ed. Jammy (Lione: 1652), XVI, 710.

24 Storella certainly must have known the Achillini edition, as well as the abbreviated edition by Franciscus Taegius, published at Pavia in 1516, which Storella precisely mentions in his Preface. See Storella, *Preface*, in *Secretum secretorum*, 2v–3r.
25 See Storella, *Preface*, in *Secretum secretorum*, 2v–3r.
26 Achillini, also wrote a *Quaestio de subiecto physionomiae et chyromantiae*, published in 1503 in Bologna, to which Storella explicitly refers in the *Secretum secretorum*. According to Achillini, physiognomics and chiromancy have man as their object and are sciences subordinated to the natural philosophy of Aristotle. In addition to the Achillini's edition of the *Secretum secretorum*, Storella certainly knows that of Taegius, which he cites in his preface, but he tries above all to reconstruct the text starting from what are variously defined 'Vetera exemplaria', 'vetustissima exemplaria', 'Vetustissimus codex' and 'antiquissimus codex'. See Schmitt, *Francesco Storella and the Last Printed Edition of the Latin Secretum secretorum (1555)*. On Achillini, see also Paola Zambelli, 'Aut diabolus aut Achillinus. Fisiognomica, astrologia e demonologia nel metodo di un aristotelico', *Rinascimento* 18 (1978): 58–86.
27 Cf. Averroes, *In De cael.*, in *Nove transaltioni librorum de celo et mundo . . . ab Averroi Cordubensi commentate*, s.l., 1483.
28 See Peter of Abano, *Problemata* (Mantue, 1475): 25, especially 20.
29 Pietro d'Abano, *Lucidator dubitabilium astronomiae*, ed. Graziella Federici Vescovini (Padua: Programma e 1+1, 1988), 122. See also Fabio Seller, *Scientia Astrorum* (Naples: Giannini Editore, 2009).
30 As is known, the debate concerning the theoretical legitimacy of physiognomics dates back to at least the twelfth century, with the rediscovery of the anonymous *De physiognomonia liber*. It is a long process that continues into the thirteenth century with the circulation of the second treatise of the *Liber Almansoris* by Razi, the writing of the *Liber phisionomiae* by Michael Scot, the diffusion of the *Secretum secretorum* and the version of the pseudo-Aristotelian *Physionomia* by Bartolomeo da Messina. See Jole Agrimi, *Ingeniosa scientia nature. Studi sulla fisiognomica medievale* (Florence: Sismel, Edizioni del Galluzzo, 2002), 63.
31 Bartolommeo Cocles, *Chyromantiae et Physionomiae Anastasis* cum approbatione magistri Alexandri de Achillinis (Bononiae, 1504), Liber primus, chp. 1, p. n.
32 Storella, *Secretum secretorum* Aristotelis, c. 61r–64v: c. 61r.
33 See Chiara Crisciani, *Ruggero Bacone e l' 'Aristotele' del* Secretum secretorum, in *Christian readings of Aristotle from the Middle Ages to the Renaissance*, ed. Luca Bianchi (Turnhout: Brepols, 2011), 37–64.
34 On Pietro Bono's arguments, see Chiara Crisciani, '*Aristotele, Avicenna e* Meteore *nella* Pretiosa Margarita *di Pietro Bono*', in *Aristotele chemicus. Il IV libro dei* Meteorologica *nella tradizione antica e medievale*, ed. Cristina Viano (Sankt Augustin: Verlag, 2002), 165–82.

35 Storella, *De utilitate logices*, f. 10rv. *Tractatulus quinquaginta contradictionum*, Quadracesima tertia, f. 10r.

36 A very similar definition can be also found in Agrippa's *De incertitudine*. See Agrippa, *De incertitudine et vanitate scientiarum* (Coloniae: 1585), 202.

37 Benedek Láng, *Unlocked Books. Manuscripts of Learned Magic in the Medieval Libraries of Central Europe* (University Park: Pennsylvania University Park, 2020), 55.

38 See Albertus Magnus, *Liber aggregationis seu liber secretorum. De virtutibus, herbarum, lapidarum et animalium quorundam*, Impressum quidem est hoc opusculum per Magistrum Iohannem de Annunciata de Augusta, 1478. See Isabelle Draelants and Antonella Sannino, *Albertinisme et Hermetisme dans une anthologie en faveur de la magie, le Liber aggregationis: prospective*, 'Archives et bibliothèques de Belgique', *Numéro spécial* 83 (2007): 223–51. On Della Porta and his relationship with the Pseudo-Albertus Magnus, see Verardi, *La scienza e i segreti della natura a Napoli nel Rinascimento*. On the presence of the pseudo-Albertus in Bruno's work, see in particular G. Bruno, *De Magia mathematica*, in *Opere magiche*, 4–139, and the relative annotated notes of the editors, 141–58.

39 Pseudo-Aristotle, *Lapidarium Aristotelis*, or *De lapidibus* (two versions), in 'Aristoteles *De lapidibus* und Arnoldus Saxo', *Zeitschrift für deutsches Altertum und deutsche Literatur* 18, no. 6 (1875), 321–455, 349–82 and 384–97.

40 Albertus Magnus, *De mineralibus et rebus metallicis libri quinque* (Cologne, 1569), 4.

41 *Secretum secretorum Aristotelis*, 80.

42 Albertus Magnus, *De natura loci*, II, chp. I, edidit Paulus Hossfeld (Monasterii Westfalorum: in Aedibus Aschendorff, 1980), 24.

43 See Albert the Great, *Book of Minerals*, trans. Dorothy Wyckoff (London: Oxford University Press, Ely House, 1967), II, iii, 3, 63: 'Of all the ancients, Hermes gives the most probable reason for the powers of stones, since we know for a fact that all the powers of things below come from above. For [the stars] above, by their substance and light, position, motion, and configuration pour down into things below all the noble powers they possess. Nevertheless, this statement is not enough for natural science, although perhaps it may be sufficient for astrology and magic', Albert the Great, *Book of Minerals*, trans. Dorothy Wyckoff (London: Oxford University Press, Ely House, 1967), II, iii, 3, 63. On Albertus Magnus's magic and astrology, see H. Darrel Rutkin, 'Astrology and Magic', in *A Companion to Albert the Great: Theology, Philosophy, and the Sciences*, ed. Irven M. Resnick (Leiden: Brill, 2013), 451–505; Saif, *The Arabic Influences on Early Modern Occult Philosophy*, 78–82.

44 See Paola Zambelli, *White Magic, Black Magic in the European Renaissance* (Leiden and Boston: Brill, 2007); H. Darrel Rutkin, 'The Physics and Metaphysics of

Talismans (Imagines Astronomicae) in Marsilio Ficino's *De vita libri tres*: A Case Study in (Neo)Platonism, Aristotelianism and the Esoteric Tradition', in *Platonismus und Esoterik in Byzantinischem Mittelalter und Italienischer Renaissance*, ed. Helmut Seng (Heidelberg: Universitätsverlag Winter, 2013), 149–74.

45 On Della Porta's astrological and empirical approach and his distance from the metaphysical one, see Verardi, *La scienza e i segreti della natura a Napoli nel Rinascimento*, 83–120; Eamon, *Science and the Secrets of Nature*, 194–233. On Della Porta's science see also Sergius Kodera, 'Giambattista Della Porta's Histrionic Science', *California Italian Studies* 3/1 (2012): 1–27. On Della Porta's experimental attitudes, see the recent study by Arianna Borrelli, 'Giovan Battista Della Porta's Construction of Pneumatic Phenomena and His Use of Recipes as Heuristic Tools', *Centaurus* 62/3 (2020), Special Issue: *The Creative Power of Experimentation: Bacon and Della Porta* (eds Doina-Cristina Rusu and Dana Jalobeanu): 406, especially 24.

46 *Secretum secretorum Aristotelis*, chp. XLII, p. 90.

47 Gio. Baptista Porta, *Dei miracoli et maravigliosi effetti dalla natura prodotti libri IIII* (Venice: Avanzi, MDLX), I, 10, c. 18rv. Io. Baptistae Portae *Magiae naturalis sive de miraculis rerum naturalium libri IIII* (Neapoli: Matthias Cancer, 1558), I, 10: 17; Porta, *Natural Magick in Twenty Books* (London: T. Young and S. Speed, 1658), I, 13, 18–19; Portae *Magiae naturalis libri XX Ab ipso autore espurgati, et superaucti, in quibus scientiarum Naturalium divitiae, et delitiae demostrantur [. . .] cum privilegio* (Neapoli: apud H. Salvianum, 1589), I, 13, 13–14. Della Porta certainly has the *Secretum secretorum* in mind, attributing it to Aristotle. See the chapter of the *Secretum secretorum*, *De puella nutrita veneno* (ed. Storella, c. 37), taken up in the *Magiae naturalis libri XX*, VIII, 15. See Della Porta, *Della Magia naturale libri XX, Tradotti da Latino in Volgare, e dall'istesso autore accresciuti sotto nome di Gio De Rosa* (Naples: Buliffon, 1677), VIII, 15, 288.

48 See Ambr. S. 79 sup., ff. 233r–234r.

49 Schmitt, 'Francesco Storella and the Last Printed Edition of the Latin *Secretum secretorum* (1555)', 127.

50 See Burnett, 'Arabic, Greek and Latin Works on Astrological Magic attributed to Aristotle', 84–96.

51 On the chapters taken from Aristotle's *Astrological Judgements* (*Iudicia*) in the *Liber Novem Iudicum*, and the corresponding chapters in the separately occurring Aristotle's *Iudicia*, see Burnett, 'Aristotle as an Authority on Judicial Astrology', 41–62.

52 If Storella's attention to natural magic dates back to his Paduan doctorate, his astrological interests resulted from frequent exposure to these topics at home growing up, which he confirms in the *Explanatio in digressione undecimi commenti Averrois* published in Naples in 1553. See Francesco Storella, *Explanatio in digressione undecimi commenti Averrois* (Naples: Cilium Allifanum, 1553), f. 17v.

53 Storella also discusses some alchemical works. He does not comment on the authenticity of the *Liber perfecti magisterii* and the *Liber de rabis*. The *Lumen luminum*, on the other hand, he believes is authentic, while he does not seem to believe in the authenticity of *De alchimia ad Arda seu Ardagotum discipulum*. See Ambr. S. 79 sup. ff. 239v–243v. With regard to astrology, in the *Enumeratio* Storella attributes four works to Aristotle: *Astronomia, Astrologia, Libellus de viginti octo mansionibus Lunae* and *Liber de regiminibus coelestibus*. See Ambr. S. 79 sup. ff. 245v–246v.

54 Cornelius Agrippa, *De incertitudine et vanitate scientiarum*, chp. xliiii, 1536, [s.l.] [s.n.], f. hiiv.

55 Girolamo Cardano, *De subtilitate*, xviii, in *Opera omnia* (Lugduni: Ioannis Antonii Huguetan & Marci Antonii Ravaud, 1663), t. 3, 646.

56 See Jean Bodin, *De la démonomanie des sorcieres*, eds Virginia Krause, Cristian Martin and Eric MacPhail (Genèvre: Droz, 2016), 459–60. See Verardi, *La scienza e i segreti della natura a Napoli nel Rinascimento*, 126–32.

57 See Agrippa, *De incertitudine*, chp. xliiii, ff. hiiv–hiiiv.

58 The 'agnostic' interpretation of *veneficium* proposed by Della Porta in *Magia naturalis* finds different points of contact with that of Storella, proof of a profoundly rationalist interpretation of the magic in vogue in the Neapolitan context of the time, both within the university and outside of it. See Verardi, *La scienza e i segreti della natura a Napoli nel Rinascimento*, 123–45.

59 F. Storella, *Libellus de utilitate Logices*, f. 26v.?

60 See Giovanni Pico della Mirandola, *Conclusiones sive theses DCCCC Romae anno 1486 publice disputandae, sed non admissae*, éd. par Bohdan Kieszkowski (Genève: Droz, 1973), 79.

61 See Vittoria Perrone Compagni, 'Le opere magiche di Giordano Bruno: Note di lettura', *Rivista di Storia della filosofia* 2 (2002): 201–24.

62 See Ambr. S. 79 sup. ff. 239v–243v. Peter of Abano, following the author (believed by some to be Albertus Magnus) of the *Speculum astronomiae*, condemns the *Mors animae*, linking it, in *Lucidator dubitabilium astronomiae*, to the *Secretum secretorum*. It should be noted that the doctrines attributable to the *Mors animae* – a work that already evokes in the title the complex problem of the immortality of the soul – were present in the first Latin version of the *Secretum secretorum* attributed to Philip of Tripoli (of uncertain dating, before 1237 or between 1262 and 1271). Some chapters, such as the one on onomancy, were subsequently suppressed by the ecclesiastical authorities, on account of their necromantic character. See Graziella Federici Vescovini, *La scienza bizantina e latina: la nascita di una scienza europea. Lo pseudo-Aristotele e le tradizioni affini*, in *Storia della Scienza* (Rome: Istituto della Enciclopedia Italiana, 2001), 307–12. In the Renaissance, Peter of Abano's fame as a necromancer was fuelled by the circulation, to which Storella also alludes, of

apocryphal necromantic texts attributed to him. On this problem, see Jean-Patrice Boudet, *Magie et illusionnisme entre Moyen Âge et Renaissance: Les 'Annulorum experimenta' attribués à Pietro d'Abano*, in *Médicine, astrologie et magie entre Moyen Âge et Renaissance: autor de Pietro d'Abano*, eds Jean-Patrice Boudet, Frank Collard, Nicolas Weill-Parot (Florence: Sismel, Edizioni del Galluzzo, 2013), 247–94 ; Julien Véronèse, *Pietro d'Abano magicien à la Renaissance: Les cas de l'Elucidarius Magice (ou Lucidarium artis nigromantice)*, in *Médicine, astrologie et magie entre Moyen Âge et* Renaissance, 295–330. It is important to underline Storella's familiarity with the position of Peter of Abano expounded in the *Lucidator*, citing this text and its author among the authorities who recognized the Aristotelian authorship of the text. See, Storella, Preface, in *Secretum secretorum*, 3r.

63 We will find a very similar formulation, which insists on the morally reprehensible character of venefical magic, in Bruno's *De Magia Naturali*, where, in fact, Bruno claims that the magician is defined as evil if he tends to Evil, while if he tends to Good, he is a kind of doctor. If the magician tries to enact extreme evil and death – Bruno continues – we can define him as a 'venefical magus'. See Bruno, *De magia naturali*, in *Opere magiche*, 165.

64 See Germana Ernst, 'I poteri delle streghe tra cause naturali e interventi diabolici. Spunti di un dibattito', in *Giovan Battista Della Porta nell'Europa del suo tempo*, ed. Maurizio Torrini (Naples: Guida, 1990), 167–97.

65 I. B. Portae *Magiae naturalis libri viginti, Ad lectore praefatio*, 2. See Verardi, *La scienza e i Segreti della natura a Napoli nel Rinascimento*, 130–2.

66 John Wier, *De praestigiis daemonum et incantationibus ac veneficiis libri sex* (Basilea: Ex Officina Oporiniana, 1568), 273.

67 See Michaela Valente, *Johann Wier. Agli albori della critica razionale dell'occulto e del demoniaco nell'Europa del Cinquecento* (Florence: Olsckhi, 2003).

68 Storella's distrust of the possibility that a venefical magic could exist through an implicit diabolical pact is confirmed by him in the commentary on the *Secretum secretorum*. Commenting on the chapter entitled 'De puella nutrida veneno', which tells of a girl who, fed on snake venom, had changed her own nature into that of a snake, Storella does not seem to look favourably on 'demonological' arguments. The witchcraft interpretation of the notion of *veneficium* is strategically resized. He shows greater sympathy for the doctrines of Galen and Averroes, which would show the natural reason of this marvellous phenomenon reported by the *Secretum*. In this passage, Storella also lavishes himself in a praise of natural magic, citing, among other works, the *Conclusiones* by Giovanni Pico, and the *De vita* by Marsilio Ficino as evidence of the nobility of the true magic of the wise, that is, the magi. Doing evil is a possibility that, although offered by the *scientia*, is programmatically excluded by the magi, who are dedicated to wisdom. See *Secretum secretorum*, f. 21rv.

4

Making and unmaking marvels in early modern Europe

William Eamon

4.1 Introduction

Before Renaissance magic sparked renewed interest in the occult, the mysterious and hidden forces of nature were deemed beyond human capacity to know and were strictly off-limits to philosophers. To medieval scholastics, there were occult properties that God had intentionally hidden from humankind. Thomas Aquinas wrote in a treatise on magic that magnetism was an 'occult quality' that humans are incapable of explaining.[1] Like the ne plus ultra of the geographical world that prohibited anyone to venture beyond the familiar territory bounded by Hercules's Pillars, the world of the occult was forbidden intellectual territory. That changed with the rise of natural magic.

What is magic? To most moderns, magic is about creating illusions. Magical tricks performed onstage astonish and delight us but are otherwise harmless. But early modern Europeans didn't think of magic that way. While they were as familiar with magic tricks as we are, since they witnessed them regularly on street corners and plazas, they also knew there was a different kind of magic that we moderns have long since disavowed. It was a form of magic that tapped into nature's secret forces and used them to create 'marvellous' effects – not illusions, but real effects – that nature cannot accomplish on its own, without the intervention of a magus. Historian Valerie Flint defines magic as 'the exercise of a preternatural control over nature by human beings, with the assistance of forces more powerful than they'.[2] By 'preternatural', she refers to the large and nebulous domain of anomalous phenomena 'suspended between the mundane and the miraculous', which had long resisted philosophical explanation. Medieval and early modern natural philosophers never disputed the existence of marvellous or occult phenomena, nor doubted that such phenomena might arise from natural causes. However, with few exceptions they excluded such phenomena from the purview of natural philosophy as neither regular nor demonstrable.[3] Only a miracle – a divine suspension of natural law – can break the natural order. So much for the intellectual's magic. Alongside it, there was also a vast body of everyday magic.

4.2 Magic in everyday life

For centuries people had turned to magic for aid in addressing life's problems. In pre-industrial Europe magic, like religion, was a part of everyday life. People didn't just believe in the efficacy of magic, they used magic themselves. Farmers employed magic to bring rain during a drought or fair weather when gathering the harvest. Animal breeders used magic to ensure the fertility of livestock, sprinkling water from shrines on the genitals of stallions and mares, for example. Midwives used special magical plants such as motherwort to ensure a successful delivery.[4] Even priests used magic when they anointed a sore with holy water. Clerics used magic in other, more consequential ways too, as the example of Don Bartolomeo, a priest in the rural Italian village of Stuffione illustrates. In 1598, Don Bartolomeo was charged by the Inquisition of Modena for having performed a baptism on a *calamita*, or lodestone (magnet), which he then used to entice the favour of his patron, whom he'd offended. 'I did believe that the baptized *calamita* had the power to induce persons touched by it to wish me well, so I touched the clothing of my patron with it', he confessed. Early modern people, including lower clergy like Don Bartolomeo, depended on the goodwill of patrons, and the prospect of losing one's benefactor caused deep anxiety. Resorting to magic was a kind of insurance against such a catastrophe. As punishment for his infraction, the aged friar was essentially given a slap on the wrist: his sacramental functions were suspended, and he was confined under house arrest in his convent in Bologna.[5]

Of all forms of common magic, treasure hunting had the most direct economic impact on everyday life. In the absence of banks, people hid their wealth, and the dream of finding buried treasure was no illusion. Professional treasure hunters drew on a vast arsenal of magic. They had spell books and amulets and lead tablets etched with magical signs. Treasure hunters devised ways to communicate with the spirits that were said to guard treasures. To the horror of ecclesiastical authorities, they invoked angels and saints. They talked to ghosts.

Some even tried to conjure demons. Yet, although thousands of treasure hunters practised in early modern Europe and almost all used magic, very few were ever accused of witchcraft or consorting with demons. Usually treasure hunters just paid a fine or did a few days of penal labour. Common people simply didn't see treasure magic as witchcraft, and most judges agreed.[6]

Miners in early modern Germany believed that deep in the bowels of the earth lurked mountain spirits and mining gnomes (*Bergmännlein*). The German mine supervisor Georgius Agricola wrote an entire book about them and other creatures that dwelled underground, *De amantibus subterraneis*, and discussed them, though sceptically, in his authoritative treatise, *De re metallica* (Figure 4.1). To early modern people, the earth was not inert but teemed with forces that were responsible for the generation of minerals and metals. Like all living and growing things, metals breathed, giving off distinct fumes that miners, using a

Figure 4.1 Dowsing for minerals, from Agricola, *De re metallica* (Basel 1556). Although highly sceptical of dowsing, Agricola gave a detailed description of the art, supposing that the ancients (Homer's Minerva and Circe for example) knew magical dowsing and had passed it down to miners. Public Domain Source: Wikimedia Commons.

special form of magic, could detect. The dowsing or divining rod, like special mirrors and crystal balls, functioned as an instrument of sorcery that detected mineral breaths and revealed hidden knowledge of the underworld. A forked stick usually made of hazelwood, the dowsing rod was believed to be (in expert hands) particularly sensitive to the sounds of the underworld and the vapours emanating from ores. Though not a machine, the dowsing rod was a technology, one that employed magic to harness hidden forces of nature.[7] It was an ancient practice that straddled the border between legitimate and prohibited magic. Was dowsing a form of expertise learned by apprenticeship and long experience? Or was it an art practised by a 'wise man' or magus who possessed secret knowledge and power? Was dowsing a form of divination, like astrology, or was it an empirical practice that involved employing only natural forces? Dowsing shaded into those practices the Church regarded as 'superstitious', that is, as a form of false belief. But, like similar magical practices, it was creatively assimilated rather than rejected outright. Although in 1580 the Catholic witchcraft scholar Jean Bodin identified mining spirits with Satan, he regarded dowsing as legitimate because the attraction between the dowsing rod and metal was commonly experienced by prospectors even though the mechanism underlying it was imperceptible.[8] Dowsing rods worked only in the hands of experts. The artisan was, in this sense, like a magus.

Magic wasn't practised just in the countryside, where farmers and miners dwelled. In cities and towns across Europe, professional sorcerers and sorceresses plied their trade, providing aid and comfort in dealing with common ailments and everyday problems.[9] Cunning men, as they were called in England, used magic to divine treasure in abandoned monasteries and ancient burial mounds, to detect thieves and find lost property. Amulets, carried on one's person or laid on the doorstep, protected against venomous snakes. Charms could be used to entice a lover. Popular magic was a way of coping with real problems and fears of everyday life. None of these practices were thought to involve satanic forces or pacts with demons, although some offenders may have used prayers in unorthodox ways. Magic brought reassurance and a sense that things weren't completely out of one's control. Although the Church was serious about eradicating 'superstitious' practices, to a large degree clerics tolerated common magical arts, regarding them as part of the lore of the *illiterati* and the *rustici* but not demonic.

As the witch hunts picked up steam during the sixteenth century, the art of dowsing, along with other forms of everyday magic, fell under the watchful gaze of ecclesiastical and civil authorities. Some Protestant preachers insisted that dowsing involved making an implicit (though not explicit) pact with Satan. The Wittenberg professor of philosophy Johan Sperling mused whether the dowsing rod dipped because of an occult quality that accounted for the attraction of the hazelwood rod with metal, but he rejected that explanation and concluded that the dowser made an implicit pact with the Devil.[10] There was no doubt in Sperling's mind: dowsing was a form of witchcraft. But the question Sperling pondered was at the core of early modern discussions about magic. What did he mean by an 'occult quality'? Intellectuals of Sperling's time recognized that certain physical properties – for example, the lodestone's attraction to iron – could not be deduced from the object's tangible properties, such as the coldness and hardness of a stone. It's obvious to all that magnets attract iron, but by what cause? To explain such phenomena, intellectuals distinguished between manifest and occult or hidden properties of things, both considered real properties of nature. The difference lay in whether the cause of a given phenomenon was observable. For example, characteristics such as hotness, wetness, hardness and roughness are tangible, whereas, occult properties, including planetary influence, the action of poison or the attraction of a lodestone to iron, are imperceptible. You could see the effects of such a property, but its cause was hidden. As a Jesuit scholar jesuitically explained, although occult qualities are 'manifest to the intellect, they are not apparent to the senses'.[11] For the most part, scholastics agreed that occult properties could not be explained by Aristotelian principles and they therefore placed such properties outside the boundaries of natural philosophy. Banished from the territory of natural philosophy, occult properties were exiled to the domain of magic.[12] They were the tools, so to speak, of the magus, the powers a sorcerer used to produce the impressive 'marvels' of his art, causing nature to do out-of-the-ordinary things it can't do without intervention. But the Devil was also a worker of occult properties. The Devil too made marvels. That was the rub: How do you tell one from the other?

The Church's traditionally tolerant stance towards common magic was completely reversed in the sixteenth century, as hysteria over witchcraft took hold. It's difficult to imagine the terror the witch craze inflicted on people. Anyone, even the most unsuspecting, could be caught up in the vise of the witch hunts. The astronomer Johannes Kepler's aged mother Katharina was one of the estimated 80,000 persons, mostly women, who were accused of witchcraft in Europe. Although the old widow was eventually acquitted, her trial, which commenced in 1615, lasted six years while the great astronomer, at the height of his career, was completing his masterpiece, *Astronomia nova*.[13] Katharina escaped execution, thanks to her son's connections. But tens of thousands of others were murdered for their supposed crime. As the terror spread, intellectuals who were curious about magic (a group that included Johannes Kepler) were put on the defensive and forced to defend the kind of magic they regarded as legitimate. In doing so, they made a distinction between a 'natural magic' that only harnessed the forces of nature and a demonic magic that instead relied on the invocation of angels and demons.[14] While the latter should be forbidden, they argued, natural magic was a legitimate science that held high promise for making improvements beneficial for human welfare.

4.3 The Renaissance of ancient magic

Intellectual magic flourished in the Renaissance. While medieval theologians viewed magic with fear and loathing, in the late fifteenth-century magic had a stunning rebirth and remained at the centre of attention among humanists and philosophers for nearly 200 years.[15] The Florentine humanist Marsilio Ficino (1463–94) set the stage for the revival with his translation of an eclectic and barely coherent collection of Greek texts believed to contain the magical doctrine of Hermes Trismegistus, a Greek version of the ancient Egyptian god Thoth. The pseudonymous Hermetic treatises, which were printed in 1471, enlivened curiosity about magic among intellectuals – not the common sort of magic practised by ordinary people but a kind of magic that carried a long and respected (though fake) pedigree. Hermetic magic presented a lofty vision of humanity as embodied in the figure of the magus, one whose power resides in knowing how to manipulate nature's hidden forces to produce wondrous effects. Created in the image of God, a divine craftsman (demiurge) who fashions the universe from formless matter, the human magus too is an artisan – one who, having scrutinized God's handiwork, knows the material he works with and makes wondrous art by joining the mind and hand.[16] Enshrined in the Hermetic doctrine was the Neoplatonic conception of nature as a reservoir teeming with hidden forces that the magus could tap into. It also inherited the idea of a correspondence between the human microcosm and the universal macrocosm, an analogy that in one of the Hermetic works is expressed as, 'What is Above is like what is Below, what is Below is like what is Above': the fundamental principle of all magic and a maxim familiar to magical adepts from Hermes Trismegistus to Madame Blavatsky.[17]

No one knew the sublime promise and terrifying danger of magic better than the German physician and philosopher Heinrich Cornelius Agrippa von

Nettesheim (1486–1535). His notorious magic manual, *De Occulta Philosophia* (*On Occult Philosophy*), was printed in 1535, having circulated in manuscript since 1510. It's no wonder Agrippa hesitated to publish the work. In it he made an audacious claim: that natural magic was 'the pinnacle of natural philosophy'; indeed is 'the supreme and holiest science'. He exalts the occult philosophy as a grand unified theory that brings together physics, mathematics and theology, joining earth to heaven to produce marvellous works:

> Helped by the mutual and timely application of natural virtues, it produces works of incomprehensible wonder. Observing the powers of all things natural and celestial, probing the sympathy of these powers in painstaking inquiry, it brings powers stored away and lying hidden in nature into the open. Using lower things as a kind of bait, it links the resources of higher things to them, so that astonishing wonders occur, not so much by art as by nature.[18]

Agrippa's book became the desk reference for all intellectuals who wrote about magic. And all agreed that some forms of technology – burning mirrors, automata and flying machines, for example – belonged to the realm of magic.[19]

4.4 The wizard of Naples

The concept of natural magic played a secondary role in the natural philosophy of medieval scholasticism, which was mostly about normal events that occur naturally and with regularity.[20] Although the term *magia naturalis* appears for the first time in William of Auvergne's *De legibus*, William associated the concept with necromancy in order to account for demonic power. For him, natural magic was primarily a theological rather than a natural philosophical concept.[21] The Renaissance notion of natural magic, which was a direct challenge to the natural philosophy and the demonology of the inquisitors, emerged in the late fifteenth century alongside – and in radical opposition to – the criminalization by the Church and state of the ritualized practices people used to enlist the help of occult powers to navigate everyday life. In the sixteenth century, the concept of natural magic became fashionable in intellectual circles, discussed in salons and academies from Naples to Paris. Largely responsible for the sudden popularity of natural magic was a blockbuster book by the Neapolitan aristocrat, philosopher and playwright Giambattista Della Porta, who was by far the most celebrated proponent of natural magic in early modern Europe. The book, bearing the title *Magia naturalis* (*Natural Magic*), described all manner of experiments in agriculture, optics, magnetism, hydraulics, distillation, cosmetics and a bunch tossed into a disordered chapter titled 'Chaos' because its subjects didn't fit any of the other categories – such things as how to freshen sea water and make a hearing aid, an instrument that Della Porta assures 'is confirmed in the principles of natural philosophy' – all meant to demonstrate the myriad ways of exploiting the awesome hidden power of nature. First published in Latin in 1558, Della Porta's book grew as his experiments multiplied. By 1589 he had accumulated so many secrets (as he called his experiments) – including many supposedly done in the 'academy of secrets' that met in his home – that he more than doubled the size of his book in a new edition brought out that year. *Natural Magic* was printed in more than fifty early modern editions, including translations into French, Italian, English, Dutch, Spanish and the last, a German edition of 1714. His sensational book was for four generations the theoretical and experimental foundation of natural magic for intellectuals all over Europe. No one who kept up with developments in the sciences of secrets could ignore it.[22] No wonder it was said that the two biggest tourist attractions of Naples around the year 1600 were the baths of Pozzuoli and Giambattista Della Porta.[23]

The Della Porta residence in Naples made the city a mecca for literati from all over Europe and a necessary stop on the customary Grand Tour.[24] Della Porta wrote on a multitude of subjects – cryptology, astrology, physiognomy, horticulture and much more. And he was an engaging wit, as his comic plays bear witness. But people came not just to engage in learned conversation with the wizard of Naples but also to witness his extraordinary demonstrations of magic: mirrors that reflected outlandish visions, fireballs shot into the air, lighting the night skies, invisible writing, water clocks, 'wonders of the lodestone' and a mirror that displayed images of viewers suspended in the air, 'like birds in flight' – all the awesome productions of the novel Renaissance science of natural magic.[25]

Although Della Porta was a talented performer of magical experiments, to him natural magic wasn't just smoke and mirrors. It was a serious science that demonstrated how to discover nature's inner forces and put them to work. If you understood nature's inner powers you could apply them to improve on nature, whether in growing better crops, making stronger metals or beautifying women. Della Porta's experiments were also *demonstrations* – not of the theoretical principles of natural magic but of the awesome power of occult forces and the magus's ingenuity and skill in manipulating them. Manifestations of marvellous but natural forces, they are preternatural events choreographed by the magus.[26] Although not the inventor of the scientific demonstration – Archimedes, one of Della Porta's idols, claims that title – he was the inventor of the scientific performance. He was a scientific magus for a new, public audience curious about the wonders of natural magic.

Natural magic was thus a science of making, but also, as in the case of popular errors and witchcraft, a science of unmaking. To Della Porta natural magic's most urgent task was to demonstrate the folly of the witchcraft delusion. To that end he composed a treatise bearing the title *Criptologia*, in which he vowed to 'smash the superstition' of witchcraft. The tract was a head-on challenge to the Church's conception of popular magic. 'In this book I treat the most deeply hidden secrets buried in the intimate bosom of nature', he wrote. 'Science cannot explain them, but they are not for that reason vain superstitions'. Popular magic conceals great truths, he said. But its truths were distorted by popular superstitions and learned demonology alike. On the one hand, the common people foolishly believe that the effects of natural magic are caused by the invocation of supernatural aid. But Della Porta argued that the seemingly supernatural forces that witches and cunning men manipulated were in fact natural forces, whereas the magic spells connected with them were useless and blasphemous. On the other hand, philosophers and theologians were just as credulous in attributing magical effects to demonic agencies. Scholastic natural philosophy of demonologists was hopelessly inadequate to account for popular superstitions, said Della Porta, and hence contributed to the propagation of error. Indeed, popular and 'theological' opinions about witchcraft were equally superstitious. Both rested on false assumptions. He wanted to eradicate both kinds.[27] In unmaking demonic marvels and relegating them to the junk heap of 'superstitions', Della Porta created a strategy for attacking witchcraft delusion, thereby delegitimizing the witchcraft persecutions and their devastating impact on the people. Although he never published his treatise on demonic magic, the vast network of correspondence among the literati ensured that Della Porta's views were widely known, indeed conventional among avant-garde intellectuals.

4.5 The Renaissance of machines

The magus was not the only new power figure to strike wonder in early modern Europeans. In cities all over Europe, engineers thrived, making all manner of mechanical inventions that thrilled people by their complexity and power. Early modern Europeans were surrounded by machines, mills grinding grain, pumps draining mines, cranes muscling up huge stones to erect buildings and even 'living machines' – that is, automata, which adorned the facades of churches and clocks, fascinating onlookers who gazed on mechanical birds and lifelike puppets marching and banging on drums as if in a real parade.[28] One of the most awe-inspiring mechanisms was the spectacular astronomical clock on the façade of the Strasbourg Cathedral, completed in 1574 and fitted with a celestial globe, an astrolabe and automata driven by the clockwork, including a mechanical cock that flapped its wings and crowed to the accompaniment of mechanically played hymns[29] (Figure 4.2). Such devices, and more, also graced the groaning tables and magnificent gardens of princes. But machines invaded the homes and daily lives of ordinary people as well. Once confined to the wealthy, the market for domestic clocks expanded to include merchants and the bourgeoisie.[30]

The engineers who accomplished these feats drew on ancient technologies described in the works of Archimedes and Hero of Alexandria, not spells. Yet to the unwary they could appear marvellous, even magical. Engineers, like their rivals the magicians, loved to baffle and amaze people with mechanical gadgets. In the theatre of court culture, entertaining a prince with whirring automata might land you a place in the court, as it did engineers like Aristotele Fioravanti of Bologna, whose ingenious machines made him sought after by princes throughout the Italian peninsula, and whose fame took him all the way to Moscow, where he worked for the tsar of Russia.[31] To prove that the despots of Renaissance cities and states had power over nature as well as their subjects, engineers built spectacular pageant wagons that seemed to move without horses to pull them, while hidden teams of soldiers cranked their wheels.[32] Machines were also prominent in the gardens of the wealthy. Grottos concealed hydraulic devices that powered dancing puppets and automata playing flutes and drums, while clever booby traps drenched unsuspecting visitors with water from hidden pipes – a practical joke that delighted witnesses. As Anthony Grafton writes, 'Not just princes and city governments but every master of a great house could now display his ability to make dead matter move.'[33]

Engineers dreamed big. They envisioned great projects and invented visionary devices to carry them out. One of the most spectacular engineering feats of the period took place on 15 September 1586, when a huge crowd gathered in St Peter's Square Rome to witness the raising of the Vatican Obelisk, which had already been lowered from its previous position in a dark corner near the square and transported on a platform to a more visible site in the centre of St Peter's, where it would be lifted onto its new pedestal (Figure 4.3). Centuries before, in 41 CE, the Emperor Caligula had the 360-tonne block of carved stone transported from Egypt, one of about fifty of the great monoliths brought to

Figure 4.2 The astronomical clock on the Strasbourg Cathedral (constructed 1571–4). Woodcut by Tobias Stimmer (b. 1539–d.1584). Public Domain Source: Wikimedia Commons.

Figure 4.3 Lowering the Vatican obelisk. Woodcut from Domenico Fontana, *Della trasportatione dell'Obelisco Vaticano* (1590). Fontana's method called for lifting the gigantic obelisk with a mammoth scaffold, lowering it on its side onto a gurney, then moving it by rollers via a horizontal ramp to the new site some 275 yards away and reversing the process. On 28 September 1586, the scaffolding was removed and the obelisk stood on its pedestal at the location where it still rests, in the centre of St Peter's Square. Public Domain Source: Wikimedia Commons.

Rome during the imperial age as trophies of conquest. Eight hundred workers, some leading horses, took their places around forty capstans, each turned by three horses, attached by ropes to a maze of pullies positioned on an immense structure named 'the castle' (*castello*), which within which lay the giant obelisk wrapped in sheathing. At the blare of a trumpet, the horses tugged on ropes tied to the capstans. The crowd hushed. As the capstans turned the colossal stone slowly inched upward. By sundown, the obelisk hung vertically over the new pedestal built for it, to be lowered the following morning.[34]

The engineer who accomplished the spectacular choreography of moving the obelisk to its new location was the architect Domenico Fontana, who stationed himself on a specially constructed command tower to direct the undertaking. It was an extraordinarily risky venture, one that could make or break an engineer's reputation. Michelangelo declined the job. Asked why, he replied, 'And what if it breaks?'. Fontana described the feat in a work published in 1590, *Della trasportatione dell'Obelisco Vaticano* (Rome 1590). Illustrated gigantic *castello* and the other machines Fontana invented to complete the task. A proliferation of texts and images describing the feat were printed in the decades that followed. Pamela Long writes, 'No other sixteenth-century engineering project was depicted in such dramatic and prolific detail.' Some observers claimed that the obelisks promised to provide the deepest knowledge of the natural world that was assumed to be possessed by the Egyptians – perhaps even the ancient magical knowledge of Hermes Trismegistus. if only someone could decipher the hieroglyphs carved into the monoliths.[35]

Machines like the ones Fontana invented to move the Vatican obelisk put on public display the power of the engineer. But did the people who looked on register the event as an act of magic? Did they think the engineer was a magus? It seems unlikely. They may have been amazed at seeing such powerful forces being yoked – and who wouldn't be? – but it's doubtful they perceived Fontana as a sorcerer. Waving his hands and barking out orders from his platform high above the piazza, he must have seemed more like a general directing a siege. Most onlookers knew he was an engineer whose special powers came not from magic but by harnessing the forces of nature.

4.6 Imaginary machines: The pseudo-Aristotelian *Mechanica*

While some Renaissance engineers built impressive machines, others dreamed up new and ever more complicated mechanical devices. They left a record of their dreamt-up machines in a new genre of technological literature, the 'theaters of machines', lavish, expensive and profusely illustrated books. The exquisitely engraved images of the theatres of machines display, in the words of historian Paolo Galluzzi, 'Herculean, redundant contrivances, intricately assembled so as to provoke astonishment'. These hefty, pricy books reflect the baroque taste for the curious, rare, surprising and exaggeratedly complicated.[36] Of course, none of these imaginary machines were ever built, except as, much later, models for museum exhibitions. As Alex Keller writes, 'Here for the first time was a literature which portrayed not what was, but what might be; not in terms of spiritual improvement or social reform, but as the machines of a possible, mathematically guided future.'[37] The 'daydreaming engineers' of the early modern period may not have built anything, but the visionary inventions they dreamed up created expectations and aspirations of technological progress. The real message of the theatres of machines was to show that the fruits of engineering are endless, even utopian.

One of the earliest works of the genre was Jacques Besson's *Theatrum Instrumentorum* (1571–2). Besson (*c.* 1540–73) was no engineer but was a French Huguenot who worked primarily as a mathematics teacher. The work for which he is best known was not a description of machines already in use, as previous machine books tended to be, but of new inventions Besson envisioned might be built. It was, in other words, a work of 'imaginary engineering'. The book was generously illustrated with stunning engravings, including designs for an array of machines ranging from drawing instruments to lathes, stone cutters, cranes and horse carriages. A raft of theatres of machines followed.[38] The grandest of all was Agostino Ramelli's *Le diverse et artificiose machine*, published in 1588.[39] Ramelli (1531–1600) was a military engineer in the service of the Duc d'Anjou (later Henri III) with the title of *ingénieur du roi* (King's engineer). With more than 200 etched plates, Ramelli's *Le diverse et artificiose machine* is the most extravagant and sumptuous of all the Renaissance treatises of imaginative engineering on paper. Its baroque depiction of colossal, complex and superhuman machines demonstrated the possibility that technology could outdo magic (Figure 4.4).

The authors and engineers who composed the theatres of machines found a potent, if unlikely, ally in the ancient philosopher Aristotle – or at least an author everyone assumed was Aristotle. Among the vast library of classical manuscripts dug up by the humanist movement was an obscure work ascribed to Aristotle titled *De mechanica* (or *Problemata mechanica*), a treatise on the mathematical principles of mechanics. This foundational work was almost certainly not by

Figure 4.4 A crane for lifting heavy objects. This complex machine, with intricate multiple pulleys, is effortlessly powered by one person turning a crank. From *Le diverse et artificiose machine del capitano Agostino Ramelli* (Paris, 1588). Public Domain Source: Science History Institute.

Aristotle but was probably by one of his pupils, perhaps Strato. Unknown in the Middle Ages, the *Mechanical Problems* was first made available in the sixteenth century in editions by humanists. In the opening chapter of the *Mechanica*, the author distinguishes between two kinds of phenomena that excite wonder: those that occur 'according to nature' and whose cause is unknown and those that come about by means of art for the benefit of human beings.[40] 'Remarkable things occur in accordance with nature, the cause of which is unknown, and others occur contrary to nature, which are produced by art for the benefit of mankind', he asserts.[41] Following this introduction, the work claims that mechanical marvels are to be explained by the marvellous properties of the circle, which in turn underlie the characteristics of the balance and lever, which underlie most other mechanical movements. The remainder of the text discusses some thirty-five problems to which these principles are applied, such as the balance, lever, pulley, wedge, oars, rudders and projectile motion.[42]

The first Latin translation of the *Mechanica* was made by the Venetian humanist Vittore Fausto (1480–1551) and published in 1517. Other editions followed, as well as an influential commentary on the work by Alessandro Piccolomini (1508–79), published in 1547 to an enthusiastic audience of architects and engineers. The Italian metallurgist Vannoccio Biringuccio translated Piccolomini's commentary into Italian in 1550.[43] The *Mechanical Problems* soon became a standard work for engineering writers, taking a place alongside classics by Euclid, Archimedes and Hero of Alexandria. Giovanni Branca, writing in 1628, spoke for many authors who produced theatres of machines: 'Underlying all these machines are those principles which Aristotle discussed and proposed in his *Mechanica*, a work of which man will always be able to avail himself as the foundation for the invention of machines suitable for meeting any needs that may arise.'[44] The *Mechanica* also found its way into the university curriculum, notably at the University of Padua, where Galileo occupied the chair of mathematics from 1592 until 1610, when he took the post of mathematician and philosopher to the Grand Duke of Tuscany. Like other professors before him, he lectured on the *Mechanical Problems*. In a study manual he wrote for students, Galileo defines mechanics as 'the faculty that teaches the explanations and renders the causes of marvellous effects that we see produced with various machines, such as the moving and lifting of the greatest weights with the smallest forces'.[45] Galileo's conception of the scope of mechanics aligned well with the tradition of Renaissance commentaries on the *Mechanical Problems*.

Marvels that occur against nature were also the subject of natural magic. As Della Porta explained, the aim of natural magic is to reveal the hidden secrets of nature and to put them to practical use.[46] The magus is like a superior artisan who possesses an intimate knowledge of the secrets of materials and the forces acting upon them. Substituting philosophy for the artisan's cunning, he makes nature do what nature cannot do on its own. Della Porta wrote:

> Art being as it were Nature's Ape, even in her imitation of Nature, effects greater matters than does Nature. Hence it is that a magician being furnished with art, as it were another nature, searching thoroughly into those works which nature accomplishes by many secret means and close operations, works upon Nature, and partly by that which he sees and partly by that which he conjects and gathers

from thence, takes his sundry advantages of nature's instruments, and thereby either hastens or hinders her work, making things ripe before or after their natural season, and so indeed makes nature to be his instrument.[47]

Through natural magic, Della Porta claims, art does not merely imitate nature but is made to surpass nature.

Gradually during the seventeenth century, machines and mathematics pushed aside the mystery of occult forces. The 'new philosophers' didn't deny the existence of occult qualities (Newton's formulation of gravity was a deeply problematic occult force); instead, they sought to make such forces mechanical. If occult forces can be explained by a mechanics that rests on the certainty of mathematics such powers are magical only in the sense that they may, to some people, seem marvellous. That at least was the contention of the sober Anglican clergyman John Wilkins (1614–72), the author of the popular *Mathematical Magic* (1648), one of a growing body of 'fun with mathematics' books for bourgeois readers that appeared in the seventeenth century.[48] Wilkins explained that he used the term in his title merely 'in allusion to vulgar opinion, which doth commonly attribute all such strange operations unto the power of Magick'.[49] The work is largely a discussion of mechanical and optical devices crafted by celebrated engineers such as Archytas, whose wooden dove 'flew cheerfully forth as if it had been a living dove'; Archimedes's celebrated mirror that focussed the sun's blazing rays to set fire to enemy ships during the siege of Syracusa; and, not to be outdone by the ancients, England's own Roger Bacon, who, according to legend made a brass fortune-telling head.[50] Such widely disseminated works removed the wonder from engineering and transferred it to mathematics, which gave it a cool reception. Mathematics is the realm of certainty, not mystery. Even if the theatres of machines seem more like extravagant coffee table books than manuals for building things, they served a singular purpose by aligning technology with mathematics instead of magic.

4.7 Conclusion: Taking the wonder out of nature

Harnessing the forces of nature to produce wonders that ease the burden of human labour and increase society's material wealth and well-being was the technological dream of the Renaissance engineers. It was also the dream of the Renaissance magus. The concept of occult power was present in both traditions: the problem of occult qualities vexed the new philosophers as much as it did the natural magicians. Occult power is invisible; the only way to know it is by observation of its effects. We can't see magnetic force; but we can observe its unusual effect of attracting iron, a property specific to the lodestone. But when the infallibility of mathematics was added to engineering (in some measure through the influence of ps.-Aristotle's *Mechanica*), it became easier to separate the magical from the mechanical. Machines enabled people to visualize another kind of power: not of spells but of pullies, levers and other simple machines made comprehensible by mathematics. In other words, magic is a trick; mathematics is a certain truth.

Machines, mechanisms, gadgets and devices were ubiquitous in the everyday lives of early modern Europeans. Whether you lived in a city, countryside or court you were surrounded by whirring and clanking mechanical devices. The machine (particularly the mechanical clock) provided natural philosophers with a powerful metaphor. As historian Steven Shapin explains, the clock was a supreme exemplar of uniformity and regularity, and it served as a visible model of natural order. Moreover, machines had a determinate, intelligible structure. There was nothing mysterious or magical and nothing unpredictable or capricious about a machine.[51] Shapin argues that the machine metaphor was a vehicle for 'taking the wonder out' of our understanding of nature, in other words what the sociologist Max Weber characterized as the 'disenchantment of the world'. Shapin writes: 'The allure of the machine, and especially the mechanical clock, as a uniquely intelligible and proper metaphor for explaining natural processes not only broadly follows the contours of daily experience with such devices but also recognizes their potency and legitimacy in ordering human affairs.'[52]

The seventeenth-century English virtuoso Robert Hooke, a fellow of the Royal Society of London and the society's Keeper of Experiments, was an avid reader of Della Porta's *Natural Magic*. Hooke found in the work a way of thinking about the occult forces of nature in mechanical terms and envisioned a scientific method that would enable instruments, particularly the microscope, to reveal the inner machinery that made nature tick. Hooke was optimistic that the microscope would reveal the mechanical causes of phenomena, enabling natural philosophers to 'discern all the secret workings of Nature, almost in the same manner as we do those that are the productions of Art, and are managed by wheels, and engines, and springs that were devised by humane wit'. By revealing the interior 'machinery' of nature, Hooke thought, the microscope would confirm the principles of the mechanical philosophy and resolve the ancient problem of occult qualities. By means of instruments to aid the senses, Hooke wrote, the virtuosi 'find reason to suspect that those effects of bodies that have been commonly attributed to *Qualities*, and those confessed to be *occult* are performed by the small Machines of Nature, which are not to be discerned without these helps'.⁵³

In that age of Baconian visions of a world transformed through science and technology, the figure of the magus was a powerful symbol.⁵⁴ Even as the link between technology and magic began to dissolve in the seventeenth and eighteenth centuries, the dreams and fantasies of engineers soared to unimagined heights. Although the rise of the mechanical philosophy dealt a blow to the long-standing relation between technology and magic, it was by no means fatal. For as long as people are capable of wonder, human invention will retain its magic.

Notes

1. Keith Hutchison, 'What Happened to Occult Qualities in the Scientific Revolution?', *Isis* 73 (1982): 233–53, especially 237. In addition, see Nicolas Weill-Parot, *Points aveugles de la nature. La rationalité scientifique médiévale face à l'occulte, l'attraction magnétique et l'horreur du vide (XIIIe – milieu du XVe siècle)* (Paris: Les Belles Lettres, 2013).
2. Valerie Flint, *The Rise of Magic in Early Medieval Europe* (Princeton: Princeton University Press, 1991), 3.
3. Lorraine Daston and Katharine Park, *Wonders and the Order of Nature, 1150–1750* (New York: Zone Books, 1998), 14, 159–60.
4. Stephen Wilson, *The Magical Universe: Everyday Ritual and Magic in Pre-Modern Europe* (London: Hambledon and London, 2000), 174.
5. Mary Rose O'Neil, *Discerning Superstition: Popular Errors and Orthodox Response in Late Sixteenth Century Italy* (PhD diss., Stanford University, 1981), 245–6.
6. Johannes Dillinger, *Magical Treasure Hunting in Europe and North America: A History*, Palgrave Historical Studies in Witchcraft and Magic Series (London: Palgrave Macmillan, 2012).
7. Warren Alexander Dym, *Divining Science: Treasure Hunting and Earth Science in Early Modern Germany* (Leinden and Boston: Brill, 2011).
8. Jean Bodin, *De la demonomania des sorciers* (1580); Dym, *Divining Science*, 70.
9. See, for example, for Spain, María Tausiet, *Abracadabra Omnipotens: Magia urbana en Zaragoza en la Edad Moderna* (Madrid: Siglo XXI Editores, 2007).
10. Dym, *Divining Science*, 62–3.
11. Duarte Madeira Arrais, *New Philosophy and Medicine concerning Occult Qualaities* (Lisbon, 1650), quoted by Dym, *Divining Science*, 63.

12 Edward Grant, *A History of Natural Philosophy from the Ancient World to the Nineteenth Century* (Cambridge: Cambridge University Press, 2007), 178.
13 Ulinka Rublack, *The Astronomer and the Witch: Johannes Kepler's Fight for His Mother* (Oxford: Oxford University Press, 2015).
14 Arianna Borrelli, 'Giovan Battista Della Porta's Construction of Pneumatic Phenomena and His Use of Recipes as Heuristic Tools', *Centaurus* 62 (2020): 406–24.
15 Brian Copenhaver, 'Magic', in *Cambridge History of Science*, vol. 3, Early Modern Science (Cambridge: Cambridge University Press, 2006), 518–40, especially 518.
16 *Hermetica*, ed. and trans. Brian Copenhaver (Cambridge: Cambridge University Press, 1992), 2.
17 In Latin, *Quod est superius est sicut quod inferius, et quod inferius est sicut quod est superius*. Ps.-Apollonius of Tyana, *Emerald Table*.
18 Copenhaver, 'Magic', 519 (with alterations).
19 Anthony Grafton, *Magic and Technology in Early Modern Europe* (Washington DC: Smithsonian Institution Libraries, 2005), 35. In addition, see William Eamon, 'Technology as Magic in the Late Middle Ages and the Renaissance', *Janus* 70 (1983): 171–212.
20 Grant, *History of Natural Philosophy*, 171.
21 William of Auvergne, *De legibus*, chp. 24 (*Opera*, I, p. 69b). In addition, see Richard Kieckhefer, *Magic in the Middle Ages* (Cambridge: Cambridge University Press, 2000), 12. I am grateful to Donato Verardi for alerting me to William of Auvergne's work and for helping me avoid some errors.
22 Among the many studies of Della Porta's natural science and magic, see in particular Donato Verardi, *La scienza e i segreti della natura a Napoli nel Rinascimento. La magia naturale di Giovan Battista Della Porta* (Florence: Firenze University Press, 2018); Luisa Muraro, *Giambattista Della Porta mago e scienziato* (Milan: Feltrinelli, 1978); and William Eamon, *Science and the Secrets of Nature: Books of Secrets in Medieval and Early Modern Culture* (Princeton: Princeton University Press, 1994).
23 Louise George Clubb, *Giambattista Della Porta Dramatist* (Princeton: Princeton University Press, 1965), XI.
24 William Eamon, 'A Theater of Experiments: Giambattista Della Porta and the Scientific Culture of Late Renaissance Naples', in *The Optics of Giovan Battista Della Porta (1535–1615): A Reassessment*, eds Arianna Borrelli, Giora Hon and Yaakov Zik, Archimedes: New Studies in the History and philosophy of Science and Technology, vol. 44 (Dordrecht: Springer, 2017), 11–38.
25 Giambattista Della Porta, *Natural Magick* (1658), ed. Derek J. Price (New York: Basic Books, 1957), book 7, 356–7.
26 Sergius Kodera, 'Giambattista Della Porta's Histrionic Science', *California Italian Studies* 3 (2012): 1–27.

27 Giambattista Della Porta, *Taumatologia e Criptologia*, Edizione Nazionale delle Opere di Giovan Battista della Porta, vol. 17, ed. Raffaele Sirri (Naples: Edizioni Scientifiche Italiane, 2013), 158.
28 On the tradition of medieval automata, see Elly R. Truitt, *Medieval Robots: Mechanism, Magic, Nature, and Art* (Philadelphia: University of Pennsylvania Press, 2015).
29 Grafton, *Magic and Technology*, 24; Francis Haber, 'The Clock as an Intellectual Artifact', in *The Clockwork Universe: German Clocks and Automata, 1550–1650*, eds Klaus Maurice and Otto Mayr (New York: Neale Watson Academic Publications 1980), 9–18, especially 16.
30 Silvio A. Bedini, 'The Mechanical Clock and the Scientific Revolution', in *Clockwork Universe*, eds Maurice and Mayr, 19–26, especially 20.
31 Paolo Galluzzi, *The Italian Renaissance of Machines* (Cambridge, MA: Harvard University Press, 2020), 6–7.
32 Grafton, *Magic and Technology*, 24.
33 Grafton, *Magic and Technology* 36.
34 Pamela Long, *Engineering the Eternal City: Infrastructure, Topography, and the Culture of Knowledge in Late Sixteenth-Century Rome* (Chicago: University of Chicago Press, 2018), 89–90.
35 Long, *Engineering the Eternal City*, 209.
36 Galluzzi, *Italian Renaissance of Machines*, 183.
37 Alex Keller, 'Renaissance Theaters of Machines', *Technology and Culture* 19 (1978): 495–508, especially 495.
38 Among the most important works are: Ambroise Bachot, *Le govvernail . . . Lequel conduira le curieux de geometrie en perspectiue dedans l'architecture de fortifications, machine de guerre & plusieurs autres particularitez y contenues* (Melun, 1598); Jacques Besson, *Theatrum instrumentorum et machinarum* (Lugdini, 1578); Joseph Boillot, *Modelles, artifices de feu et divers instrumens de guerre avec les moyens de s'en prévaloir* (Chaumont-en-Bassigny, 1598); Georg Andreas Böckler, *Theatrum machinarum novum* (Nuremberg, 1661); Giovanni Branca, *Le machine* (Rome, 1629); Jean Errard, *Le premier livre des instruments mathématiques méchaniques* (Nancy, 1584); Gaspard Grollier de Servière, *Recueil d'ouvrages curieux de mathematique et de mecanique* (Lyon, 1719); Agostino Ramelli, *Le diverse et artificiose machine* (Paris, 1588); Heinrich Zeising, *Theatri machinarvm* (Leipzig, 1607); Vittorio Zonca, *Novo teatro di machine et edificii* (1570).
39 Agostino Ramelli, *Le diverse et artificiose machine del capitano Agostino Ramelli* (1588).
40 Mark J. Schiefsky, 'Art and Nature in Ancient Mechanics', in *The Artificial and the Natural: An Evolving Polarity*, eds Bernadette Bensaude-Vincent and William R. Newman (Cambridge, MA: MIT Press, 2013), 67–108, especially 75. For my

treatment of the *Mechanical Problems*, I follow Walter R. Laird, *The Unfinished Mechanics of Giuseppe Moletti. An Edition and English Translation of his* Dialogue on Mechanics, *1576* (Toronto: University of Toronto Press, 2000). I used the Loeb Classical Library edition of the *Mechanica* in Aristotle, *Minor Works*, ed. and trans. Walter Stanley Hett (Cambridge, MA: Harvard University Press, 2015).

41 Pseudo-Aristotle, *Mechanica*, 331 (with one modification: Hett renders technè as skill rather than art).
42 Walter R. Laird, 'The Scope of Renaissance Mechanics', *Osiris*, 2nd series 2 (1986): 43–68, especially 47.
43 Paul Lawrence Rose and Stillman Drake, 'The Pseudo-Aristotelian *Questions of Mechanics* in Renaissance Culture', *Studies in the Renaissance* 18 (1971): 65–104, especially 96; Laird, 'Scope of Renaissance Mechanics'.
44 Rose and Drake, 'Pseudo-Aristotelian *Questions of Mechanics*', 96.
45 Laird, 'The Scope of Renaissance Mechanics', 62.
46 Della Porta, *Natural Magick*, 19.
47 Della Porta *Natural Magick*, 73–4 (slightly modified).
48 The prototype of all such works was the popular *Recreations mathematiques* (1624) by the French Jesuit priest and mathematician Jean Leurechon (1591–1670), a book that went through more than thirty editions in French and was translated into English in 1633 by William Oughtred.
49 John Wilkins, *Mathematicall Magick*, 'To the reader'.
50 John Peacham, quoted in Peter Zetterberg, 'The Mistaking of the Mathematics for Magic', 93; Eamon, 'Technology as Magic', 184–5; Truitt, *Medieval Robots*, 69–70.
51 Steven Shapin, *The Scientific Revolution* (Chicago: University of Chicago Press,1996), 36.
52 Shapin, *Scientific Revolution*, 33.
53 Robert Hooke, *Micrographia* (orig. ed. 1665; New York: Dover Publications, 1961), Preface.
54 Eamon, 'Technology as Magic'; Grafton, *Magic and Technology*.

5

Aristotelianism, chymistry and mechanics in early seventeenth-century Europe

The techno-magical approach

Arianna Borrelli

5.1 Magic and technology in the Renaissance

'Any sufficiently advanced technology is indistinguishable from magic'[1]: This often-quoted statement by science-fiction author Arthur C. Clarke illustrates well today's popular images of technology and magic, both of which are linked to a sense of wonder in front of unusual effects whose explanation remains obscure to the non-experts. According to some historians, this same sense of wonder was one of the common features between magic and technology in the European Middle Ages and Renaissance.[2]

Despite this similarity, today's 'magic' and 'technology' are very different in conceptual and practical perspective from those of the pre- and early modern period, and especially of the Renaissance. The notion of technology is the most problematic of the two, since term and concept emerged only in the course of the late seventeenth and eighteenth century in context of a systematization of and reflection on skills in planning, constructing and operating automata, pneumatic and steam devices, optical instruments, as well as various kinds of military and defensive equipment.[3] The crystallization and professionalization of the figure of the engineer was an element of these developments.[4] In the Renaissance, as in the medieval period, the term 'engineer' (*ingegnere* (it), *Ingenieur* (dt.), *ingénieur* (fr.) and *ingeniero* (sp.)) could be used to indicate very different persons and activities, and the relatively few individuals engaged in what we would call engineering had no predetermined social and economic role, so that their position was very different from that of traditional artisans, who were strictly organized in corporations. Therefore, it is not surprising if Renaissance practitioners who specialized in creating new kinds of apparatuses took advantage of their unclear status and presented their work as something different from traditional artisanal products, connecting it with magical, philosophical or theological frameworks. How deep the connection was depended from the interests and capabilities of the individual authors. As we shall see, the Dutchman Cornelis Drebbel (1572–1633) made an in-depth and plausible argument linking the perpetual motion machine he built to the principle of motion and life in nature.

Because of the conceptual issues sketched earlier, I prefer to speak of 'technical artefacts' rather than of 'technology' when discussing the Renaissance. This choice has historiographical significance, because the modern notion of technology conveys the idea of a unitary field of activities systematically aimed at enlarging the realm of the practically possible and is also closely linked to the modern notion of progress. These views were not there in the Renaissance and what we a posteriori may see collectively as Renaissance technology appeared in fact to historical actors rather as a collection of diverse apparatuses and methods including cranks and pulleys, pumps and self-playing musical instruments, explosives, talismans and (fake) precious stones, as well as clocks and automata. Between the late Middle Ages and the Renaissance such disparate objects and experiences started being presented side by side, and this often happened in texts about the 'secrets of nature', or natural magic. In this sense, one might argue that the modern notion of technology somehow also has its roots in magic.[5] Historians of the Renaissance are of course well aware of this situation when employing the term 'technology' to describe technical artefacts, but I believe that, despite all care, this use might still involuntarily lead to a projection of the modern, unitary notion of technology to a time where it did not yet obtain.

Other than technology, magic was part of medieval and early modern culture. Term, notions and practices of magic were an important component of the European Renaissance, yet the magical landscape was very complex and fragmented, ranging from popular rituals and traditions, to new learned literature inspired by ancient Neoplatonic, Hermetic, Aristotelian or pseudo-Aristotelian writings to the experimentally oriented 'natural magic' usually connected to the work of Giambattista Della Porta (1535–1615) and his *Natural Magic*, a collection of experiences of very different kinds described in recipe format, some taken from traditional literature and artisanal practice, other newly developed.[6] In my contribution, I will focus on this latter kind of magic, which is also the one most often connected to technology. Besides magic and technology, there is a third notion which will play an important role in my analysis, namely science. Some historians have convincingly argued that at least some facets of Renaissance magic contributed to the development of the notions and practices from which modern science emerged, although this view has not been generally accepted, and a distinction between allegedly 'irrational' magic and 'rational' science is often still upheld.[7] Instead, artisanal practices and new technical artefacts and methods have been widely recognized as having contributed to the emergence of science, though usually not in connection with the magical context.[8] In recent years, though, historians have recognized that the emergence of science has to be understood as a long and many-layered process in which different factors played a role, including not only artisan knowledge and engineering innovations but also magical practices and concepts.[9] Within this constellation, the question of the relationship between magic and technical artefacts becomes particularly interesting, since the sense of wonder associated to some magical and technical displays also characterized natural philosophical investigation in the Renaissance, when scholars and practitioners started regarding the study of extraordinary phenomena as a path to the discovery of nature's secrets.[10]

In the following pages I will argue that, in the Renaissance, technical artefacts and the magical framework could be linked by much more than a sense of wonder and that what may appear today as a confusing combination of the two could be the expression of a heuristically fruitful approach in view of the emergence of science. I will refer to this specific approach to investigating nature as 'techno-magical', because I believe it is helpful to introduce new terminology to make explicit the difference between the subject being studied and concepts that emerged later, like science or technology. My hypothesis is that, for some authors, Renaissance natural magic provided a flexible conceptual framework for combining experimental and theoretical searches for nature's secrets using the workings of chosen technical artefacts as a guideline.

I will present my argument using as an example the perpetual motion device built by Cornelis Drebbel at the beginning of the seventeenth century, an apparatus in which a mass of water moved back and forth inside a glass tube reacting to changes in atmospheric air. This device, combined with other simpler experiences, provided Drebbel with a starting point to reflect on phenomena which today are seen as pertaining to thermodynamics, meteorology and climatology. However, these knowledge fields started emerging only more than a century later, and I will argue that, in the course of the seventeenth century, the growing differentiation between mathematical, mechanical, (neo-)Aristotelian and the chemical philosophy let devices and phenomena like those Drebbel was focussing on appear as less relevant for understanding the principles of nature's workings.

In this case, the heuristic potential of the techno-magical approach turned out to be greater than that of later, more specialized frameworks. This is the reason why the case study is particularly illuminating for better understanding the specific features of early seventeenth-century techno-magic, as opposed to later practical and philosophical disciplines. In the next section, I will review some previous research on the relationship between magic and technology in the early modern period as a starting point for my own analysis. After that, I present the case study: a short overview of Drebbel's life and work (Section 5.3), a discussion of his *perpetuum mobile* (Section 5.4) and its interpretations by contemporary scholars (Section 5.5), and finally the framework in which Drebbel himself interpreted his creation, as an example of the productivity of the techno-magical approach (Sections 5.6 and 5.7). Section 5.8 summarizes my argument and conclusions.

5.2 The techno-magical approach

An early, but today still seminal contribution to investigating the relationship between magic and technical artefacts in the pre- and early modern period is William Eamon's paper 'Technology as Magic in the Late Middle Ages and the Renaissance' (1983).[11] Eamon argued that in the late medieval and the Renaissance period '[m]agic, far from being incompatible with technology, was seen as its sister art. It not only gave technology a needed theoretical context, but it also served to promote the technological ambitions of engineers by constructing an image of man as a *magus* who, through his inventions and his manipulations of nature's secrets, gains mastery over the world'.[12] According to Eamon's analysis, one reason why the builders of innovative apparatuses presented them as magical marvels was that magic provided explanations for the functioning of those devices which other directions of natural philosophy could not deliver.[13] In this context, Eamon argues, it was useful to explain newly developed apparatuses in terms of 'occult forces and energies' pervading the universe, and authors like Della Porta even came to see natural magic as 'nothing more than ordinary technology', that is, the practical application of knowledge about nature.[14] However, once more elaborate theoretical frameworks were developed, especially making use of mathematical methods, magical explanations were not necessary anymore and were accordingly discarded.[15] Thus, according to Eamon, the magical framework had a heuristically fruitful function in promoting the creation and diffusion of new technical artefacts but was eventually replaced by more specialized approaches later on.

Another author arguing in the same direction as Eamon is Jan Lazardzig, who focuses on the link between 'white magic' and 'mechanics' during the seventeenth century.[16] What Lazardzig calls 'white magic' is very similar to what I have so far referred to as natural magic, namely magical activities which, other than black magic, aimed at generating effects without the intervention of demonic powers. The term 'mechanics', instead, requires some attention because its meaning rapidly changed during the Renaissance.[17] In medieval times, any kind of manual labour could be seen as part of the 'mechanical arts', but between the late Middle Ages and the Renaissance the term 'mechanical' increasingly often referred more specifically to the construction of machines of different kinds which could produce artificial movements, that is motions which, in the Aristotelian framework, were seen as going against the natural tendencies of bodies. Finally, in the late seventeenth century, 'mechanics' came to indicate the practical and theoretical discipline dealing with devices that we today would describe as mechanical in a more strict sense, as opposed, for example, to hydraulic or pneumatic apparatuses. Appreciating this difference is important to better understand the transformation discussed by Lazardzig.

Like Eamon, Lazardzig argues that the Renaissance connection between mechanics and white magic helped practitioners both to attract attention to their marvellous creations and to develop general principles of mechanics.[18] In the course of the seventeenth century, though, texts presenting machines increasingly focussed on 'useful' ('nützlich') devices, and the themes of magic and wonder became marginalized, with the exception of works dealing with theatrical apparatuses.[19] This was because in that period increasing attention was devoted to specific groups of apparatuses and the possible principles of their functioning, and practitioners realized that a number of – though not all – devices could be explained in terms of relatively few principles. These instruments would eventually be described as 'mechanical' in a more strict sense.[20] At the same time, technical marvels that did not lend themselves to such explanations became less and less interesting for natural philosophers and engineers proposing a mechanical world view and were marginalized as mere devices of wonder. As an example of the emerging 'epistemic division' (*epistemische Zäsur*)[21] between marvellous and useful mechanics, Lazardzig discusses John Wilkins' (1614–72) work *Mathematical Magick: Or the Wonders That May Be Performed by Mechanical Geometry* (1648).[22] The book was divided into two parts: the first one presented simple machines illustrating the principles of a (new) science of mechanics dealing primarily with automata – principles which Wilkins, following Francis Bacon (1561-1626) and René Descartes (1596–1650) saw potentially as the basis of all natural phenomena.[23] The second part offered an overview of (mainly) marvellous apparatuses, many of which could not really be explained according to the principles expounded in the first section of the work.[24] Apparently, what could be explained according to the principles of the emerging discipline of mechanics could not be seen any more as a marvel.

In conclusion, both Eamon and Lazardzig see the Renaissance natural magical framework as having helped technical practitioners promote and reflect upon their creations, before being abandoned during the seventeenth century, when more focussed, often mathematical methods for conceptualizing the functioning of technical apparatuses emerged. These results correctly depict the rise and fall of natural magic as an epistemically fruitful framework for developing and reflecting on technical artefacts. On this basis, though, one may wonder about the specific epistemic role of magic in the period before its demise: How exactly did the magical framework help reflect on the new devices? This question is not at the centre of Eamon's and Lazardzig's studies, but I believe their analyses deliver material and motivation to further reflect on the role that magic played in the Renaissance, not just as a generic motivation to marvel at and experimentally investigate the secrets of nature but as a heuristically fruitful framework for the conceptualization of new experiences. An indication in this sense is also given by Maarten Van Dick and Koen Vermeir's analysis of Wilkins' *Mathematical Magick*, where they argue that Wilkins did not oppose mathematical to wonderful machines, but rather suggested that some wonders have mathematical character and can help scholars understand and develop new mechanical devices.[25] Mathematical magic was not just a catchy title, but a real possibility.

I believe that this observation, together with Eamon's and Lazardzig's results, suggests that, when considering the relationship between Renaissance magical frameworks and technical artefacts, one should pay attention to the growing diversification between different kinds of apparatuses and the explanations fitting their workings. For example, mathematical or geometrical explanations turned out to be useful to understand the function of optical instruments, or of devices which in today's terms are described as mechanical, such as automata, but were less good when trying to account for the workings of pumps or dyeing methods. On the other hand, Paracelsian alchemy or more generally what Allen Debus called the 'chemical philosophy' was capable of making sense of experiences which we today regard as chemical, but did not offer explanations for the workings of automata.[26] During the seventeenth century, a synergy was established between specific sets of experiences and given natural philosophical approaches, leading to rapid developments in both areas, as argued by various authors for the mechanical and chemical philosophy, and as can be seen for example in Wilkins' work.[27] Yet how could such a synergy be established? Natural magic had in this respect a special role, as it provided a flexible, multiform framework that could be heuristically fruitful for a broad range of devices. Some authors, like Della Porta and Drebbel, had in this context the possibility of speculating about experiences by combining and modifying a diverse spectrum of theoretical frameworks, using as a guideline the results of their experimentation.

I believe that similarities exist between this techno-magical approach and contemporary constellations in the development of mechanics, for which Domenico Bertoloni Meli has introduced the notion of 'thinking with objects' to describe how simple mechanical instruments like lever and pendulum provided a template for conceptualizing more complex apparatuses and experience, allowing mechanical knowledge to be constructed through a combination of top-down and bottom-up reflections.[28] Building upon Bertoloni Meli's notion I have suggested that a similar development also took place in optics, when around 1600, experiences with mirrors and glass spheres helped 'think' about the properties of more complex optical systems, such as lenses or telescopes, and thus led to the emergence of early modern geometrical optics.[29] I will argue that, within the techno-magical approach, devices like Drebbel's *perpetuum mobile* provided a template for conceptualizing more complex phenomena involving heat and air, up to and including meteorological and climatological ones. However, other than in the case of mechanics, optics or chemistry, these developments did not have broad reception and resonance and both the science of heat and meteorology only emerged much later. This is a case in which the heuristic potential of the techno-magical approach was not matched by later developments of the seventeenth century.[30]

When seen a posteriori, techno-magical writings and activities may give the impression of asystematic, not to say chaotic, endeavours: the alleged irrational element in the early modern study of nature which had to be overcome for the construction of scientific knowledge. On the contrary, techno-magical practices represented a fertile ground for the development of new methods of natural philosophy precisely thanks to their open, exploratory character which allowed to search for new ordering principles in nature by creating, transforming, combining or rejecting both experiences and philosophical frameworks.[31] This context promoted the emergence of both mechanical and chemical philosophies, as well as the revision and transformation of the Aristotelian framework. The term 'magic' could be used to describe techno-magical practices, though this was not always the case. As we shall see, Drebbel did not speak of his activities as having magical character, while Della Porta did. Another Renaissance author who used the term in a similar sense was Francis Bacon. Doina-Cristina Rusu and Dana Jalobeanu have discussed the differences and similarities between Della Porta's and Bacon's notions of natural magic, stating that for the Neapolitan scholar: 'magic is interwind with natural philosophy. It is the operative side of all our knowledge of nature [...] Della Porta's magician acquires the knowledge of causes and of relations between causes and effects through experience'.[32] The epistemic role of experience was characteristic of various directions of Renaissance magic, but in Della Porta's case experience was often specifically understood as the performance of experiments aided by devices which we would describe as technological, and he was largely free from conceptual commitments, combining ideas from different conceptual frameworks.[33] This is why I see him as representing the techno-magical approach, which was also an important factor in shaping Bacon's natural philosophy, as Rusu and Jalobeanu argue. Part of Bacon's plan for a reform of natural philosophy was the project of a 'high kind of natural magic'.[34] Although the project was never realized, the material Bacon had collected for it was posthumously published in 1626 or 1627 as the *Sylva sylvarum*, a collection of more or less complex experiences which, despite its rather unsystematic character, was quite popular in the seventeenth century. As Rusu and Jalobeanu show, the *Sylva sylvarum* not only contained many experiments taken from or inspired by Della Porta's *Natural Magic* but also followed Della Porta's example in tentatively grouping and comparing experiments in an empirically driven search for general working principles of nature. This knowledge could in turn be deployed to new ends, as in the society of learned men called 'House of Solomon' envisaged by Bacon in the *New Atlantis* (1627). The House of Solomon was a model for the Royal Society and other academies founded in the seventeenth century, and historians have argued that figures like Drebbel were in part an inspiration for Bacon in conceiving it.[35] In this sense, the House of Solomon might be seen as an idealization of what I have called techno-magical practices.

In the late seventeenth century, the techno-magical approach to the study of nature provided starting points for the development of more specialized natural philosophical areas like mechanics, optics or chemistry. At this point, the study of phenomena which did not fit any of the emerging disciplines was increasingly neglected, to be taken up again only under very different circumstances in the modern age. This is what happened to the study of the moving power of heat, of what would later be called phase transformations and of their role in weather and climate, which played a central role in the work of Drebbel.

5.3 Cornelis Drebbel's life and works

Cornelis Drebbel was born in 1572 in the town of Alkmaar in the Netherlands and died in London in 1633.[36] He came from a family of wealthy landowners with no known connection to the artisanal trade but eventually decided to become an apprentice and then assistant of the engraver Hendrik Goltzius (1558–1617) in Haarlem, and in 1595 he married Goltzius' sister Sophia.[37] Goltzius was a practitioner of alchemy and was probably an important influence on Drebbel's interests. Beside engraving pictures and maps, Drebbel also practised what we would call engineering, among other things building a fountain and patenting a perpetually moving clock. At the beginning of the seventeenth century, he moved to London, where in 1607 he presented a perpetual motion machine to King James I (1566–1625), eventually obtaining the patronage of James' son Henry Prince of Wales (1594–1612). Between 1610 and 1613 Drebbel was in Prague at the court of the Holy Roman Emperor Rudolf II (1552–1612), where he also built a version of his perpetual motion device. Rudolf II died in 1612, and Drebbel probably left – or fled from – Prague in 1613, although his exact whereabouts in these years remain unclear. In any case, from 1620 onward he was mainly in London and occasionally in the Netherlands. In London, he built various devices, among them self-playing musical instruments, a submarine, optical instruments (microscopes and magic lantern), self-regulating ovens, and explosive weapons for the British Navy. In the 1620s, Drebbel joined forces with the three Kuffler brothers, one of whom, Abraham, married his daughter Anna. The Kufflers devoted themselves to marketing Drebbel's creations among wealthy, though not royal, patrons, both in England and on the continent. Especially successful were optical instruments and smaller copies of the *perpetuum mobile*, which appeared in a number of Dutch Kunstkammer paintings.[38] Drebbel was also versed in alchemy, and, besides explosives, he invented a method to purify the air within his submarine, as well as a new dyeing procedure. In the last years of his life, he was apparently impoverished and ran an alehouse under London Bridge, attracting clients thanks to his submarine.

Drebbel provides a good example of the figure of an engineer in the Renaissance thanks to his broad range of competences, as well as to his ambiguous status as an engraving artist, court philosopher, mechanical practitioner and innkeeper.

This ambiguity has to be kept in mind before trying to describe him primarily as engineer, philosopher or natural magician, although a posteriori all these labels would seem to fit him.[39] Other than many practitioners of his time, Drebbel never described his creations in writing, but instead published a small number of relatively short texts of a more general, abstract character: a *Treatise on the Nature of the Elements*, published in Dutch in 1604, later in German (1608) and in Latin (1621) translations; a letter addressed to James I in which the *perpetuum mobile* and other creations are praised, originally written in Dutch (1607) and later translated into Latin (1621); a Latin treatise *On the Quintessence* (1621), describing the extraction of essences from different substances with medical aims.[40] These texts were very successful both in England and on the continent and were translated and reprinted until the eighteenth century, providing the basis for a wide reception of Drebbel's work as part of the alchemical and occult tradition.[41] Interestingly, though, scholars who read Drebbel's work in alchemical context were with time less interested in the actual functioning of his perpetual motion machine, as we shall see later on. Perhaps because of this development, in the modern period Drebbel often came to be regarded as a charlatan whose creation did not really fulfil the promises he made and were only tricks to attract the attention of monarchs interested in the occult arts.[42] Only in the course of the twentieth century, a reassessment of the sources has allowed to compensate this bias, showing that most of Drebbel's inventions actually worked, including the perpetual motion machine.

In the following pages I will focus on Drebbel's *perpetuum mobile* and its relationship to the Dutchman's natural philosophy as expressed in the *Treatise on the Nature of the Elements*. I will argue that in Drebbel's world view a number of experiences, some of them instrument-aided, were connected to each other within a flexible overarching natural magical framework and from there used to grasp and explain the principles behind phenomena of weather and climate as well as of what would be later known as thermodynamics. Because of this, I believe that Drebbel's activities may be seen as an example of the techno-magical approach.

5.4 Drebbel's *perpetuum mobile*

Since the early twentieth century, historians of science and technology have collected evidence on the structure and function of Drebbel's *perpetuum mobile*, and my discussion is based on their results, to which I refer readers for details on extant sources.⁴³ Like most natural philosophical instruments and texts, the *perpetuum mobile* and its presentation, too, had a substantial political dimension.⁴⁴ For the aims of this chapter, however, I will focus on the various interpretations of the causes of its movement.

We do not know when exactly Drebbel conceived his perpetual motion machine, but it was certainly already planned, if not built, in 1604, when he published the first, Dutch edition of the *Treatise on the Nature of the Elements*. Around this time Drebbel had inherited some money from his widowed mother and apparently used it to finance the printing of the treatise, and possibly also the construction of the perpetual motion device which he in 1607 presented to James I. An account of Drebbel's display of the machine at the London court is extant in the recollections of the Bohemian gentleman Heinrich Hiesserle von Chodaw (1557–1665), which are preserved in the form of a German-language illustrated manuscript in the Prague Natural Museum.⁴⁵ Hiesserle recalls being present at a royal dinner during which Drebbel knelt down in front of the king and offered him the *perpetuum mobile* which he had brought with him. The Bohemian gentleman provides in his recollection an image of the machine (Figure 5.1) as well as the following description of its appearance:

> AA is a round gilded globe, which indicates by two different hands the month and the day and in which sign of the zodiac the sun and moon are. B is a round globe representing the moon, and how it waxes and wanes, how old it is, and the connection between high and low water. CD is a glass ring. C is above and D is below the water, which moves all the time, up and down, twice every twenty-four hours, like the sea. All these movements proceed of their own accord, and without doing anything, which is to be seen as the most wonderful thing on earth.⁴⁶

Hiesserle did not specify what the letters *E* and *G* in the drawing represented, but they clearly stood for the hands and dials mentioned in the description, one indicating day, month and solar sign and the other the sign in which the moon was located. Again, according to Hiesserle, the king appreciated the present, but tested Drebbel's claims by keeping the device locked up and isolated for two months, to see whether it would really keep on working. The *perpetuum mobile* stood the test: after two months of isolation, it was not only still moving, but its dials also showed the correct astronomical data. According to the historians who have studied the topic, this feat was definitely plausible and in this respect Drebbel's machine was much superior to the astronomical clockworks of the time, which required not only regular winding up but also

Figure 5.1 The *perpetuum mobile* presented by Cornelis Drebbel to King James I in 1607, drawing from the illustrated recollections of Hiesserle von Chodaw (1557–1665). Image from the manuscript: Heinrich Hiesserle von Chodaw, *Rais-Buch und Leben* (1612), Prague National Museum MS vi A 12, f. 49r. Public DomainSource: http://en.wikipedia.org/wiki/User%3APortolanero / Wikimedia Commons/CC BY 3.0.

continuous adjustments to keep correct time – not to mention the fact that they also stopped and had to be repaired.[47] Therefore, Hiesserle was not exaggerating when describing the capacity of the device to keep on moving without external intervention as 'the most wonderful thing on earth'. James I was satisfied by the experience, and Drebbel entered the service of the Henry Prince of Wales. The machine was exhibited to the public in Eltham palace and there are eyewitness accounts of its continued motion, and references to it in theatre plays testify to its popularity.[48] As already mentioned, smaller, less elaborated versions of the machine were marketed later on.

Drebbel never published an account of how the machine was built and how it worked, but thanks to the various contemporary accounts its key features could be established. As can be seen in Figure 5.1, the centrepiece of Drebbel's *perpetuum mobile* was a hollow metal sphere whose inner space was connected to a round glass tube running around the sphere in the vertical plane. The other extremity of the glass tube was open and from there the tube could be partially filled with water in such a way that a certain amount of air remained trapped between the walls of the sphere and of the tube and the inner water surface. The other water surface was in contact with atmospheric air outside the machine and so the water mass could be seen slowly moving left and right along the tube in response to changes in those properties of the environment which we today describe as atmospheric pressure and temperature.

As will be discussed more in detail later on, though, it is important to note that the modern notions of pressure and temperature did not exist in Drebbel's time. When using modern terms, though, the shifting position of the water in the tube was such as to constantly maintain a balance between the pressure on its two surfaces. On one surface acted atmospheric air pressure, which was of course fully independent of what happened inside the device. The pressure on the other surface, instead, followed from a combination of the expansion or contraction of the air trapped in the sphere due to changes in temperature and outer air pressure. In this sense, it would be too reductive to regard the motion as purely due to the thermal contraction and expansion of the trapped air, because the weather conditions (high- and low-pressure air masses) also played an important role. Nonetheless, it is plausible to assume that the temperature excursion between night and day was responsible for the daily movement back and forth of the mass of water which observers often described as a kind of ebb and flow. If the mass of water regularly moved to the left and right during the day-night cycle, this motion could be used to move each day one step forward the hands of the solar and lunar clocks described by Hiesserle, although there is no positive evidence that the machine actually worked in this way. The exact structure of the astronomical part is, however, not of primary importance for my argument, which focuses on the ultimate source of the moving power of the whole construction as described by contemporary authors, including Drebbel. I will start by presenting the way in which the workings of the perpetual motion machine were understood by various philosophers of the time, and afterwards turn to Drebbel's own views on nature's principle of motion and life.

5.5 Interpretations of Drebbel's *perpetuum mobile* in the early seventeenth century

The decades around 1600 were a very productive period for European natural philosophy. Historians have traditionally traced back to those years the beginning of mechanics and mechanical philosophy, remarked on the entrance of practices and theories of alchemy in the academic community and the beginnings of chemical philosophy, and noted the wealth of approaches to transforming Aristotelianism and the growth of interest in performing and reflecting experiences of various kinds.[49] However, most of these apparent novelties were based on the developments of the previous decades, if not centuries, and only fully enfolded later on. Therefore, one should be wary of classifying authors active in the late sixteenth and early seventeenth century as strictly adhering to 'mechanical', 'chemical' or 'Aristotelian' views, as they often combined different approaches, albeit with varying degrees of commitment for or against one or the other framework. As I argued earlier, scholars and practitioners deploying a techno-magical approach were particularly free in piecemeal choosing or rejecting elements of broader natural philosophical frameworks. In this section, I will present an overview of how the workings of Drebbel's *perpetuum mobile* could be interpreted by authors from the early seventeenth century who had a somehow stronger commitment to the mechanical, chemical or Aristotelian world view.

In 1612 Daniello Antonini (1588–1616), one of the many friends and disciples of Galileo Galilei (1564–1642), while in Brussel, saw a drawing and heard descriptions of Drebbel's perpetual motion machine and wrote to Galileo about it.[50] Antonini proudly explained that he had understood the way in which Drebbel's machine worked and that it was based on a phenomenon which Galileo had demonstrated to his students and friends already some years before: the expansion and contraction of air due to heat and cold. Antonini even built a copy of the machine and presented it to the governor of the Netherlands. Interestingly, once the *perpetuum mobile* had been understood to be based on air's properties, Antonini and Galileo apparently did not think that further investigations were necessary, as though thermal expansion and contraction of air would not hide any natural secrets worth discovering.

Was the phenomenon really so trivial? This was hardly the case, although the effect was known since Antiquity and accepted within Aristotelian natural philosophy. However, already Hero of Alexandria (first century BCE), in his treatise on pneumatics, had realized that the standard Aristotelian framework was not sufficient for explaining the functioning of pumps and suction cups.[51] Accordingly, Hero postulated the existence of what he called 'interstitial vacua' within air, which could expand and contract, modifying the amount of space occupied by the same mass of air. When heat was also involved the situation was more complex and Heros' solution combined interstitial vacua with a change in the form of air. However, Hero denied the possibility of vacua which were not embedded in a substance and so remained at least partially within the Aristotelian framework. In Renaissance Europe, Hero's pneumatic treatise was rediscovered and translated into Latin, while a growing number of hydraulic and pneumatic systems like pumps and fountains were constructed. In this context, speculations on the nature and properties of air and heat increased, often combining Aristotelian notions with Stoic or atomistic views and with the new knowledge of practitioners. Between the late sixteenth and the early seventeenth century, the question of the thermal expansion and contraction of air was often discussed using as an example a very simple experience which had appeared in print for the first time in the first edition of Della Porta's *Natural Magic* (1558) and which I have elsewhere suggested to refer to as the 'inverted glass experiment'.[52]

In the inverted glass experiment, an empty, transparent glass vessel with a long neck is heated, and then its mouth is plunged into a basin full of water. The heated air inside the glass cannot escape, slowly cools down and, exactly as in Drebbel's *perpetuum mobile*, decreases both in volume and in pressure, so that the water rises up the neck of the glass vessel. If fire is brought near the belly of the glass, the air heats up again, and one can see the water level go down again. Similar experiences had been described since Antiquity, but Della Porta's version was the first one to involve a glass container, through which the moving water level could be observed. This was the experience to which Antonini referred in his letters to Galileo about Drebbel's *perpetuum mobile* and, indeed, by the early seventeenth century the inverted glass experiment was well known.

Della Porta described the experiment in much more detail in his treatises on pneumatics (1601, 1606) and on meteorology (1610).[53] In the meteorological treatise *On the Transformations of the Air* (1610), he presented the inverted glass experiment as a demonstration of the origin of winds, which were due to the expansion and contraction of air following from the changing heat of the sun.[54] As we shall see, Drebbel offered the same explanation in his *Treatise on the Nature of the Elements*. The connection between the inverted glass experiment and meteorology became particularly evident in the Netherlands and England in the early seventeenth century, where the rising and lowering of the water level in the apparatus was used to predict weather changes, and the device was referred to as a weatherglass.[55] Della Porta devoted much attention to the inverted glass experiment and similar ones, not only underscoring their relevance for understanding weather but also searching for a fitting conceptualization that allowed to grasp the common features of apparently different phenomena.

At the same time, in the hands of scholars who chose to remain closer to the Aristotelian framework, like the physician Santorio Santorio (1561–1636) or the Jesuit mathematician Giuseppe Biancani (1566–1624), the inverted glass experiment became a way to visualize the degree of heat and cold which, according to the Aristotelian-Galienian tradition, quantitatively determined the special balance (temperament or temperature) between heat and cold in living or non-living bodies and in environments.[56] In this context, the experimental setup eventually came to be called first a 'thermoscope', then a 'thermometer', although these terms, like 'degree of heat' and 'temperature' by the later seventeenth century, had become largely decoupled from their Aristotelian-Galenian origins. Although the experiment could easily be embedded in the Aristotelian framework, in that context it was difficult to find an explanation for its specific causes. Changes in volume of the air inside the weatherglass could not be explained by an increase in the quantity of matter, since no air could penetrate the glass, or by a change in quality, since air remained air.[57] Because of this, some Aristotelian scholars like the Jesuit Niccolò Cabeo (1585–1650) proposed to reform Aristotle's physics and meteorology in such a way as to accommodate this and other experiences, including Drebbel's *perpetuum mobile*, which Cabeo regarded as an object worth being studied.[58]

Let us now turn back to Galileo. When he exchanged letters with Antonini in 1612 he was familiar with the inverted glass experiments and, soon after that, he received news about Santorio's use of a similar apparatus from his Venetian friend Giovanfrancesco Sagredo (1571–1620).[59] Sagredo had copies of the device made and experimented with them, corresponding with Galileo on the subject, yet we know very little about Galileo's activities and reflections, since he never published anything on the topic. Matteo Valleriani, in his detailed discussion of Galileo's changing views on the nature of heat and its action on air and other substances, has shown that the lack of publications was not due to a disinterest for the topic on the part of Galileo, but rather to the fact that he never could develop a fully satisfactory theory of how the inverted glass experiment and similar experiences worked.[60] Galileo's reflections on heat and air were based both on his experience creating hydraulic and pneumatic devices for the gardens in Pratolino and on his reception of ancient and modern thoughts, among them those by Aristotle, Hero and the engineer Giovanni Battista Aleotti (1546–1636). Aleotti had explained the thermal expansion of air by assuming that heat is a substance made out of extremely thin particles which are able to penetrate glass and any other material, increasing the volume of air and other bodies in which they penetrate. In correspondence with his friend Sagredo in 1615 Galileo used the same explanation for the instrument: heat particles are able to pass through the glass and diffuse within the air, increasing both its temperature and its volume. Sagredo criticized this explanation as based on the existence of heat particles which had not and possibly could not be perceived by the senses. According to Valleriani, because of this critique Galileo tentatively developed another explanation for the working of the thermoscope, which is preserved in an undated manuscript fragment, probably written between 1615 and 1623.[61] The fragment contains only a rather sketchy explanation of the behaviour of the thermoscope and combined the heat particles with Aristotelian elements. Later on, though, Galilei went back to a fully atomistic conception of heat, whose particles were distinguished from other kinds of matter only by their shape and motion. Following Valleriani, we can therefore conclude that Galileo was definitely interested in the thermal expansion and contraction of air, but encountered difficulties in finding an explanation for it which would fit to the atomistic-mechanistic or Aristotelian framework in which he was developing his natural philosophy. Therefore, he never published anything on the workings of the thermoscope – or of Drebbel's *perpetuum mobile*.

What about the followers of the chemical philosophy? This topic has been dealt with in great detail by Vera Keller, who has shown that it was in those circles that Drebbel's work was most positively received.[62] Despite being no scholar or gentleman and having devoted himself to what was essentially manual labour, Drebbel came to be seen by alchemists like Johann Hartmann (1568–1631) and Andreas Libavius (1555–1616) as a philosopher, and images of his *perpetuum mobile* adorned the pages of alchemical texts, albeit often as a symbol of knowledge rather than an object to be investigated. As I have argued elsewhere, Drebbel's perpetual motion machine, and more in general devices demonstrating the moving power of heated air or steam, when interpreted in terms of the activity of air, could be connected to explanatory templates based on traditional and new notions of 'spirits' as active principles and middle instances between material body and immaterial soul.[63] This kind of explanation fit chemical philosophy and was helpful in making sense of weather and climate, highlighting their global dimensions and letting them appear as a fundamental manifestation of natural order alternative to celestial motion. An example of such a productive connection between chemical philosophy and weather and climate phenomena is the natural philosophy of Robert Fludd (1574–1637), who chose the weatherglass as a symbol of cosmic order.[64] Fludd's work can be seen as part of the chemical philosophy of the early seventeenth century, just as Galileo's was part of the mechanical one, yet in both cases those philosophical approaches were not yet as sharply delineated as would be the case later in the century. However, in the chemical philosophy of the early seventeenth century, Drebbel's perpetual motion could be interpreted not only as due to the activity of fire and air: the Paracelsian philosopher Thomas Tymme (d. 1620) explained that Drebbel 'extracted a fierie spirit out of the mineral matter, joyning the same with his proper Aire, which enclued in the Axeltree, being hollow, carrieth the whells, making a continuall rotation or revolution, except issue or vent be given to the Axeltree, whereby that imprisoned spirit may get forth'.[65] Another kind of explanation which was proposed by alchemists in the early seventeenth century connected Drebbel's *perpetuum mobile* with what they called 'magnetism', a term which at the time could refer not only to the loadstone and earth's magnetism but also to the property of a substance referred to as 'magnesia'.[66] These interpretations were, however, not generally accepted among chemical philosophers and, as shown by Vera Keller, during the seventeenth century Drebbel's perpetual motion machine was a sensual demonstration of the activity of a cosmic spirit on which different natural philosophical views could be projected. It had thus become rather a symbol of philosophical reflection that an object to think with in Bertoloni Meli's sense.

I would like to argue that the reason for this development was that in the course of the seventeenth century, both the mechanical and the chemical philosophy became more sharply defined disciplines, with the latter focussing more on those phenomena and explanatory templates which we today would refer to as chemical. These were fitting for understanding a broad range of new experience, but not the moving power of fire and air, and in this sense, the situation was similar to that obtained within the mechanical and Aristotelian framework. Keller has expressed a similar opinion, stating that Drebbel's *perpetuum mobile* was difficult to grasp for both mechanical philosophers and alchemists because it combined mechanical and non-mechanical elements.[67] I agree on this point, although I think that conceiving Drebbel's device as a combination of mechanical and non-mechanical parts somehow obscures the significance of the machine and of Drebbel's reflection, as I shall discuss later on.

5.6 Drebbel's dynamic conception of natural phenomena and the relationship to the *perpetuum mobile*

Let us now consider the way in which Drebbel interpreted his perpetual motion machine and embedded it in his natural philosophical reflections. In the letter he wrote to James I Drebbel explained that, thanks to his activities as an inventor and constructor of devices of various kinds, he had been able to grasp the principle of motion in the universe, which he referred to as the 'cause of the *primum mobile*'.[68] The fact that Drebbel underscores how his knowledge of the origin of motion was derived from his practice has been interpreted as a connection to the 'artisanal epistemology' described by Pamela Smith, which played an important role in early modern magical and occult traditions. Drebbel described his perpetual motion device as 'a little twig of the perpetually-moving tree', an image which has a very specific significance, as I will argue later on.[69] Both in the letter and in his treatise, Drebbel took extreme pains to underscore how the aim of all his investigations of the secrets of nature was to better understand God's creation, and he never spoke of magic or occult science. As to ancient authorities, he explicitly prided himself to refrain from quoting them. In conclusion, it was important for Drebbel to underscore the freedom of his reflections from any pre-existing framework, an attitude that can be seen as characteristic of the conceptual flexibility of natural magic of the early seventeenth century and especially of the techno-magical approach to the study of nature.

Focus of Drebbel's *Treatise on the Nature of the Elements* was the question of motion, life and change in the universe. In this work, Drebbel made use of Aristotelian notions in so far as he formulated his views in terms of the four elements and their properties, but the similarities to the Aristotelian framework were rather superficial. First of all, the fundamental Aristotelian concepts of matter and form played no role in Drebbel's discussions of elements and their transformations. More importantly, the four elements and their qualities served not as ontological reference points to explain phenomena, but rather as simple means to describe more or less complex meteorological and climatological dynamics in terms near to everyday experience. Indeed, the main feature of Drebbel's elements was very much non-Aristotelian, namely their ability to act upon each other. To describe this interplay of the elements, Drebbel made use of a vocabulary borrowed from alchemy, speaking of 'clarification'. Once again, this language may have been a reason to classify his work as pertaining to the alchemical tradition, although, as we shall see, Drebbel did not count himself among the alchemists. In conclusion, Drebbel's elements were both sensually perceivable substances and active principles and this flexibility allowed him a bottom-up construction of knowledge about natural phenomena. Instead of trying to a priori define the principles of his natural philosophy, he used well-known terminology as a provisional starting point to describe the interplay of the elements, which in the end were characterized primarily in terms of their actions and transformations. In the first chapter of the work, the four elements were introduced by describing how God had created and distributed them, in a version of the 'chemical creation' also present in Paracelsian literature.[70] After that, the elements were further characterized by the way they acted upon each other, transforming and being transformed, with an initial focus on how fire clarifies air:

> [Fire] gives all things life and without it all things are dead, as we see every day and especially in winter. We see that fire first clarifies the air and makes it have a clarity equal to its own, and it illuminates it from all darkness and makes apparent what was hidden in darkness, and clarifies it from vaporous damp and all earthly clouds. [. . .] In summa the fire makes the air equal to itself in everything, so that there is no distinction between the two.[71]

We note here that fire is described as clarifying air by heating it up, by purifying it from water vapours or by making things visible in obscurity. Drebbel also explains that fire goes out for lack of air because it cannot live on without purifying it. Thus, a broad range of phenomena are unified as resulting from the clarifying action of fire on air. In the second chapter, the action of fire on water and earth is discussed. Here Drebbel uses the example of coal for earth and of *aqua vitae* (alcohol) and oil for water. As in the previous chapter, these are not simply literary references to illustrate some abstract theoretical principles but are there to help readers grasp how the principles of nature work in practice. In this sense, the examples can be seen as a form of 'thinking with objects' in Bertoloni

Meli's sense. This reading is supported by the way in which Drebbel takes pains to describe the processes in detail and to anticipate practical objections. For example, he realizes that the idea of fire clarifying water may seem counterintuitive since the two elements are traditionally seen as opposites which cannot interact. Accordingly, he explains that fire can only clarify water if a mediating instance is also present, as in the case of distillation: 'Therefore the water cannot be unified with the fire without the subtlety of the air and the dryness of the earth, which mixture occurs in the form of an Aqua Vita, or oil.'[72] Drebbel's conclusion is that fire is life, a notion often picked up in later alchemical discussions of his work, where, as discussed above, the workings of the *perpetuum mobile* could be explained in terms of a 'fierie spirit' which Drebbel had distilled from 'mineral matter' and imprisoned in the machine. However, in his treatise, Drebbel never spoke of spirits as active principles distinct from the elements, and his natural philosophy was based on principles and actions perceivable to the senses.

After the discussion of fire, chapter three of the treatise went one step further and explained that all elements were capable of acting on each other, clarifying and bringing life. In this way, Drebbel made away with any hierarchy of natural forces and instead introduced the theme of a constant circulating dynamics of nature in which all elements are equally involved as both active and passive participants. Once again, this feature of nature is not stated as an abstract principle but introduced by describing phenomena which provide a template for conceiving the universal dynamics of life and motion. In this case, the evaporation and condensation of water help conceptualize the daily and seasonal life cycle of plants, where earth moisture turns into air, then into clouds and rain, eventually mixes with earth to penetrate the roots of plants and give them life, before ascending to their upper branches and once again dissolving into air thanks to the action of heat.

In the sixth chapter Drebbel focussed on further ways in which the elements could act and interact, namely the effects of cold. Here it is worth noting that, as also in other parts of the treatise, he makes use of the term 'reflection of earth' to indicate a lower, warmer layer of the atmosphere and distinguish it from a higher, colder one. He provides no nearer explanation of this terminology, but it is plausible to assume that he was referring to the (optical) reflection of the rays of the sun on the earth's surface, which heats up the air nearer to the soil. It is a phenomenon today referred to as albedo, but which had already been described in the medieval Islamic-Arabic culture and, in Europe, by Bernardino Telesio (1509–88) and by Della Porta.[73] This is another intriguing link between Della Porta's and Drebbel's meteorological treatises, about which unfortunately no further information is extant. It is, however, potentially significant that in this same chapter the other connection between the two works appears, namely the discussion in word and image of the inverted glass experiment as a means to conceptualize the origin of winds. Drebbel's version of the experience involves a retort hanging from a tree over fire, as shown in the only image included in the whole treatise. Drebbel explains that, when the fire heats the retort, and thus the air contained in it, air escapes through the mouth and the bubbles coming out of the water correspond to a wind rising. When the fire is removed, the air cools down and becomes thicker, and the water rises along the neck of the retort. Drebbel offers no explanation of this effect in terms of overarching principles and instead uses it in chapters five and six as a starting point to make sense of rather complex occasional, seasonal and local wind occurrences, including specific references to weather in Holland.

Precisely because he was not trying to connect his reflections to any preestablished natural philosophical framework, Drebbel was able to take the inverted glass experiment and other experiences as starting points for 'thinking' weather and climate in their global dimensions, which nowadays are at the centre of both scientific and political attention. This connection was much more problematic for authors working in the Aristotelian tradition, because in that framework the elements, and in particular air, were not regarded as being active and capable of self-motion, and the Aristotelian theory of meteorology underscored rather its local than its global dimension, for example, linking specific wind phenomena to the quality of local soil and waters.[74] In a similar way, Galileo's attempts to conceptualize heat phenomena in terms of atomistic and mechanical principles besides being largely unsuccessful also prevented him from considering the possible relevance of the interaction of solar heat and air for meteorology.[75] Taking experiences on the motive power of heated air or water as a starting point rather than as an explanandum is precisely what engineers from the late eighteenth to early nineteenth century did, when studying the workings of steam engines and pumps, and this turned out to be a heuristically fruitful approach in view of the later development of thermodynamics.[76] A further important contribution to those development, and in particular to the formulation of the principle of energy conservation, were natural philosophical views postulating the existence of a universal force which was globally conserved and manifested itself in a very broad range of motions and transformations.[77] It is of course not my intention to draw a linear connection between Renaissance techno-magic and these modern developments, but I wish to underscore similarities in the epistemic approaches, in the same way in which one may claim that, despite all differences, there were some similarities between Renaissance and modern mathematical or mechanical philosophers.

Let us turn back to Drebbel's treatise. Chapter seven is devoted to thunder and lightning, which are described as resulting from the evaporation, condensation and sudden, extreme expansion of water in air. Drebbel here does not claim that saltpetre is directly involved in the process, as others did following Paracelsus, but he uses experiences with explosives and other technical artefacts to explain how thunder and lightning are formed, and in particular how the loud noise of thunder results from the sudden expansion of dense matter, just as is the case with explosives.[78] Chapter eight summarizes the topics developed in the previous ones by showing how they are mutually connected in a perennial cycle of life and death:

> Consider [God's] good and wonderful ordinance which we discover in all creatures, note how wonderful (as can be seen in the previous causes) it is that the thick water becomes invisible through the sun and is rarefied and expanded into the form of air which also causes the motive power of the wind. Then it sails and expands over the lands, where through the lack of water there is no condensation and coarsening, and there it is pulled upwards through the heat of the Sun up to the cold air above the Reflection of the Earth where it is once again coarsened and condensed like a fog through which the quiet of the evening is caused, and the air which appears foggy becomes coarser and thicker through the clouds and is changed into water drops, and moistens the thirsty Earth, which melts and rots in it, and through the wetness the earth penetrates the plant, but through the heat of the sun the wetness is pulled up to the uttermost part of the plant and since the water is more flighty than the nutriment of the Earth, the water dries into the air and leaves behind the nutriment which through the life of things is changed into the nature of the plant and thus all the creatures of the Earth are sustained and multiplied out of this single substance. Therefore they once again through putrefaction are changed into earth. This is something everyone sees, but hardly a single person out of a thousand properly understands. If this were known many alchemists would not struggle so pitifully to discover their materia. But when the evaporated fog again sails into very hot places it causes thunder and lightning (through the sudden expansion) and wind: But when the air naturally becomes just a bit hotter than the fog, it gives out only wind and rain as we explained previously at greater length.[79]

Chapter nine provides a final short summary of the nature and dynamics of the four elements, while chapter ten describes how to use this knowledge to make matter cleaner, purer and subtler through a procedure of distillation and clarification based on 'reiteration', as is the case in nature. Finally, chapter eleven asks whether and how far it is legitimate to assume that one can, through man-made procedures, obtain matter more clarified than in nature: 'How could we clarify through fire more than God through the Sun?'[80] Drebbel's answer is that no clarification by human hand can go beyond what God created but may still enhance the purity which is ordinarily found in natural phenomena. The treatise concludes with an encouragement to love and honour God by researching the secrets and wonders of the nature he created.

5.7 Drebbel's natural philosophy and his *perpetuum mobile*: A reassessment

The overview of the contents of Drebbel's *Treatise on the Nature of the Elements* has shown how the Dutchman's conceptual framework for understanding natural phenomena focussed on dynamics: motion, transmutation of elements, changes between hot and cold, dense and rare and dry and humid. Moreover, it was a dynamics driven by inner active principles which pervaded the whole creation and constantly worked upon each other and not by specific parts of the universal structure. Although Drebbel spoke of a '*primum mobile*', it was in the sense of a moving force which was equally distributed in the universe and was itself in constant motion: apart from divine creation, there was no top-down hierarchy in his universe. Because of this primarily dynamical conception of nature, its workings could not be explained in terms of static definitions but had to be grasped by observing and connecting phenomena as they cyclically enfolded and by learning to use the dynamic power of the elements to create new ones. This was what Drebbel, in his letter to James I, claimed to have done during his career as an artisan, inventor and engineer.

The perpetual motion machine was a result of his studies, and from this background its significance as a means to understand the secrets of nature becomes clearer. The device was no model; it was not a small-scale demonstration of large-scale structures but a direct manifestation of those structures. Because of this, although I fully support Vera Keller's argument for the philosophical significance of the *perpetuum mobile*, I cannot agree with her interpretation of it as 'a moving microcosm or compendium of natural knowledge'.[81] This way of looking at the perpetual motion machine is biased by the views of late seventeenth-century alchemists, and in my opinion especially by an implicit analogy with mechanical, that is, clockwork, machines of the time, which indeed were a moving microcosm representing celestial motions and at the same time summarizing the mathematical-geometrical knowledge acquired about them. In Drebbel's own view, instead, the *perpetuum mobile* was no stand-alone device presenting in table-top version the cosmic dynamics of the elements: it was an instrument actually allowing its spectators to observe first-hand a small portion of cosmic dynamics. Other than clocks and automata, the machine in Eltham palace and its variants moved without external intervention because they were part of the slow, but perennial cycle of motion and transformation which Drebbel had described in his treatise. This is why he characterized his device as 'a little twig of the perpetually-moving tree'. A branch can move and live because it is part of the tree, and its motion and life are at the same time evidence of those of the tree. In the same way, Drebbel's machine functioned because it was embedded in the global dynamics of the elements which it demonstrated: it was not a stand-alone *perpetuum mobile*, but a part of the perpetual motion of nature. In this sense, Keller is fully right in underscoring how Drebbel's devices were 'living instruments'. This is an important difference between the techno-magical approach and early modern mechanical philosophy, which also made use of instrument-aided experiences and demonstrations. An astronomical clock embodies knowledge about celestial motion that can be read off its dials, but its inner workings say little about the way the cosmos works, despite all claims by mechanical philosophers to the contrary. In the case of Drebbel's devices, instead, by understanding the function of the machine and asking about the origin of its moving power, it was possible to learn the principle of motion and life in nature.[82]

As we saw earlier, seen from today's perspective, the secrets Drebbel was hinting at could be interpreted, first, in terms of the moving power of heat which, in context with the development of steam-power technologies, captured the attention of engineers and scholars at the turn to the nineteenth century, and, second, of the dynamic interplay of rotating air masses with lower and higher pressure and temperature, whose role in global weather and climate became clear only from the later nineteenth century onward.[83] At the same time, when looking at Drebbel's reflections from a modern perspective, it is easy to regard them as too simplistic. To appreciate the epistemic effort behind them, one must keep into account how difficult it was in the Renaissance to conceptualize the natural phenomena and instrument-aided experiments on which Drebbel, like other practitioners of his time, focussed his attention. Today, a refined set of scientific notions exists to express knowledge in the fields of pneumatics, thermodynamics and meteorology, but these concepts only slowly emerged in the course of the early modern and modern period. Although the terms density, pressure and temperature were partly already in use in the Renaissance, the modern notions had to be slowly constructed in a long-term interplay between theoretical and experimental practices. The idea of energy and its conservation was even further away in time. Being aware of this situation is extremely important when dealing with natural philosophy and natural magic of the Renaissance, because it is easy a posteriori to interpret some experiences and reflection in terms of concepts which emerged only later on.[84] Of course, this is a perfectly legitimate strategy from a heuristic perspective, but only as long as one realizes that notions which seem evident to us today were very difficult to construct. Otherwise, one runs the risk of either trivializing past developments or writing off as 'irrational' or plain wrong conceptual frameworks which do not fit modern concepts but, when considered in their own context, were self-consistent and plausible, and often constituted an important phase in long-term conceptual developments. I have argued in this sense using as an example Della Porta's writings on pneumatics and optics.[85] My thesis is that Della Porta had a key role in some processes of concept formation because, using the recipe format, he developed new strategies for expressing in standardized words and images knowledge about a broad range of so far often unrelated experiences. In this way, concepts could emerge as the shared features of a number of experiences. Drebbel was of course much different: he did not attempt to systematically describe and collect experiences, but he, too, focussed on the common features of apparently different phenomena and highlighted their connections. Like Della Porta, Drebbel made use of traditional terminology to express notions which, although innovative, were in no way modern ones and should not be set equal to them in the historical analysis if one wishes to do justice to the work of Renaissance authors.

Keller is aware of this fact and, in her in-depth discussions of Drebbel's writings and his 'living instruments', she notes how important it is to 're-entangle' them, meaning that one should recognize that Drebbel's creations combine elements of what would later be distinct disciplines like chemistry and mechanics, each with its own philosophical principles.[86] Indeed, Keller has shown in great detail how Drebbel's treatise and his *perpetuum mobile* could be read very differently by the persons she refers to as 'mechanical' and 'chemical' philosophers.[87] According to her analysis, chemical philosophers better appreciated Drebbel's focus on cyclic transmutations of active principles, which instead appeared trivial to mechanical philosophers. I fully agree with this assessment, yet I believe that the sharp contrast between mechanical and chemical approaches, while it helps understand Drebbel's reception in the later seventeenth century, also hides those aspects of Drebbel's work that do not fall into one or the other class, but somehow straddle their border, and which I, for lack of better ideas, have (anachronistically) described as thermodynamics. Keller writes that Drebbel in his *perpetuum mobile* 'fused mechanics and the transmutation of the elements within his machine', but this description still gives the impression that the later distinction mechanical/non-mechanical was already given, and that Drebbel was 'fusing' the two.[88] Instead, what Drebbel was focussing on was a specific area of inquiry in its own right which only a posteriori appears as a combination of distinct fields. However, I am not here proposing to add a third category to the mechanical and chemical ones, but rather that, fully in the spirit of Keller's critique to earlier historiography, Drebbel's work should be looked at in its own right and not as a combination of later notions.

In this respect, it is interesting to note that Keller describes the contents of Drebbel's treatise referring to the 'hidden energy supply of the universe', claiming that he had an '"energetic" rather than compositional view of heat' and noting the 'emphasis upon "energy" in Drebbel's philosophy'.[89] Here there are two points to be noted. In the first place, using the modern, and extremely complex notion of energy to describe Drebbel's theory is a very serious and problematic anachronism, and surprising in a research putting so much emphasis on a precise historical and cultural contextualization of Drebbel's work. At the same time, it is clear that Keller, when using the term 'energy', has no intention of placing Drebbel as antecedent in the long history of thermodynamics and energy conservation but was only trying to find appropriate expressions to characterize Drebbel's approach to natural philosophy. This is indeed a problem, and I tried to solve it by using the terms 'dynamics' and 'dynamical', which, although far from ideal, at least do not immediately connect to modern notions. Keller apparently spoke of energy because she (in my opinion correctly) recognized in Drebbel's text some elements of what would be (much later on) the notion of energy. Yet I believe that she did not appreciate enough the difficulty which Drebbel faced in expressing his views, and the way in which the techno-magical framework, thanks to its flexibility, allowed him to use the inverted glass experiment not as an explanandum in context of a given natural philosophical system but rather as a template to conceptualize other phenomena, such as in weather and climate. Here another remark by Keller is of interest: she points out that Heinrich Dove (1803–79), an important contributor to the emergence of modern meteorology, acknowledged Drebbel's early realization of large-scale meteorological dynamics.[90] However, Keller mentions this point only briefly and seems not to realize how this tribute witnesses to the originality of Drebbel's views as opposed to other early modern notions of weather and climate.[91]

In conclusion, Drebbel's (and Della Porta's) reflections on the properties of air cannot be seen as having contributed to the much later development of thermodynamics or meteorology, but they at least had the potential to have a greater impact than actually was the case, and that this was also thanks to the flexible magical framework in which they were embedded.

5.8 Summary and conclusions

Building upon developments of the previous centuries, the European Renaissance saw the rapid increase in variety and epistemic relevance of new instruments and man-made experiences which shaped and were shaped by cultural, social and economic changes. On this basis, during the seventeenth and eighteenth century, specialized areas of learning like mechanics, chemistry or mathematical analysis emerged, in combination with new approaches to the philosophy of nature. At the same time, practical knowledge about the new apparatuses and procedures was systematized and codified. One may speak in this context of the emergence of technology and its practitioners, the engineers.

Historians of science and technology have noted how, while these developments enfolded, also notions, practices and the epistemic status of magic changed. During the seventeenth century, magic was increasingly often linked to what was called black magic, that is, the commerce with demons – a trend which some authors tried to counter by distinguishing between black and white, or natural magic. In the course of the seventeenth century, natural magic, too, lost its appeal as a method to investigate the secrets of nature and came to be regarded at best as a superficial endeavour focussed on the production of marvellous effects, and at worst as an irrational practice which represented an obstacle to attaining true knowledge of natural principles. This view also dominated historiography until the late twentieth century, when investigations started underscoring the role of magic for the emergence of what would later be called science and technology. However, the magical framework has been often presented as an epistemic field which was, at least from some perspective, a deficient, or primitive form of science and/or technology. From this background, it seems self-explanatory that the magical framework was discarded as soon as allegedly better methods for the construction and application of knowledge about nature had been formulated.

I have instead argued that the magical framework was more than that, and that its fruitfulness in promoting reflection on the products of the mechanical arts and their working principles can best be appreciated by realizing how difficult it was in the Renaissance to construct and express knowledge which we a posteriori easily conceive of in later, techno-scientific terms. My claim is that the strength of the multiform and flexible field of magic resulted from a combination of two factors. The first one was a focus on and appreciation of the methods and products of artisanal and 'mechanical' practices – with mechanical here understood in its wider pre-modern meaning. The second factor was the wish to speculate about the connections and causes of these experiences without feeling bound by either acceptance or rejection of pre-existing philosophical frameworks. As seen in Drebbel and Della Porta, explanations could be formulated by combining and transforming terms and notions from different philosophical schools. This was the productive context from which some, though of course not all, later techno-scientific development emerged, and which I suggested to refer to as the techno-magical approach.

To support this thesis, I offered an analysis of some of the practical creations and writings by the Dutchman Cornelis Drebbel, in particular his perpetual motion machine and his *Treatise on the Nature of the Elements* (1st ed. 1604). By looking more closely at the key principles expressed in the treatise and at the way in which these principles were implemented in the *perpetuum mobile*, I have argued that, although the later reception of Drebbel's work among practitioners of chemical philosophy was quite positive and among mechanical philosophers negative, both groups failed to grasp some of Drebbel's reflection on the principle of nature's activity – reflections which instead resonate with later, modern theories in physics and meteorology. With this, I do not mean that Drebbel was formulating modern notions but rather that, thanks to his flexible techno-magical approach to the investigation of nature, he had individuated some areas of interest which would have deserved further explorations at least as much as mechanics or chemistry. That they did not receive such attention until much later is in my opinion evidence of how the techno-magical approach had a special heuristic power which cannot and should not be judged by the criteria of later science and technology, although it did contribute to the emergence of both.

Of course, one might ask how far Drebbel's natural philosophical reflections and engineering feats should be regarded as belonging in a natural magical context, given that Drebbel did not use the terms 'magic' or 'occult' and never referred to himself as a *magus*. Vera Keller has significantly avoided connecting him to the natural magical tradition and rather underscored how he combined artisanal epistemology in Pamela Smith's sense with more abstract philosophical reflections.[92] Indeed, Drebbel did not call himself a magician, but he also did not claim to be an alchemist, and even less an Aristotelian philosopher, a mathematician or an atomist. He preferred to do without references to ancient and contemporary authorities, and his use of Aristotelian or alchemical vocabulary did not imply any adherence to the general principles of those schools of thought. His conceptual framework was largely shaped by more or less complex experiences which he had both practised and reflected upon. In this respect, he was acting like natural magicians should according to the view expounded and enacted by Della Porta. A *magus* acquired knowledge of the secrets of nature by creating effects that looked, smelled, sounded and generally felt like natural phenomena to their observers. Being able to do so implied and demonstrated that the *magus* understood and mastered the secrets of nature. This attitude is expressed also in Drebbel's treatise and his letter to James I, and Keller has described his philosophy as a knowledge 'found in the body, although delivered in texts', although I would here add that the knowledge, although it took its starting point and justification from the body and from the empirical realm, was also a complex knowledge of the book, since it was only in textual form that the full connection between the different experiences could take place.[93] One might argue that the techno-magical approach was further developed by Francis Bacon, who regarded Della Porta's natural magic as insufficient, and wished to create a 'high kind of natural magic', for which Drebbel's techno-magical activities provided an inspirations.[94]

Within the techno-magical approach, knowledge was a performative endeavour that involved body and mind in one, and was as such particularly effective in promoting reflection on the broad spectrum of artefacts which we today may collectively label as technology. In this context, the workings of these artefacts were the starting point for a sense of wonder that guided the search and discovery of nature's secrets. Led by this sense of wonder, techno-magicians asked in practice and in theory about the workings of the machines, and were open to accepting any answer, regardless of the philosophical framework it came from, while at the same time never taking any principle for granted. To use Bertoloni Meli's notion, this attitude gave them the freedom to 'think with objects' and experiences of the most disparate kinds, using them not only as empirical starting points but also as conceptual templates for the investigation of nature. It was this flexibility which promoted the beginnings of disciplines as different as mechanics, optics or chemistry; and it was this flexibility which allowed Drebbel to productively speculate about the moving power of heat demonstrated by the inverted glass experiment and similar apparatuses and to realize the potential relevance of these speculations for the study of weather and climate.

To support this claim, it is also worth mentioning again the similarities between Drebbel's and Della Porta's discussions of pneumatic and meteorological phenomena. Given the different personal background, social position, cultural context and audience between the two authors, the shared features of their work may appear surprising, and it remains an open question how far they were due to parallel developments, mutual influences or common sources. However, for the topic at hand, I believe that both the similarities and the differences may be seen as supporting the argument that what I called the techno-magical approach was an important factor in shaping reflections on new devices and experiences. Eventually, during the seventeenth century, the emergence of specialized areas of theoretical and experimental natural philosophy let some of the insights gained with the techno-magical approach appear uninteresting. Jan Lazardzig has sketched these developments in the case of mechanics, showing how, in the early seventeenth century, the framework of white magic helped promote reflection and develop general principles of the functioning of clockwork apparatuses, but then the development of those principles in turn contributed to the exclusion of magical discourse from mechanics. In this context, devices whose functioning could not be explained in terms of levers, gears or falling weights were increasingly often marginalized. This was the case of Drebbel's *perpetuum mobile*, which was only briefly mentioned in Wilkins' *Mathematical Magick* and described as a 'chemical' apparatus. I find it fitting to conclude this contribution by quoting Wilkins' description of Drebbel's machine:

> Amongst the Chymical experiments to this purpose [i.e. to realize perpetual motion (AB)] may be reckoned up that famous motion invented by *Cornelius Dreble*, and made for King *James*; wherein was represented the constant revolutions of the Sun and Moon, and that without the help either of spring or weights. Marcellus Vranckeim, speaking of the means whereby it was performed, he calls it, *Scintilla animae magneticae mundi, seu Astralis et insensibilis spiritus* [Spark of the magnetic soul of the world, or an astral and unperceivable spirit (AB)]; being that great secret, for the discovery of which, those Dictators of Philosophy, *Democritus, Phythagoras, Plato*, did travel unto the Gymnosophistists, and Indian Priests. The Author himself in his discorse upon it, does not at all reveal the way, how it is performed. But there is one *Thomas Tymme*, who was familiar

acquaintance of his, and did often pry into his works, (as he professes himself) who affirms it to be done thus; *By extracting a fiery spirit out of the Mineral matter, joyning the same with his proper air, which included in the Axle-tree* (of the first moving wheel) *being hollow, carrieth the other, making a continual rotation, except issue or vent be given in this hollow axle-tree, whereby the imprisoned spirit may get forth*. What strange things may be done by such extractions, I know not, and therefore dare not condemn this relation as impossible; but methinks it founds rather like a chemical dream, than a Philosophical truth. It seems this imprisoned spirit is not set at liberty, or else is grown weary, for the instrument (as I have heard) hath stood still for many years.[95]

This passage vividly demonstrates how, within a few decades of its creations, Drebbel's *perpetuum mobile* had become lost in a hopeless tangle of contrasting mechanical and chemical interpretations. As shown by Van Dyck and Vermeir, Wilkins took pains to reconstruct whether and how the machines he described in the *Mathematical Magick* could be actually built or not.[96] In the case of Drebbel's *perpetuum mobile*, though, he was unable to find reliable information on the original device and its workings, and so concluded with the open verdict that he 'dare not condemn this relation as impossible'. In a similar way, scholars of this period had started losing sight of the productivity of the earlier techno-magical approach.

Acknowledgement

The research presented in this chapter was funded by the Institute for Advanced Study on Media Cultures of Computer Simulation (MECS), Leuphana University Lüneburg (DFG grant KFOR 1927).

Notes

1 Arthur C. Clarke, 'Clarke's Third Law on UFO's', *Science* 159, no. 3812 (1968): 255.
2 William Eamon, 'Technology as Magic in the Late Middle Ages and the Renaissance', *Janus* 70 (1983): 171–212; Jan Lazardzig, 'Gottesfaden und Weltenhebel. Zum Verhältnis von Weißer Magie und Mechanik im 17. Jahrhundert', in *Naturmagie und Deutungskunst. Wege und Motive der Rezeption von Giovan Battista Della Porta in Europa*, eds Rosemarie Zeller and Laura Balbiani (Bern: Peter Lang, 2008), 113–35.

3 Torsten Meyer, 'Technologie', in: *Enzyklopädie der Neuzeit Online* (Leiden: Brill, 2005–12 online since 2019) http://dx-1doi-1org-1008930k005f7.erf.sbb.spk-berlin.de/10.1163/2352-0248_edn_COM_363085; Claus Zittel, 'Introduction', in *Philosophies of Technology. Francis Bacon and His Contemporaries*, eds Claus Zittel, Gisela Engel, Romano Nanni and Nicole Karafyllis, vol. 1 (Leiden: Brill, 2008), XIX–XXIX. This process is often described as a 'scientification', but I wish to avoid this terminology, since science is also a notion that was emerging in that period.

4 Marcus Popplow and Wolfgang König, 'Ingenieur', in: *Enzyklopädie der Neuzeit Online* (Leiden: Brill 2005–12, online 2019) http://dx-1doi-1org-1008930k005f7.erf.sbb.spk-berlin.de/10.1163/2352-0248_edn_COM_284595

5 Brian Copenhaver, when discussing Della Porta's innovation of magic, writes that part of it was 'to treat what we would call technology as practical magic', a quote which prompts reflection on how natural magic could let technical artefacts appear as 'what we would call technology' (Brian P. Copenhaver, *Magic in Western Culture: From Antiquity to the Enlightenment* (New York: Cambridge University Press, 2015)), 315; a similar argument could be made on the basis of Eamon's discussions in: William Eamon, *The Professor of Secrets: Mystery, Medicine, and Alchemy in Renaissance Italy* (Washington: National Geographic, 2010).

6 On Renaissance magic and on Della Porta's natural magic, see: Copenhaver, *Magic*; Eamon, *Professor*, Eva Labouvie and Monika Neugebauer-Wölk, 'Magie', in *Enzyklopädie der Neuzeit Online* (Leiden: Brill, 2005–12, online 2019) http://dx-1doi-1org-1008930k005f7.erf.sbb.spk-berlin.de/10.1163/2352-0248_edn_COM_306126; Donato Verardi, 'Francesco Storella e l'Aristotele Negromante', *Bruniana e Campanelliana* 25, no. 2 (2019): 541–9; Donato Verardi, *La scienza e i segreti della natura a Napoli nel Rinascimento: La magia naturale di Giovan Battista Della Porta* (Florence: Firenze University Press, 2018); Paola Zambelli, *White Magic, Black Magic in the European Renaissance* (Leiden: Brill, 2007).

7 Albert Heinekamp and Dieter Mettler ed., *Magia naturalis und die Entstehung der modernen Naturwissenschaften* (Steiner: Wiesbaden, 1978); Keith Hutchison, 'What Happened to Occult Qualities in the Scientific Revolution?' *Isis* 73, no. 2 (1982): 233–53; John Henry, *The Scientific Revolution and the Origins of Modern Science* (London: Macmillan 2002); John Henry, 'The Fragmentation of Renaissance Occultism and the Decline of Magic', *History of Science* 46, no. 1 (2008): 1–48; Christoph Meiner, 'Okkulte und exakte Wissenschaften', in *Die okkulten Wissenschaften in der Renaissance*, ed. August Buck (Wiesbaden: Harrassowitz, 1992), 21–43; Lynn Thorndyke, *History of Magic and Experimental Science*, 8 vols (New York: Macmillan, 1923–58).

8 Jim Bennett, 'The Mechanical Arts', in *The Cambridge History of Science. 3, Early Modern Science,* eds Katharine Park and Lorraine Daston (Cambridge: Cambridge

University Press, 2008), 673–95; Peter Dear, 'The Meaning of Experience', in *The Cambridge History of Science. 3, Early Modern Science*. eds Katharine Park and Lorraine Daston (Cambridge: Cambridge University Press, 2008), 106–31; Pamela H. Smith, *The Body of the Artisan: Art and Experience in the Scientific Revolution* (Chicago: University of Chicago Press, 2004).

9   Katharine Park and Lorraine Daston, 'Introduction: The Age of the New', in *The Cambridge History of Science. 3, Early Modern Science*, eds Katharine Park and Lorraine Daston (Cambridge: Cambridge University Press, 2008), 5–17.

10 Lorraine Daston and Katharine Park, *Wonders and the Order of Nature: 1150–1750* (New York: Zone Books, 2012); William Eamon, *Science and the Secrets of Nature: Books of Secrets in Medieval and Early Modern Culture* (Princeton: Princeton University Press, 1994).

11 Eamon, 'Technology'. Eamon here uses the term 'technology', but I will interpret his statements in terms of technical artefacts, as it is clear from his analysis that he is using the concept of technology as a heuristic aid, and not with the intention of projecting the modern notion back in time.

12 Eamon, 'Technology', 172.

13 Eamon, 'Technology', 194–5.

14 Eamon, 'Technology', 195–8, especially 198.

15 Eamon, 'Technology', 196–7.

16 Lazardzig, 'Gottesfaden'.

17 Bennett, 'Mechanical Arts'.

18 Lazardzig, 'Gottesfaden', 114.

19 Lazardzig, 'Gottesfaden', 122–5.

20 Domenico Bertoloni Meli, *Mechanism: A Visual, Lexical, and Conceptual History* (Pittsburgh: University of Pittsburgh Press, 2019); Alan Gabbey, 'The Mechanical Philosophy and Its Problems: Mechanical Explanations, Impenetrability, and Perpetual Motion', in *Change and Progress in Modern Science*, ed. Joseph C. Pitt (Dordrecht: Springer Netherlands, 1985), 9–84.

21 Lazardzig, 'Gottesfaden', 125.

22 John Wilkins, *Mathematical Magick: Or the Wonders That May Be Performed by Mechanical Geometry* (London: Gellibrand, 1648).

23 Lazardzig, 'Gottesfaden', 126–7.

24 Lazardzig, 'Gottesfaden', 127–30.

25 Maarten Van Dyck and Koen Vermeir, 'Varieties of Wonder', *Historia Mathematica* 41, no. 4 (2014): 463–89.

26 Allen G. Debus, *The Chemical Philosophy: Paracelsian Science and Medicine in the Sixteenth and Seventeenth Centuries*, 2 vols (New York: Science History Publications, 1977).

27 Derek J. de Solla Price, 'Automata and the Origins of Mechanism and Mechanistic Philosophy', *Technology and Culture* 5 (1964): 9–23; Debus, *Chemical Philosophy*, Gabbey, 'Mechanical Philosophy', Van Dyck and Vermeir, 'Wonder'.
28 Domenico Bertoloni Meli, *Thinking with Objects. The Transformation of Mechanics in the Seventeenth Century* (Baltimore: Johns Hopkins University Press, 2006).
29 Arianna Borrelli, 'Thinking with Optical Objects: Glass Spheres, Lenses and Refraction in Giovan Battista Della Porta's Optical Writings', *Journal of Early Modern Studies* 3 (2014): 39–61; Arianna Borrelli, 'Optical Diagrams as "Paper Tools": Della Porta's Analysis of Biconvex Lenses from *De Refractione* to *De Telescopio*', in *The Optics of Giambattista Della Porta (ca. 1535–1615): A Reassessment*, eds Arianna Borrelli, Giora Hon, and Yaakov Zik (Cham: Springer International Publishing, 2017), 57–96.
30 Bertoloni Meli, *Thinking*; William R. Newman, 'From Alchemy to "Chymistry"', in *The Cambridge History of Science. 3, Early Modern Science*, eds Katharine Park and Lorraine Daston (Cambridge: Cambridge University Press, 2008), 497–517.
31 The role of exploratory practices in modern science has been discussed by recent studies, and I believe the notion may be useful also for pre- and early modern historiography. References on topic are: Richard Burian, 'Exploratory Experimentation and the Role of Histochemical Techniques in the Work of Jean Brachet, 1938–1952', *History and Philosophy of the Life Sciences* 19 (1997): 27–45; Grant Fisher, Axel Gelfert, and Friedrich Steinle, 'Exploratory Models and Exploratory Modeling in Science: Introduction', *Perspectives on Science* 29, no. 4 (20 August 2021): 355–8; Friedrich Steinle, *Exploratory Experiments: Ampère, Faraday, and the Origins of Electrodynamics* (Pittsburgh: University of Pittsburgh Press, 2016).
32 Doina-Cristina Rusu and Dana Jalobeanu, 'Giovan Battista Della Porta and Francis Bacon on the Creative Power of Experimentation', *Centaurus* 62, no. 3 (2020): 381–92, especially 385.
33 Rusu and Janobeanu note how Della Porta referred to the theory of sympathies and antipathies in the introduction of the *Natural Magic* (Rusu and Jalobeanu, 'Experimentation', 385), but in the discussions of experiences Della Porta had a syncretic approach to theorizing (Arianna Borrelli, 'Giovan Battista Della Porta's Neapolitan Magic and his Humanistic Meteorology', in *Variantology 5. On Deep Time Relations of Arts, Sciences and Technologies*, eds Siegfried Zielinski and Eckhard Fürlüs (Cologne: Walther König, 2011): 103–30, especially 123–9).
34 The following discussion is based on: Rusu and Jalobeanu, 'Experimentation', especially 386–8.
35 Rosalie L. Colie, 'Cornelis Drebbel and Salomon de Caus: Two Jacobean Models for Salomon's House', *Huntington Library Quarterly* 18, no. 3 (1955): 245–60.

36 Drebbel's life and work have been discussed in a number of papers and monographs. For this contribution I made use of the following texts: Arianna Borrelli, 'The Weatherglass and Its Observers in the Early Seventeenth Century', in *Philosophies of Technology: Francis Bacon and its Contemporaries*, vol. 1, eds Claus Zittel, Gisela Engel, Nicole C. Karafyllis and Romano Nanni (Leiden: Brill, 2008), 67–130; Jennifer Drake-Brockman, 'The *Perpetuum Mobile* of Cornelis Drebbel', in *Learning, Language and Invention: Essays Presented to Francis Maddison*, eds Willem D. Hackmann and Anthony J. Turner (Aldershot: Ashgate, 1994), 124–47; Lawrence Ernest Harris, 'Cornelis Drebbel: A Neglected Genius of Seventeenth Century Technology', *Transactions of the Newcomen Society* 31, no. 1 (1957): 195–204; Lawrence Ernest Harris, *The Two Netherlanders: Humphrey Bradley and Cornelis Drebbel* (Leiden: Brill, 1961); Francis M. Jaeger, *Cornelis Drebbel en Zijne Tijdgenooten* (Groningen: Noordhoff, 1922); Vera Keller, 'Cornelis Drebbel (1572-1633): Fame and the making of modernity' (PhD diss., Princeton University, 2008) https://www.proquest.com/openview/46d508a8fb098be3311 e899c267b26ca/1?pqorigsite=gscholar&cbl=18750&diss=y; Vera Keller, 'Drebbel's Living Instruments, Hartmann's Microcosm, and Libavius's Thelesmos: Epistemic Machines before Descartes', *History of Science* 48, no. 1 (2010): 39–74; Vera Keller, 'How to Become a Seventeenth-Century Natural Philosopher: The Case of Cornelis Drebbel', in *Silent Messengers: The Circulation of Material Objects of Knowledge in the Early Modern Low Countries*, eds Sven Dupré and Christoph Lüthy (Berlin: LIT Verlag, 2011), 125–51; Vera Keller, 'Re-Entangling the Thermometer: Cornelis Drebbel's Description of His Self-Regulating Oven, the Regiment of Fire, and the Early History of Temperature', *Nuncius* 28, no. 2 (2013): 243–75; Gerrit Tierie, *Cornelis Drebbel (1572–1633)* (PhD diss., Rijksuniversiteit Leiden, 1932). Further references are given at specific places.

37 Tierie provides no birth or death date for Sophia Golzius, and only states that she was 'a little older than Drebbel' (Tierie, *Drebbel*, 3).

38 Henri Michel, 'Le Mouvement Perpetuel de Drebbel', *Physis* 13 (1971): 289–94, especially 290–1; a comprehensive discussion of Dutch Kunstkammer paintings showing Drebbel's *perpetuum mobile* is found in: Floor Koeleman, 'Visualizing Visions: Re-viewing the Seventeenth-Century Genre of Constcamer Paintings' (PhD diss., University of Luxembourg, 2021) https://orbilu.uni.lu/handle/10993/48720 and I am very grateful to her for informally sharing with me information on this topic.

39 On Drebbel's multifacted image see Keller, 'Drebbel', 88–172.

40 No copy of the Dutch edition of the *Treatise* is at present known as extant (Keller, 'Drebbel', 109). The first German edition is: Cornelis Drebbel, *Ein Kurzer Tractat von der Natur der Elementen* (Leiden: von Haesten, 1608). The letter to King James I was published in its Dutch original in: Cornelis Drebbel, *Wonder-vondt van de*

eeuwighe bewegingh (Alkmaar: Jacob de Meester, 1607). The Latin translation of the Treatise, the text on the quintessence and the Latin translation of the letter to James I were published in 1621: Cornelis Drebbel, *Tractatus Duo: Prior de Natura Elementorum, . . . Posterior de Quinta Essentia . . . Accedit Ejusdem Epistola . . . De Perpetui Mobilis inventione* (Hamburg: Carstens, 1621). Keller, 'Drebbel', 499–532 contains a trascription and English translation of the German version of the Treatise and of the Durch version of the letter to James I, and in the following pages I will quote her translation.

41 On Drebbel's reception, see: Keller, 'Drebbel', Keller, 'Living Instruments'.
42 Harris, 'Drebbel'.
43 The following description is based on: Borrelli, 'Weatherglass'; Arianna Borrelli, 'Pneumatics and the Alchemy of Weather: What Is Wind and Why Does It Blow?', in: *Variantology 3. On Deep Time Relations of Arts, Sciences and Technologies in China and Elsewhere*, eds Siegfried Zielinski and Eckhard Fürlus (Cologne: Walther König, 2008): 27–72; Drake-Brockman, '*Perpetuum Mobile*'; Harris, 'Cornelis Drebbel'; Harris, *Netherlanders*; Michel, 'Mouvement'; Tierie, *Drebbel*.
44 Keller, 'Living Instruments'; Keller, 'Philosopher'.
45 Heinrich Hiesserle von Chodaw, *Rais-Buch und Leben (1612)*, Prague National Museum MS vi A 12, ff. 48v–50r, figure fol. 49r. The manuscript is available online: http://www.manuscriptorium.com/hub/browser/#/gallery?repo=mns &docid=AIPDIG-NMP___VI_A_12_____1XHFIVF-cs&fromDetail=true &highlightCanvasId=ID0050r. The transcription of the passages devoted to Drebbel's device can be found under https://drebbel.net/wiki/index.php?title =PDF:1612_Heinrich_Hiesserle_von_Chodaw. Phil Roger's English translation of the German original of the discussion of Drebbel's machine is printed in Drake-Brockman, '*Perpetuum Mobile*', 128–9.
46 Hiesserle, *Rais-Buch*, ff. 48v, English translation from Drake-Brockmann '*Perpetuum Mobile*', 128.
47 On Renaissance clocks and their problems see Jim Bennett, 'Mechanical Arts', 680–61; Manfred Schukowski, *Wunderuhren: Astronomische Uhren in Kirchen der Hansezeit* (Schwerin: Helms, 2006), 12–13.
48 Drake-Brockman, '*Perpetuum Mobile*', 131.
49 Dear, 'Experience'; Matteo Martelli, 'Chemistry in Renaissance Sciences', *Encyclopedia of Renaissance Philosophy*, ed. Marco Sgarbi (Cham: Springer International Publishing, 2015); Sergio H. Orozco-Echeverri, 'Mechanics in Renaissance Science', in *Encyclopedia of Renaissance Philosophy*, ed. Marco Sgarbi (Cham: Springer International Publishing, 2020). Historians have often discussed whether one should speak of alchemy, chemistry of chymistry to describe early modern practices and theories (Newman, 'Alchemy'): in this contribution I will follow the use in the secondary literature I employed, using the term 'chemical'

in the sense of Allen Debus' chemical philosophy (Debus, *Chemical Philosophy*) and describing some early modern scholars as alchemists following Keller (Keller, 'Philosopher'; Keller, 'Living Instruments').

50 Borrelli, 'Weatherglass', 107–8; Drake-Brockman, '*Perpetuum Mobile*', 136–8.
51 The following discussion follows Matteo Valleriani, 'From Condensation to Compression: How Renaissance Italian Engineers Approached Hero's Pneumatics', in *Übersetzung und Transformation,* eds Hartmut Böhme, Cristof Rapp and Wolfgang Rösler (Berlin: De Gruyter, 2007), 333–53; Matteo Valleriani, *Galileo Engineer* (Cham: Springer, 2010), 175–7.
52 The following discussion is based on: Borrelli, 'Weatherglass'.
53 Giovan Battista Della Porta. *Pneumaticorum Libri Tres, I Tre Libri de' Spiritali* ed. Oreste Trabucco (Naples: Edizioni scientifiche italiane, 2008); Giovan Battista Della Porta, *De Aeris Transmutationibus,* ed. Alfonso Paolella (Naples: Edizioni scientifiche italiane, 2000). I discussed Della Porta's pneumatic and meteorological work in Borrelli, 'Meteorology'.
54 Borrelli, 'Pneumatics', 60–3.
55 Borrelli, 'Weatherglass', 116–17; Henri Michel, 'Le Baromètre Liégeois', *Physis* 3 (1961): 203–12.
56 Borrelli, 'Weatherglass', 109–11, 117–21.
57 Valleriani, *Galileo,* 175–7.
58 Drake-Brockmann, '*Perpetuum Mobile*', 141–2; Craig Martin, *Renaissance Meteorology* (Baltimore: John Hopkins University Press, 2011), 10–24; Craig Martin, 'The Aeolipile as Experimental Model in Early Modern Natural Philosophy', *Perspectives on Science* 24, no. 3 (2016): 264–84, especially 273.
59 Borrelli, 'Weatherglass', 112–14.
60 The following discussion is based on Valleriani, *Galileo,* 155–80.
61 Valleriani, *Galileo,* 184.
62 Keller, 'Living Instruments'; Keller, 'Philosopher'.
63 Borrelli, 'Weatherglass', 93–100; Borrelli, 'Pneumatics', 70–1.
64 Allen G. Debus, 'Key to Two Worlds: Robert Fludd's Weather-glass', *Annali dell'Istituto e Museo di Storia della Scienza di Firenze* 7 (1982): 109–43.
65 Drake-Brockman, '*Perpetuum Mobile*', 132, quoted from Thomas Tymme's *A Dialogue Philosophicall* (1612).
66 Keller, 'Living Instruments', 47–50.
67 Keller, 'Living Instruments'; Keller, 'Thermometer'.
68 From Drebbel's letter as edited and translated in Keller, 'Drebbel', 502.
69 From Drebbel's letter as edited and translated in Keller, 'Drebbel', 503.
70 Allen G. Debus, 'The Paracelsian Aerial Niter', *Isis* 55 (1964): 43–61, especially 52.
71 Here and in the following I quote from Keller's English translation of the German original (Keller, 'Drebbel', 612).

72 Keller, 'Drebbel', 513.
73 Borrelli, 'Meteorology', 123–5; Arianna Borrelli, 'Heat and Moving Spirits in Telesio's and Della Porta's Meteorological Treatises', In *Bernardino Telesio and the Natural Sciences in the Renaissance*, ed. Pietro Daniel Omodeo (Leiden: Brill, 2019), 66–95, especially 84. Telesio was possibly the first to refer to the phenomenon in print in the Western world, and I have argued that Della Porta took up and expanded upon his discussion, although he never quoted him, since Telelsio's works were by that time on the Church's index of forbidden books.
74 As already mentioned, however, some authors like Cabeo tried to adapt Aristotelian meteorology to keep into account new knowledge about weather and climate (Martin, *Meteorology,* 106–24).
75 Galileo never formulated a general theory of wind and weather, but in some statements regarded winds as made out not of air, but of earth exhalation, and linked their motion to the Earth's rotation (Borrelli, 'Pneumatics', 64–5).
76 Crosbie Smith and M. Norton Wise, *Energy and Empire: A Biographical Study of Lord Kelvin* (Cambridge: Cambridge University Press, 1989); Crosbie Smith, *The Science of Energy: A Cultural History of Energy Physics in Victorian Britain* (Chicago: University of Chicago Press, 1999).
77 Kenneth L. Caneva, 'Physics and Naturphilosophie: A Reconnaissance', *History of Science* 35 no. 1 (1997): 35–106; Thomas S. Kuhn, 'Energy Conservation as an Example of Simultaneous Discovery', in *Critical Problems in the History of Science*, ed. Marshall Clagett (Madison: University of Wisconsin Press, 1959), 321–56.
78 Debus, 'Aerial Niter'.
79 Keller, 'Drebbel', 521.
80 Keller, 'Drebbel', 524.
81 Keller, 'Living Instruments', 42.
82 Arguably, also authors studying automatas and astronomical clocks around 1600 were deploying a techno-magical approach, albeit with different focus, which only later developed into a mechanistic natural philosophical framework. It is not my intention to pursue this argument here, but I believe it is worth considering.
83 Mark S. Monmonier, *Air Apparent: How Meteorologists Learned to Map, Predict, and Dramatize Weather* (Chicago: University of Chicago Press, 2000).
84 For a discussion of the dangers of interpreting theoretical practices of the past in terms of the concepts they helped form, see Borrelli, 'Pneumatic Phenomena'.
85 Borrelli, 'Thinking'; Borrelli, 'Pneumatic Phenomena'.
86 Keller, 'Living Instruments'; Keller 'Thermometer'.
87 Keller, 'Living Instruments', 45–8.
88 Keller, 'Philosopher', 132.
89 Keller 'Drebbel', 375, 386.
90 Keller, 'Drebbel', 375.

91 In general, I believe that Keller, when contructing a sharp opposition between mechanical and chemical natural philosophies, fails to appreciate the complexity of thermodynamical and weather phenomena, which fit in neither category, and simply classifies them as 'mechanical' for reasons obscure to me. For example, in (Keller, 'Living Instruments', 44), she writes that Drebbel's treatise '[r]ead mechanically' would 'offer innovative ideas, including laws of storms, a new theory of the winds'. However, these ideas cannot be described as mechanical, neither in the sense of modern mechanics, nor in the more qualitative sense of 'bodies that pressed against each other'. The same is true for the transformations of bodies 'from one state to the other', which can also not be understood in mechanical terms, as was very clear to early modern natural philosophers operating primarily within the mechanical paradigm, like Galilei or Descartes. Using this later opposition to interpret Drebbel's writing is certainly helpful to understand their reception in the later seventeenth century but obscures their significance in the earlier period.

92 Keller, 'Philosopher'; Keller, 'Thermometer'.

93 Keller, 'Philosopher', 133. I discussed the role of the written word in this context in the case of Della Porta and the recipe format in Borrelli, 'Pneumatic Phenomena'.

94 Rusu and Jalobeanu, 'Experimentation'.

95 Italics in the original. I quote from the fourth edition of the work John Wilkins, *Mathematical Magick: Or the Wonders That May Be Performed by Mechanical Geometry,* 4th edn (London: Baldwin, 1691), especially 229–31.

96 Van Dyck and Vermeir, 'Wonder', 16.

6

Aristotelianism, magic and experiments in early modern English meteorology

Jennifer Mori

6.1 Making weather instruments

In 1631, an unknown artisan based at the sign of the Princes Arms in Leadenhall Street published a single-sheet advertisement 'plainly teaching the making and use of the wetherglas' (Figure 6.1). These were thermoscopes of a kind purportedly invented by Galileo: in this case made of bulb-topped tubes filled with 'fair Water' and blue cupric sulphate or Roman vitriol. What makes a thermometer is a moot point, for the addition of a scale to the tube is only the beginning. This facilitates the comparison of relative quantities but is of limited use without a commonly recognized set of standards. True thermometers are therefore deemed to have emerged c. 1700. The 1631 tubes are inverted into inkwells through 'close corks', and register marks are painted or pasted onto the glass. The ad describes in general terms, how the instrument is made and to be used, though its explanation is far from 'plain'. It has omitted to mention that the bulb must be heated to create a vacuum in the tube before its insertion into the inkwell and that the liquid therein must always cover the bottom of the tube. We are told that the water in the tube ascends with cold and descends with heat, that a drop in the water level presages rain and that a steady glass signifies no change in the weather. Through 'diligent Observac:yn', the user may 'foretell frost Snow or Seed wether [sic]'. The target market was merchants and gentleman farmers.[1]

This tradesman could have learned about the weather glass from Francis Bacon's *Novum Organon* (1620), although its original appearance in Giambattista Della Porta's *Magia Naturalis* (1589) suggests several histories for the instrument: the magical, the empirical and something in between. According to the Paracelsian physician Robert Fludd, the weather glass illustrated universal connections

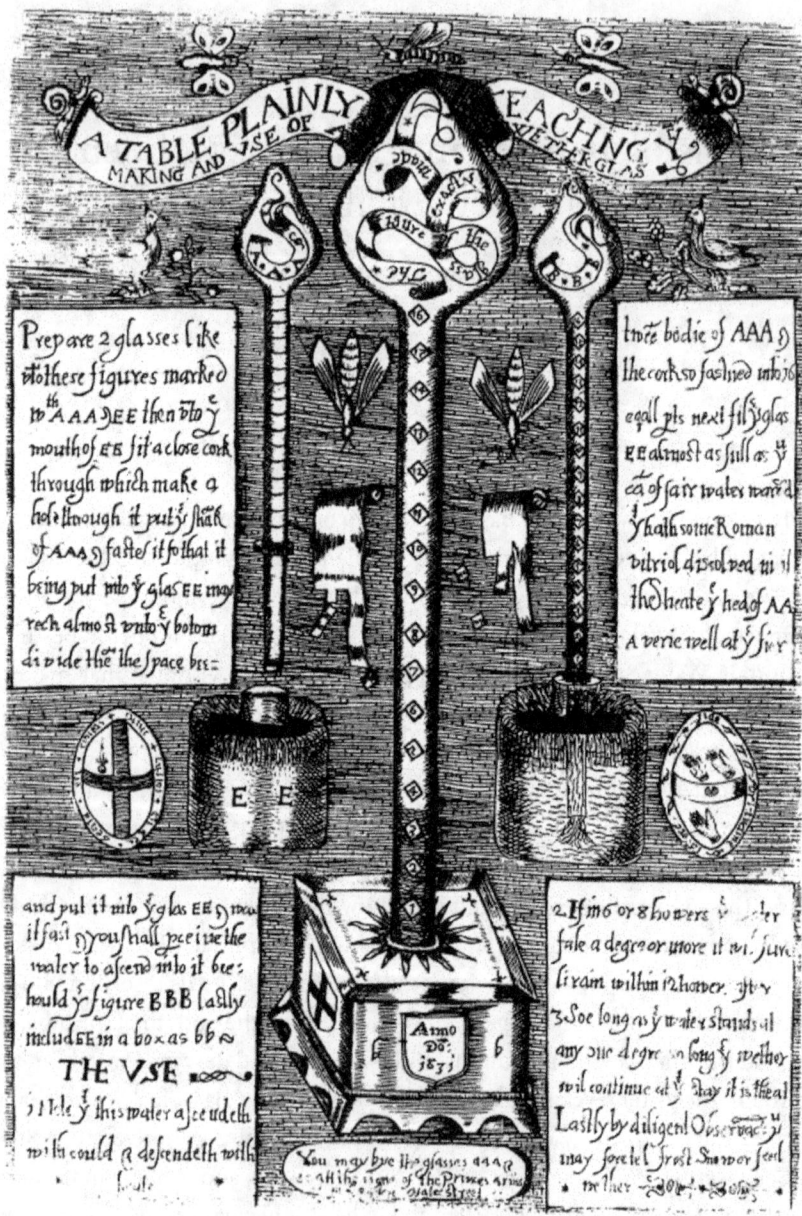

Figure 6.1 Folio advertisement for weather glasses, London 1631. STC (2nd ed.), 23636. Image published with permission of ProQuest. Further reproduction is prohibited without permission. Image produced by ProQuest as part of Early English Books Online. www.proquest.com.

between the microcosm and macrocosm. Jan Golinski and Hasok Chang have chronicled the instrument's intellectual and philosophical histories with less attention to its late medieval and early modern roots.[2] Tradition, it is argued in this paper, was more important than the new sciences to the practical adoption of weather instruments in seventeenth-century England. This chapter traces a history of meteorology that runs through vernacular print and manuscript to illustrate how empiricism built upon magic in everyday life. It is in part a history of conjuring manuals, a forgotten route through which English people learned about the making and use of modern weather technology. It is also an essay in the social history of vernacular knowledge that illustrates how books and human networks intersected to create a culture of innovation and testing in seventeenth-century England.

6.2 From sweating stones to weather glasses

In agricultural societies, the weather was and is everyone's business. Anything that purported to make it more predictable was useful knowledge.

Shepherds, say sages and almanacs, were the first astronomers and meteorologists. Some of their tradecraft informed the new natural histories of the seventeenth century though Keith Thomas observes that there were limits to this ancient lore. Piero Camporesi pays tribute to the exquisite detail of peasant empiricism but calls it a 'retarded knowledge' trapped in the cycles of agricultural time. It was therefore incapable of envisaging linear progress, let alone producing or assimilating new ideas. Golinski nonetheless points out that shepherd's weather portents continued to be used in Enlightenment England because they worked.[3] Colloquial signs, such as the closure of the pimpernel's flowers under overcast skies, constituted such oral – or common – knowledge. It began to be printed alongside classical Mediterranean weather lore in late Tudor herbals and gardening manuals.[4] The classical signs may not have been new to Northern Europe for the physician Thomas Browne observed strong similarities between these and English 'vulgar errors' or proverbial wisdom. The Mediterranean signs ranged from celestial anomalies and unusual animal behaviours to stones that sweated in humid weather. They come primarily from Aristotle's *Meteorologica* and Pliny the Elder's *Historia Naturalis*, extensive citation thereof constituting part of the humanist project to recover lost pagan knowledge.[5] Since prognostications were bestsellers in the world of popular print, all sorts of signs got into English almanacs, husbandry manuals, miscellaneous pamphlets and rhyming verse.[6]

Real English shepherds scorned forecasting by the book in favour of sky and wind watching: for the halos, horns or veils on sun, moon and stars that presaged precipitation; for the colours and shapes of clouds; and for the direction and duration of their movements. Shepherds knew that weather systems in the British Isles moved quickly from west to east, that unsettled skies were a sign thereof and that three-day-long weather conditions were likely to continue. Their long-term techniques were less reliable. These purported, for example, to foretell the severity of a coming winter from the preceding season's trends.[7] Though ostensibly based upon empirical patterns, this was similar to the Europe-wide quasi-religious weather forecasting for the coming year that took place at Christmas and the New Year. Such prognostication, says Camporesi, was driven by the peasant's obsession with the harvest, and thus grounded on subjective rather than objective experience. Bronislaw Malinowski pointed out long ago that magic took over in oral cultures where science, or empirical techniques, failed. The shepherds were, nonetheless, renowned for the accuracy of their timekeeping, which they undertook with sundials and astronomy. The Big Dipper, which they called the Charles-wain from its resemblance to an open wagon, circles Polaris every twenty-four hours.[8]

Greek natural philosophy, too, lay on a continuum between science and magic. Thanks to Aristotle, it contained an account of the physical roles played by heat and cold in what we call the water cycle. These processes – the evaporation of water, formation of clouds, their movements and precipitation – could not, however, be easily connected to the largely plant and animal signs that heralded weather events.[9] Since this logic of prediction was correlative rather than causal, Lorraine Daston calls it 'natural divination'. As Golinski has demonstrated, English meteorology never got much beyond this epistemology of signs before 1800, even when practised by savants. This guaranteed that all weather forecasting would continue to contain subjective and objective elements. It was predicated during the seventeenth century on a near-universal belief in the sublunary interdependencies of what educated men called the Aristotelian elements. Vernacular holism was based on folk ontologies ranging from empiricism to religion.[10]

Hawks and eagles, wrote Bacon in *Sylva sylvarum* (1627), flew high in the sky to presage good weather because they sensed the presence of cooling air that would balance their hot constitutions. As 'elemental' creatures of the air, birds knew the weather better than all other things. Dead kingfishers too were thus strung up 'by the bill' in England because the turning motions of their bodies were believed to show from which direction the wind blew. Browne famously hung dead birds in glass vessels 'closely stopped', to prove this false, though did not challenge the principle that there was a 'natural meteorology' in live animals.[11] Other observers concluded instead that it was the hanging strings that communicated with nature. Problem 25 of Jacques Ozanam's 1694 *Récréations mathématiques* (trans. 1708) describes an English experiment in which an artificial bird dangling from a piece of catgut 'twists by the Moisture, and retwists by the dryness of the Air'. Other such home-made instruments were promoted after 1700, their expansions and contractions measurable on yardstick scales. Although the bird had been replaced by weights, the book in which this hygrometer appears still advocated the consultation of living things.[12]

Ozanam's book constitutes a much-augmented edition of a 1624 book which, introduced to England in 1633 by Francis Malthus, went through numerous editions in French, Latin and Dutch. Its most recent historian, Albrecht Heeffer, calls the 1624 *Récréations mathématiques* a popular science blend of Italian mercantile arithmetic and medieval natural magic.[13] He attributes authorship to its printer, Jean Appier Hanzelet, rather than the usual Hendrick van Etten, whose name appears on the preface. Hanzelet, who was a printer to the University of Pont-à-Mousson, would have known the authorities from which to compile the book. A clear understanding of the contents is visible in its copperplate engravings. Many of the book's problems were what we call conjuring tricks, some of which had appeared in the works of Roger Bacon, Albertus Magnus and late medieval vernacular household manuals.[14] Sleight of hand and 'dancing' rings that exploited the volatile properties of heated mercury go back to at least the thirteenth century. Seventeenth-century readers would also have seen similarities in content between the *Recreations*, the secrets of Alexis of Piedmont and English recipe books.[15] Plagiarism was rife between natural magic, books of secrets and recipes because early modern print belonged to a mental world that reckoned intellectual legitimacy by tradition rather than novelty. Imitation was the greatest form of flattery, and all these books dealt with the manipulation of nature's secrets.

The English *Recreations* were meant for long winter evenings. Seventeenth-century England was introduced to science in part through such fireside recreational books. This, a 330-page octavo, begins with a detailed table of contents from which readers can pick and choose what they like best: 'But whoever will have the patience to read on, shall finde the end better than the beginning.' This is important in the history of books because it illustrates the beginnings of a move away from an intensive focus on a comparatively small number of texts to wider and comparative reading.[16] In the histories of science and ideas, it also bids us keep an open mind about how contemporaries perceived and related to mathematics. The *Recreations* start gently with conjuring tricks and arithmetic problems conveyed through cards and dice before moving onto discuss optics, ballistics, hydrostatics, geometry, geography and pyrotechnics. It is written in 'vulgar' English and presupposes no prior knowledge of maths and physics. The first edition was, nonetheless, expensive on account of its many illustrations. At 542 pages, Ozanam's 1708 edition too was accessible only to wealthy readers in the first instance.[17]

Problem 99 of the 1633 text explains how to make the thermometer: 'an instrument to measure the degrees of heat and cold in the aire'. Since it is made of glass, it appears alongside mirrors, lenses and prisms. The instructions are rudimentary, for it is unlikely that gentlemen would have been making the instrument themselves. Hanzelet focuses instead on its uses to observe, measure, register and compare. His guidelines say that rapid drops in the water's level foretell rain or snow while a rising liquid bespeaks fair weather.[18] The weather glass worked because it was, in part, responding to changes in atmospheric pressure. This made it, in effect, a barothermoscope. This was understood by Robert Boyle, and the instrument consequently fell out of favour with the Royal Society during the 1660s.[19] By that date, however, there were several English books describing how to make the weather glass: the *Recreations*, some other mathematical texts and two farming manuals.[20] Vernacular epistemology cared little for institutional standards. As Michael Lynn has written in the context of contemporary French attitudes to divination for water and metals, popular science satisfied common-sense criteria. It was useful, it seemed to make rational sense and could be verified by eyewitness evidence.[21]

Judging by a third English reprint of the *Recreations* in 1674, genteel readers enjoyed Hanzelet's blend of amusement, instruction and practical advice. Barbara Stafford and Patricia Fara pay tribute to the influence of such texts upon eighteenth-century science lecturing and – implicitly – their audiences.[22] More significant during the prior century was John White's *A rich cabinet, with variety of inventions; unlock'd and opened, for the recreation of ingenious spirits at their vacant houres* (1651). This is a miscellany of household tips and recreational experiments. Its author looks like a soldier because one-third of his book is devoted to pyrotechnics 'very fitting for these warlike times of action'. His title and preface direct the book's 'receits and conceits' to 'lovers of natural and artificiall conclusions'. Conceits were pursuits of wealth and leisure, and the fireworks lay well beyond the reach of common readers. The conclusions, however, referred to a 1586 threepenny tract whose contents also range from conjuring tricks to kitchen and gardening advice.[23] These recipes had been translated from Italian by the grammar-school-educated blacksmith Thomas Hill, who wrote other popular humanist manuals for the London middling sorts.[24] Trevor Hall calls this the first book of secular magic written in English and has identified other early modern conjuring books that draw attention to the hidden properties of nature. The best known of these is *Hocus pocus junior. The anatomie of legerdemain* (1634), which contained no formal science, was reprinted many times and in many formats up to 1784. Through such reading, say scholars from William Eamon to Peter Burke, readers would have learned how to start relating to the natural environment in less metaphorical and more literal, causal and consequential terms.[25]

White signed the preface of his book '*The Artist's Friend*'. This, its preponderance of household advice and the 'Mechanick way' in which technical information is presented place *A rich cabinet* partly among the artisanal books of secrets. The book's practical jokes are also drawn from the farmyard and alehouse. Over the next twenty years, White added to the riches of his cabinet. The third edition (1658) starts to feature new 'experiments' in arithmetic and geometry. These are approximate constructions of the kind used by artisans and builders up to the nineteenth century: how to take, for example, 'the Altitude of a Building by a Line and Plummer, the Sun Shining' by the application of Euclidean geometry. White's book would be plagiarized for more than a century.[26]

Since this is a recipe book, *A rich cabinet*'s directions for making a 'Thermometer, or Weather-Glasse' are much more precise than Hanzelet's. The bulb-topped tube can be bought 'ready made at the Glasseshops', of which the longest and slenderest with a small head are the best. Readers are told to make their own frames, which presupposes that they have some carpentry skills. The heating of the bulb and tube, its insertion into the cistern and the devising of the scale are described in some detail. White's design is a composite of the five glasses that appear in John Bate's *The Mysteries of Nature and Art in Four Several Parts* (1634). Bate's book is a lavishly illustrated volume of fountains, fireworks, drawing and 'extravagants' or 'divers experiments, as wel serviceable as useful'. These correspond to White's 'conceits' and are reminiscent of Hugh Plat's *Jewel House* (1594) of fancy sugar work, practical alchemy and kitchen physic. Though the *Mysteries* can be broken up into its separately paginated parts for sale, it is no popular text. Bate's glasses, some made with circular or multiple glass tubes, are delicate things whose replication is beyond the skill of most amateurs.

Master craftsmen might have bought sections of the book for reference, but it lay beyond apprentices and layfolk. Bate has placed the weather glasses among the waterworks because they operate on pneumatic principles.[27] Della Porta and Fludd had attributed the instrument's operation to heat alone. White has chosen the simplest of Bate's glasses, a single tube in which the liquid descends with heat, for reproduction along with some cheap and practical items of Bate's household advice.

White's weather glass is more than a useful tool: it is a mantelpiece ornament and conversation piece. Like Fludd's household glass, it has a decorated base (Figure 6.2)[28] covered 'with Pastboard or the like, glewing and pasting pecces of mother of Pearle shells, smiths Cinders peeces of Glasse, Antimony or other

Figure 6.2 Robert Fludd's household weather glass. *Integrum Morborum Mysterium: sive medicinae Catholicae Tomi Primi Tractatus Secundus, in Sectiones distributus duas* (Frankfurt: Wolfgang Hofmann, 1631), p. 8. Public Domain Source: Wellcome Library for the History of Medicine, London. https://wellcomecollection.org/works/m2ykf2sk/items?canvas=40.

shining things what best pleaseth your fancy; or you may cover it with Mosse, or the like, and it is finisht'. Bate's references to decoration are perfunctory, it does not appear in the illustrations and it is advocated only to cover the cistern so 'that the art may not be discerned'. Fludd hoped thereby to make his instrument seem more impressive, and White too played the magus to entertain his readers.[29]

This theme of stagecraft purporting to demonstrate mastery over nature runs through all conjuring books from the medieval encyclopaedias to the eighteenth century. They are important, say Hall and Eamon, because they represent a playful tradition of curiosity through which pre-modern investigators learned through hands-on trial and error to investigate nature's secrets. This was part of the habitus of early modern *techne*. Historians of science and secular magic illustrate how such genteel leisure pursuits were transformed into wider public knowledge during and after the eighteenth century.[30] The conversational aspect of the weather glass and fireside recreation in general are important because they helped make the observation, interrogation and applied knowledge of nature part of everyday life.

White's directions for the instrument's calibration are based on Bate's though they come from the circular glasses rather than the stick thermometers. If this glass is to be used in the summer, the initial level of the liquid should be set at one or two on a twelve-point scale White says is best for the English climate. Since Bate's scale only went up to ten, this suggests that White had actually made the glass he describes. If it was meant primarily for winter use, a setting of nine or ten was appropriate because the liquid's level was more likely to fall than rise in cold weather. Both Bate and White conclude that a fickle glass, regardless of design, signifies 'unconstant weather' or a change therein, a stable glass denotes the same, and a sudden fall of the glass 'is an evident token of rain'.[31] The first two of these rules echo the shepherds' sky-watching. According to Fludd's logic, Bate and White's weather glasses could be seen as microcosms of the wider world on Hermetic and analogical principles: 'as above, so below'. It could also be said through a reversal of inductive logic that the glasses had illustrated a hypothesis, had either man set out with weather glasses to test the shepherds' rules.[32]

Early modern technical manuals often lack accounts of causation so both explanations are possible. Bate, Hanzelet and Fludd had explained the liquid's motion in terms of Aristotelian physics. Heat, whether of the sun or a hand laid on the globe, caused the air therein to 'rarify' or expand and drive the liquid down the tube. 'Condensing' cold shrunk the air in the globe to pull up the liquid. *A rich cabinet's* lack of this language may, however, be partly responsible for its popularity. Four legal reprints and one chapbook edition of White's book had been produced by 1687.[33] The chapbook began to expose the text to a wider audience, to which it would appeal because the book contained everything from medical and gardening advice to 'A ready way to teach Children their ABC in manner of play'. By no means all of White's recipes bear evidence of testing or use. 'How to know when the Moone is just at the full by a Glasse of water' stipulates that water will 'presently boile over' its rim at the appropriate time. This information was desirable because the moon's cycles were critical to operations in folk agriculture, Galenic medicine and personal hygiene, namely planting, harvest, bloodletting and hair cutting. The moon's waxing and waning, says White, may be known by other methods, one of which is the daily increase or decrease of a house-cat's 'Eie-browes'. This supposed influence of the moon over moisture, and growth in general, was a core principle of folk natural astrology.[34] The logic of White's moonlore, specifically its emphasis on causation and quantification, is nonetheless unusual for popular rituals, even in jest. It suggests a route through which some testing and, ultimately, naturalization of common knowledge were taking place.[35]

White's medical aetiology is conventionally Galenic in its emphasis upon the four humours and their counterbalancing properties. By 1450, let alone 1650, this was arguably popular rather than learned knowledge in England because it was regularly appearing in the late medieval manuscript almanacs and vernacular household manuals owned by craftsmen, burghers, professionals and the gentry.[36] White's empiricism therefore seems largely demotic in its derivation from oral and textual sources. As a general proposition, he prefers impersonal and objective physical explanations to subjective accounts of affinity and influence. Many of his instructions are consequently more detailed than others of their ilk. He seeks through artifice to imitate nature because such activities are entertaining, thought-provoking and useful. Though operating within traditional mental frameworks, White is moving to a state of greater existential detachment from nature. In its instructions for the making and use of the weather glass, *A rich cabinet* consequently goes beyond the books of secrets and conjuring books that taught its readers to see the little patterns in nature.

As a general proposition, elucidations of nature's grander designs were aimed at the cognoscenti. This is why Fludd published primarily in Latin, his 1626 *Mosiacall Philosophy* not appearing in English until 1658. Only one popular author, Thomas Willsford, tried to convey some sense of the higher theories that underpinned meteorology in *Nature's secrets. Or, The admirable and wonderfull history of the generation of meteors* (1658). He was a student of the natural astrology that based weather predictions upon the aspects: or positions of planets relative to each other; such as quadratures (□) and oppositions (☍), of which the best-known contemporary practitioner was John Goad. This made Willsford a particular kind of mathematician and astronomer. Two published books of practical arithmetic for merchants demonstrate that he could be a competent technical writer. Another three: a geometry, a nineteen-year almanac and two histories, were never printed, though they say that his popular writing ambitions were genuine. The ephemeris would have been for other astrologers and used to track the movements and aspects of sun, moon and planets. Willsford dedicated *Nature's secrets* to his kinswoman, Lady Stafford. His nephew, the Anglican clergyman Edward Boteler, wrote a verse preamble for it. Willsford, says Golinski, was a Catholic. Despite this genteel background, he sought in *Nature's secrets* to 'please all Sexes and Ages, the Ignorant and the Learned'.[37]

Goad's *Astrometeorologia* (1686) was based in part upon thirty years of weather-journal keeping. The Royal Society never deemed this 'science', much to its author's chagrin.[38] Willsford's book was instead based primarily on 'the observations of others'. As a result, he delivers a jumbled mix of classical weather theory and causation, natural astrology and empirical weather signs. These were connected through the will of God and Aristotelian physics. Water, earth, air and fire had affinities with animals, vegetables and minerals; each element with its particular domain under the moon. The fixed and moveable stars, or planets, also had 'sympathies' with the four elements, which is the logic that made astrometeorology credible. Animals, birds in particular, can read the weather because God has given them special gifts in compensation for their lack of human reason. Though the book is modelled on older humanist natural histories, Willsford is making some room for mechanics in his cosmology. Plants have strings or nerves that move leaves and petals by 'internal vapours'. The world, states Willsford, was created by God as a machine, and God's Nature is a benevolent and consistent entity. Notwithstanding this evidence of some detachment, both from God and Nature, the older holism continued to dominate Willsford's reasoning. He paints what is probably an accurate picture of general knowledge about the weather at this time.

Willsford's technical account of how to make a weather glass made with vinegar is also correct. Like White's, it is a composite blend of other people's designs, in this case possessing a sixteen-point ascending scale. Willsford's explanation of its operation and use is, to our eyes, bizarre. He described the air in the bulb as the active agent, 'for the outward Air, being condensed with cold, that contained in the globe of the glass must ascend to avoid a vacuum'. Aristotle, after all, had denied the existence thereof. The heating of the air outside the glass would, in turn, cause a 'sympatheticall imitation of the parts here Inclos'd', whereby the air's expansion in the tube would cause the liquid's level to drop. The principle of balance underlies the physics for Willsford cites someone else's 'experiment' in which a heated glass globe of hot air bounces off a wall, preserved from breaking by the outward counterpressure of its contents. He went on to supply two pages of instructions for interpreting the motions of the liquid in the glass.[39] These are often contradictory and unlikely, particularly after testing, to have made a lasting impression upon readers. *Nature's Secrets* was never reprinted. Willsford's weather glass-manufacturing instructions were nonetheless copied verbatim into the commonplace book of one ordinary weather observer.

We don't know who owned the roughly octavo-sized notebook now known as British Library Additional MS 54487, but its contents and paleography identify the author as male, non-elite and a devotee of natural and artificial conclusions. He cites no authors or titles but the content speaks of conjuring books, books of secrets and informal knowledge networks. It ranges from conjuring tricks, metalwork, weapon care, archery, waterproof shoe polish, dyes, pigeon-keeping and fireworks to codes and invisible ink. The connection between experiment and play is explicit. There is no agricultural material, which suggests that the owner was a Londoner, and the manuscript was given to the library by the Patent Office. Add MS 54487 displays an interest in inventions, but also natural magic, namely the mythical stone supposed to come from the head of a toad which was supposed to be a universal antidote to all poisons.[40] This is important as a statement of faith in nature as an idealized state of equilibrium and as evidence of the holism that grounded this man's experiments. The manuscript is dated *c.* 1710.[41] Its owner is unlikely to have read *Nature's secrets* for its author's pneumatics, but Willsford's weather glass would have worked if made correctly, for its technology is sound. A reader, however, could ignore the glass entirely if she/he wished because the book contained thirty-two pages of natural weather signs 'from the lofty Pine to the humble Shrub, and little Vegetables, from Birds and Beasts and Fishes in the deep, down to the Minerals in the Earth'. This was more comprehensive a list than was supplied by any almanac or book of husbandry. Willsford, indeed, praises the accuracy of English weather omens but does not cite topographical weather proverbs because he dislikes experience uninformed by theory.[42] 'Vulgar' readers would, nonetheless, have focussed on this section of the book because it repeated things they already knew.

The concepts of balance and affinity were slow to disappear from vernacular knowledge, in part because elite and popular books continued to endorse the concepts of sympathy and antipathy long after they had been abandoned by elite science. Sympathy, said Ozanam's *Recreations*, was 'a Conformity of the natural qualities of Humours or Temperament, or a suitableness of occult vertues, so distributed in two things, that they easily agree and bear with one another'. The language is Galenic, subjective and metaphorical though the book says immediately afterwards that electrical bodies also have properties of attraction and repulsion. This equation of magic with science appeared elsewhere, not least in the eighteenth-century encyclopaedias,[43] while popular almanacs, trade manuals and cookbooks would continue to uphold the cosmology of four elements and their counterbalancing properties well into the eighteenth century. This preserved the central place of Aristotelianism in vernacular epistemology.[44]

Add MS 54487 contains instructions for making three weather glasses: two stick thermometers and a solution of camphor and brandy in a bottle. The origins of the last, a chemical storm glass, are lost to history but it was widely used in the mid-nineteenth century.[45] Its modus operandi stipulates that, in good weather, the camphor would crystallize into sprigs and clouds, while in bad weather it would coalesce 'like slub', or muddy sludge, at the bottom of the glass. The other thermometer shares White's four-post wooden frame, twelve-point scale and decorated base. Another hand has added a feather quill to the wax joint between the two glasses to admit air to the cistern.[46] This is necessary for the liquid in the instrument to move, and Bate had stipulated the addition of such a 'short pipe' or J-shaped cane to joints well sealed that 'nothing may come out'. The vent is an improvement to the glass's design for neither Hanzelet nor Fludd mention it or, indeed, a seal. Willsford includes the cane but White does not and instructs the maker only to 'waxe or cement' the glasses together: how closely he does not say. Air could have entered the tube through a partial joint, though too much would have affected the accuracy of the glass and the keeper of Add MS 54487 understood this.[47]

The notebook keeper liked the chemical storm glass the best: 'I have made one of these wch have done very well, & through ye forke I put a crow quill wth both ends cut of [sic] to let ye aire into ye Bottle.' The vent was clearly important to him. As far as anyone knows, this instrument emerged in the eighteenth century.[48] In 2008, a team of Japanese chemists discovered that crystallization in the camphor storm glass is governed by temperature. While its patterns cannot be used on their own to predict the weather, the chemists confirm nineteenth-century findings that this glass works as a kind of thermoscope; or more precisely, 'an apparatus affected by the history of the temperature variation'. Successive heating and cooling of the glass under laboratory conditions produces sine curves of crystal formation and dissolution. Since camphor begins to solidify in alcohol between 30 and 20 degrees Celsius, it would announce the arrival of cold air only under specific conditions. All three glasses in Add MS 54487 would, however, have been consulted in the past alongside other weather signs. Modern folk users say that its clouds form at the approach of rain or snow.[49] The Japanese findings seem to contradict the maker's instructions, but he does not tell us what his crystals looked like: only that consistently useful patterns appeared in the glass. His observations illustrate that he was comfortable with improvisation: the owner of what Antonio Perez-Ramos called the 'maker's hand'. This kind of knowledge is difficult to quantify but plays an important role in histories and making and doing.[50] So mindful was this particular hand that its owner was comfortable using the glass as Bate recommended: to 'according to your owne observation frame other rules'. In the final analysis, it looks like the notebook keeper could not envisage the glass working without physical contact between the air and the solution. This is arguably more science than magic though such syncretism is characteristic of recipe books. Willsford had not ascribed the movements of his glass to its cane. Ozanam's 1708 *Recreations*, moreover, even contained a recipe for a sympathetic ointment 'that will cure a Wound at a Distance'.[51] To what extent this is the same magic of older times is questionable when performed with new instruments and alongside new procedures.

Skilled artisans too blended objective and subjective knowledge. One unknown London clockmaker active between 1690 and 1746 kept a workshop notebook now called Guildhall MS 06619, Volume 1. His book contains recipes and diagrams: two of a mercury barometer '34 inches Long and as wyde as A Large Straw of wheat' (Figure 6.3) and one of a Newcomen steam engine. There is a page of magic here too: a list of animal parts or 'things that proquor L:[ust]'; a hagstone – a stone with a natural hole in it – to prevent nightmares in men, women and horses, and a two-part charm from 'an angel', whose written component was to be carried on the body. Coupled with a daily recitation of '3 pater nosters; [and] 3 aves' a day, the paper was supposed to protect its wearer from various threats, not least 'thunder, or Lightening, neither shall [they] be hurt with fier or water'.[52] Cryptic references indicate that this was book learning and it shares the formulaic wording of cunning-folk spells. Apart from the aphrodisiacs, the talismans are apotropaic, as is most folk magic.[53] Such charms can be found in Reginald Scot's *The discovery of witchcraft* (1584), a book famous for its denunciations of witchcraft. Because, paradoxically, the book contained so many detailed descriptions of the magic it derided, it was widely used as a grimoire.[54] The clockmaker relied upon magic in time-honoured ways to

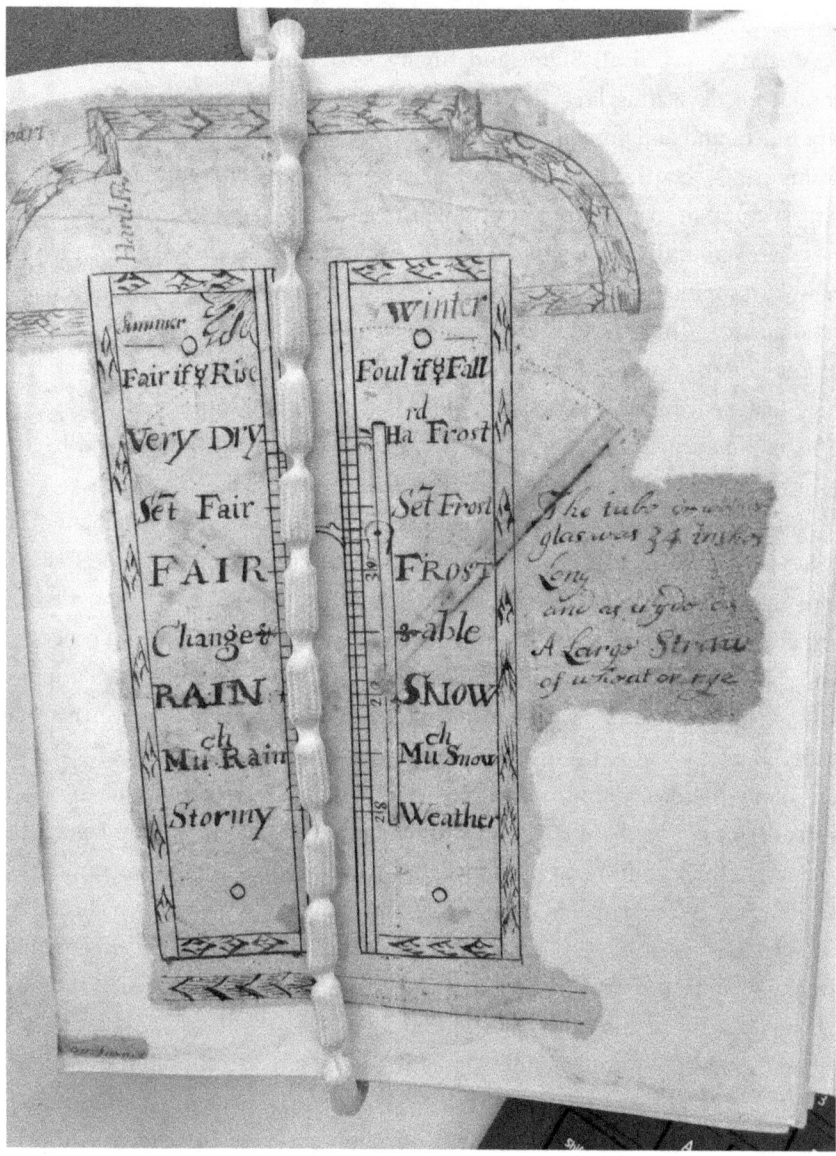

Figure 6.3 London Guildhall Library MS 06619, Vol 1, Item 31. Credit: The Worshipful Company of Clockmakers, London.

assuage anxiety. The fact, however, that he gets his magic from books says that its collection and use is, to some extent, governed by reason.

Barometers, hagstones and charms are united by religion. This was not Roman Catholic theology per se for the old liturgy remained part of English oral culture long after the Reformation, but rather an attenuated once-pagan belief in the interconnectedness of all things. English popular religion, say its scholars, was relaxed, practical, literal and highly flexible: in effect, a psychological toolkit for navigating life.[55] Seventeenth-century London popular religion was not hidebound and, in adding to it, the clockmaker has begun to move beyond Camporesi's retarded knowledge. Bad weather is an embodiment of quasi-supernatural destructive powers, while fire and water are elements as much to be feared as admired. The notebook's contents nonetheless proclaim that nature may be propitiated through faith, and better known through astronomy and mathematics. The artisan seeks to understand cyclical time through notes for 'the making and use of a new perpetual almanack' or astronomical clock. His new knowledge has not displaced older beliefs but rather merged with them. This is not surprising because the Aristotelian cosmology was upheld by the grimoires along with natural magic and, indeed, empirical experiments.[56]

Guildhall MS 06619 is part commonplace, part recipe book. Both it and Add MS 54487 are important to the histories of reading and making: the first for illustrating the interplay of textual sources that shape their keeper's thoughts; the second for the light they shed on his/her sensory perceptions, thought processes and social networks of knowledge. They illustrate what communities of popular science looked like in seventeenth-century England as well as the forms that experimentation took in ordinary people's lives. Bruno Latour once scoffed at pre-modern meteorology as a kind of 'fumbling in the dark . . . believing in all sorts of absurd myths mixed up, fortunately, with a few very sound practical recipes'. In these shifting sands of such half-truths, collective wisdom was at least as authoritative as personal experience. This is why the networks recorded by recipe books are important. What trading in such relative truths helped establish among seventeenth-century layfolk was the confidence to trust their own trials. Elaine Leong calls this 'everyday science'.[57]

Add MS 54487 was owned by someone from the lower-middling sorts, most likely a law clerk for he writes of a practical joke played on a judge with a home-made firecracker. Again, we see the connection between experiment and play. His sources included a gentlewoman for secret writing codes, a gunpowder maker for explosives and 'an old manuscript' for recipes. His notebook portrays a knowledge-exchange culture of general rather than specialized or elite learning, though much of the content is gendered as male.[58] The clockmaker's world, as depicted in MS 06619, is more socially and intellectually circumscribed. Though he records orders from elite clients, he exchanged books and recipes with other artisans. He may have seen the barometer at a coffee house or another artisan's shop and he consulted many ephemerides in search of the most accurate data he could get about the aspects of the moon and planets. This helped him to test and, ultimately, improve the accuracy of his clocks. The authorities he cites reveal that he was a largely self-taught astronomer though this was by no means unusual at the time.[59] Many authors he cited were home-grown, namely Thomas Hill, 'Samewell [Samuel]' Strangehopes, and 'Vinsent [Vincent] Wing', Thomas Streete and William Whiston. The first three were popular writers; among them Wing the best known on account of his work as the compiler of the popular almanac *Olympia Domata*. The clockmaker, however, learned through trial and error to move beyond mass-market ephemerides to mathematicians Streete and Whiston and, eventually, the making of his own.

Strangehopes' *Book of knowledge* (1664) is a perpetual almanac that assumes almost complete ignorance of mathematics in its presentation of the four arithmetical operations. It also deals with astrology, kitchen physic and farming. *The Schoole of skill* (1599) constitutes more of Hill's popular humanism simplified for a lay audience. It was 'lent me by hawe' to teach the clockmaker astronomy. The owner of Guildhall MS 06619 is more fluent a scribe of astronomical glyphs than English cursive script but must have had some Latin to consult Wing's *Astronomia Britannica* (1669). He was seeking the most accurate data he could get for the latitude and longitude of London and quoted the slightly different numbers supplied by Ptolemy, Copernicus, Tycho Brahe and Kepler for comparison and, probably, testing.[60] The clockmaker has come some way from the shepherd's methods in his astronomy.

Weather instruments were made by London clockmakers in the 1690s. Judging by the contents of MS 06619, its owner was capable of interpreting the barometer's motions in primarily pneumatic terms. Golinski points out, nonetheless, that some contemporaries saw the barometer as a prophetic as opposed to a prognostic device. It was easy, thus, to incorporate into magical weather practices and its labels of wet and dry are misleading to this day.[61] The lowest reading does not always herald torrential rain, nor the highest one good weather. The barometer, even more than the thermometer, took measurements of relative atmospheric states: both the precursors of weather events and the events themselves. It could not be used effectively without conscientious record-keeping and attention to short-term patterns in both the data and related weather conditions. In 1692, manufacturer John Patrick instructed buyers to read the glass in such relative rather than absolute terms. He ended with the admonition 'not so strictly to mind the words that are Engraven on the Plate'.[62] These maxims were still in widespread use a century later.[63] For these reasons, among others, most people continued to rely primarily on the subjective correlative meteorology of signs. Insofar as they made or bought weather instruments, these were used as adjuncts to tradition. The commonplace books of educated readers consequently disclose a consistent interest in weather signs. Thomas Jackson took three pages of notes in 1683–4 on 'natural prognostics for the judgment of the weather'. These originate with Pliny: the skies, birds, worms, moles, human aches and pains, biting fleas and sweating stones. Perpetual almanacs were another source of this information by the later seventeenth century.[64]

6.3 Conclusions

The 'natural' sources of the predictions are important because they denote that these are empirical signs, as opposed to vulgar hearsay. Oral tradition was losing some of its credibility because of its attachment to superstition. Some of William Seller's weather omens still came from 'Labouring Men and Ancient Inhabitants of Rural Places' but had been vetted by Ozanam, and consequently made respectable. Seller also took notes from Hill's *Natural and Artificial Conclusions* out of interest in the conceits that conjuring books embodied.[65] He is the kind of educated reader interested in all sorts of patterns and likely to have made toys like the weather glass for fun. Over time, however, and this is evident in how Willsford wrote the genteel section of his book, gentlemen sought to receive useful knowledge through the filter of a learned 'student'. In an expanding universe of print, gatekeepers were becoming desirable to differentiate fact from fiction. Some signs, such as forecasts of forty days of rain from showers on St Swithin's Day, were becoming less credible in England on theological grounds. Others, notably the hanging kingfishers, were undergoing naturalization. Novelties needed placement within the parameters of existing knowledge systems to be meaningful in the first instance to readers and users. Up to 1700, these encompassed mathematical exercises, Aristotelianism, natural astrology, natural magic, religion and play. Therein lies the wider importance of recreational books that popularized physics, optics and other secrets. Some were reaching the lower tiers of popular print and, thus, a wider audience.[66]

If technology is defined as the effective application of scientific knowledge for practical purposes, then the semiotics of weather in early modern England qualify in many respects. These range from the oral transmission of patterns to the making and use of instruments to better discern them. The history of weather glass manufacture and use illustrates shifts and variations in English understandings of useful knowledge and Aristotelian physics. Fludd had seen the sun's heat as the activator of the glass. Bate placed equal importance upon the expansion and contraction of its air, with which White – despite his failure to mention the vent – probably agreed. For Willsford, sympathy was the force that moved the air though he attributed the water's descent to gravity and its ascent to the avoidance of a vacuum. The owner of Add MS 54487 saw camphor and alcohol as physical registers of all four elements. The clockmaker has moved on to some awareness of atmospheric pressure but simultaneously deemed weather a concoction of air, water and fire. This was consistent with popular magic, Aristotelian meteorology and Cartesian mechanical principles.

Vernacular epistemology, as White noted, does not usually deal in absolute truths or abstract principles. Its stock in trade is results that work which begs the question why it should change at all if it satisfies human needs and wants. The answer, according to the traditional history of ideas in the West, is that the Aristotelian cosmology and its derivatives were incapable of generating new objective knowledge and that this was increasingly desired because it promised humankind a greater knowledge of, and potential control over, nature. What the history of weather instrument making in England demonstrates is that vernacular epistemology, like early modern popular culture in general, is additive rather than substitutive.[67] Insofar as the change took place in English thinking about the weather, this did not involve a significant paradigm shift in perceptions of, and attitudes to, nature. The disenchantment of the world began, practically speaking, with a slow shift along an ancient continuum away from the supernatural towards – and eventually beyond – existing conventions of natural logic within the Aristotelian framework. This began to produce notions of what we call modern, discrete, mechanical and impersonal causation before 1700. They would not, however, become uppermost in the popular mind until the nineteenth century. The process was slow in part because makers and users of weather instruments were groping towards new understandings of nature and, indeed, themselves for the new tools made perceptible things that had hitherto lay largely beyond the five human senses. In so thinking, doing and making, artificers of nature were starting, as Evernden put it, to disentangle themselves from the birds, the stars and the ancient logic associated with cyclical time.[68] Integral to this process was the identification of new enquiries, data and appropriate modes of their interpretation, which began with their understanding within – or assimilation into – familiar knowledge frameworks.

Notes

1. *A Table Plainly Teaching ye Making and Use of a Wetherglass* (London, s.n., 1631). Image produced by ProQuest as part of *Early English Books Online*. www.proquest.com; John P. McCaskey, 'History of "Temperature": Maturation of a Measurement Concept', *Annals of Science* 77, no. 4 (2020): 399–444.
2. Allen G. Debus, 'Key to Two Worlds: Robert Fludd's Weather-Glass', *Annali dell'Istituto e Museo di storia della scienza di Firenze* 7, no. 2 (1982): 109–44; Jan Golinski, *British Weather and the Climate of Enlightenment* (Chicago: University of Chicago Press, 2007), 41–3, 162–4; Hasok Chang, *Inventing Temperature: Measurement and Scientific Progress* (Oxford and New York: Oxford University Press, 2004), 25–9.
3. Keith Thomas, *Man and the Natural World: Changing Attitudes in England, 1500–1800* (London: Allen Lane, 1983), 70–5; Piero Camporesi, *The Anatomy of the Senses: Natural Symbols in Medieval and Early Modern Italy*, trans. Allan Cameron (Cambridge: Polity Press, 1994), 186–200; Golinski, *British Weather*, 67–70.
4. Linnie R. Mooney, 'Practical Didactic Works in Middle English. Edition and Analysis of the Class of Short Middle English Works Containing Useful Information' (PhD thesis, Centre for Medieval Studies, University of Toronto, 1981); *A most briefe and pleasaunte treatise, teachyng how to dresse, sowe, and set a garden* (London: John Day for Thomas Hill, 1558); *The herball, or Generall historie of plantes* (Edm. Bollifant for Bonham Norton and John Gerard, 1597). Hill and Gerard were the authors of the last two books. All books published in London unless otherwise stated.
5. Thomas Browne, *Pseudodoxia epidemica*, ed. Robin Robbins (Oxford: Clarendon Press, 1981), 2 vols., V1, 3–4, 197; S. K. Heninger, *A Handbook of Renaissance Meteorology* (Durham: Duke University Press, 1969), 103–8.
6. James Raven, *The Business of Books: Booksellers and the English Book Trade, 1450–1850* (New Haven: Yale University Press, 2009), 20, 24; *Perpetuall and Natural Prognostications of the Change of Weather* (A. Islip for Edward White, 1598); Kinki Abenezrah, *An Euerlasting Prognostication of the Change of Weather* (I. Jaggard, For M. Sparke, 1625). See the frontispiece verse preface entitled 'Infallible Signs of Rainy Weather, from the Observation of divers Animals' in the 1764 edition of a very old perpetual almanac called *The Knowledge of Things Unknown* (Allington Wilde, 1764).
7. *The shepheards legacy, or, John Clearidge, his forty years experience of the weather being an excellent treatise, wherein is shewed the knowledge of the weather* (John Hancock Junior in Cornhill, 1670), 1–7, 11; Margaret Spufford, *Small Books and Pleasant Histories. Popular Fiction and Its Readership in Seventeenth Century England* (Cambridge: Cambridge University Press, 1981), 29.

8   Camporesi, *The Magic Harvest. Food, Folklore and Society*, trans. Joan Krakover Hall (Cambridge: Polity Press, 1993), 41–3; Bronislaw Malinowski, *Magic, Science, Religion and Other Essays* (Glencoe: Free Press, 1948), 12. https://monoskop.org/images/4/41/Malinowski_Bronislaw_Magic_Science_and_Religion_and_Other_Essays_1948.pdf; Clearidge, *Shepheard's Legacy*, sig. A4, 2–8, 11, 22, 26–9.
9   Neil Evernden, *The Social Creation of Nature* (Baltimore: Johns Hopkins University Press, 1992), 20–1; Aristotle, *Meteorologica* (Loeb Classical Library Online 397, 2014), 71–6.
10 Lorraine Daston, 'Super-vision: Weather Watching and Table Reading in the Early Modern Royal Academy and Académie Royale des Sciences', *Huntington Library Quarterly* 78, no. 2 (2015): 194; Golinski, *British Weather*, 133; Keith Thomas, *Religion and the Decline of Magic* (Harmondsworth: Penguin, 1971).
11 Francis Bacon, *Sylva sylvarum: or, A naturall historie In ten centuries* (IH and Augustine Mathewes for William Lee, 1627), 823–4; Browne, *Pseudodoxia epidemica*, 196.
12 Jacques Ozanam, *Recreations mathematical and physical; laying down, and solving many profitable and delightful problems of arithmetick, geometry, opticks, gnomonicks, cosmography, mechanicks, physicks, and pyrotechny* (R. Bonwick et al., 1708), 444–6; John Pointer, *A Rational Account of the Weather* (Aaron Ward, 1738), 158–62.
13 Albrecht Heeffer, 'Récréations Mathématiques (1624) A Study on its Authorship, Sources and Influences', Ghent: Centre for Logic and Philosophy of Science, Ghent University, http://logica.ugent.be/albrecht/thesis/Etten-intro.pdf, accessed on 1 December 2020, 6.
14 Bruno Roy, 'The Household Encyclopedia as Magic Kit: Medieval Popular Interest in Pranks and Illusions', *Journal of Popular Culture* 14, no. 2 (1980): 60–70; Mooney, citation of the fifteenth century Bodleian Ashmole MS 1393 on 464.
15 Eamon, *Science and the Secrets of Nature. Books of Secrets in Medieval and Early Modern Culture* (Princeton: Princeton University Press, 1994); Allison Kavey, *Books of Secrets. Natural Philosophy in England, 1550-1600* (Urbana and Chicago: University of Illinois Press, 2007); Elaine Leong, *Recipes and Everyday Knowledge. Medicine, Science and the Household in Early Modern England* (Chicago: University of Chicago Press, 2018); Francis R. Johnson, 'Notes on English Retail Book-Prices, 1550–1640', *The Library* 5, no. 2 (1950): 95–6.
16 Hendrik van Etten, *Mathematicall Recreations* (T. Cotes for Richard Hawkins, 1633), quotation from preface, no pagination. Heidi Brayman Hackel discusses some of the issues in *Reading Material in Early Modern England. Print, Gender and Literacy* (Cambridge: Cambridge University Press, 2005), 70–80.
17 Johnson, 'English Retail Book Prices', 94. First editions of lavishly illustrated science books were double the price of unillustrated ones. Re-use of the plates dropped the price in subsequent editions.

18 Van Etten, *Mathematicall Recreations*, 110–13; Heeffer, 'Récréations mathématiques', 126.
19 Golinski, *British weather*, 112–14.
20 The farming texts were the most accessible and widely distributed. Gervase Markham, *The seconde booke of the English husbandman* (T.S. for John Browne, 1614), 2–12; John Worlidge's *Systema agriculturae* (T. Johnson for Samuel Speed, 1669), 257–9.
21 Michael Lynn, 'Divining the Enlightenment: Public Opinion and Popular Science in Old Regime France, *Isis* 92, no. 1 (2001): 36.
22 Barbara Stafford, *Artful Science. Enlightenment Entertainment and the Eclipse of Visual Education* (Cambridge, MA and London: MIT Press, 1994); Patricia Fara, *Sympathetic Attractions: Magnetic Practices, Beliefs and Symbolism in Eighteenth-century England* (Princeton: Princeton University Press, 1996).
23 John White, *A rich cabinet, with variety of inventions* (William Gilbertson, 1651), no pagination in this edition (ESTC Wing, 2nd edn, 1994, W1790A) so Early English Books Online PDF numbers used. PDF 1; Thomas Hill, *A briefe and pleasant treatise, intituled: Naturall and artificiall conclusions* (Edward Allde, 1586); Johnson, 'English Retail Book Prices', 104.
24 Johnson, 'Thomas Hill: An Elizabethan Huxley', *Huntington Library Quarterly* 7 (1943–4): 329–51.
25 There were fifteen editions of *Hocus pocus* printed between 1634 and 1742. Trevor H. Hall, *Old Conjuring Books. A Bibliographic and Historical Study with a Supplementary Check-list* (Duckworth, 1972), 31–45, 120–32; Eamon, 'How to Read a Book of Secrets', in Elaine Leong and Alisha Rankin, eds, *Secrets and Knowledge in Medicine and Science, 1500–1800* (Farnham and Burlington: Ashgate, 2011), 23; Peter Burke, *Popular Culture in Early Modern Europe*, 3rd edn (Routledge, 2009), 351–2.
26 White, *Rich Cabinet* (William Gilbertson, 1658), 173.
27 John Bate, *The Mysteries of Nature and art in Four Several Parts* (Thomas Harper for Ralph Mab, 1634), sig. A2, 29–38; White, *Rich Cabinet* (1651), PDFs 18–20, 22–3. All further citations of this work refer to the 1651 first edition. Debus, 'Key to Two Worlds', 118–19.
28 Fludd, *Integrum Morborum Mysterium: sive medicinae Catholicae Tomi Primi Tractatus Secundus, in Sectiones distributes duas* (Frankfurt: Wolfgang Hofmann, 1631), 8.
29 White, *Rich cabinet*, PDF 20, Debus, 'Key to Two Worlds', 122–3; Bate, *Mysteries of Art and Nature*, 33, 35.
30 Hall, *Old Conjuring Books*, 41; Eamon, 'How to Read a Book of Secrets', 43; J.L. Heilbronn, *Electricity in the Seventeenth and Eighteenth Centuries. A Study in Early Modern Physics* (Berkeley and London: University of California Press, 1979);

Patricia Fara, *Sympathetic Attractions: Magnetic Practices, Beliefs and Symbolism in Eighteenth-Century England* (Princeton: Princeton University Press, 1996) and *An Entertainment for Angels. Electricity in the Enlightenment* (Cambridge: Icon Books, 2002); Iwan Morus, *Frankenstein's Children: Electricity, Exhibition and Experiment in Early-Nineteenth-Century London* (Princeton: Princeton University Press, 1998); Simon During, *Modern Enchantments. The Cultural Power of Secular Magic* (Cambridge, MA: Harvard University Press, 2002); Pierre Bourdieu, *Distinction: A Social Critique of the Judgement of Taste* (London: Routledge, 1984), 471.

31 Bate, *Mysteries of Art and Nature*, 31, 38–9; White, *Rich Cabinet*, PDF 19–20.
32 The dictum comes from *The Emerald Tablet* of Hermes Trismegistus. Stanton J. Linden, ed, *The Alchemy Reader: From Hermes Trismegistus to Isaac Newton* (Cambridge: Cambridge University Press, 2003), 27–8; Clearidge, *Shepheard's Legacy*, 4–8.
33 The pirate edition was *The art of [bell] ringing . . . Also artificial fireworks . . . the art of gardening . . . [and] how to order cattle, orchards and hop-gardens*, &c. (G. Conyers, 1687?).
34 Hugh Cunningham, *Time, Work and Leisure. Life Changes in England since 1700* (Manchester: Manchester University Press, 2014), 8; White, *Rich Cabinet*, PDFs 16, 29; Patrick Curry, *Prophecy and Power. Astrology in Early Modern England* (Oxford: Polity Press, 1989), 97; Camporesi, *Magic Harvest*, 70–1; Mooney, 'Practical Didactic Works in Middle English', 356.
35 Anna Marie E. Roos, *Luminaries in the Natural World. The Sun and the Moon in England, 1400-1720* (New York: Peter Lang, 2001); Mark Harrison, 'From Medical Astrology to Medical Astronomy: Sol-lunar and Planetary Theories Of Disease in British medicine, c.1700-1850', *British Journal for the History of Science* 116, no. 1 (2000): 25–48.
36 Mooney, 'Practical Didactic Works in Middle English', 125–6, 227–8, 378.
37 Thomas Willsford, *Nature's Secrets* (Printed for N. Brooke, 1665), PDFs 2, 5–6, 8 and 199; Golinski, *British Weather*, 113.
38 Ann Geneva, *Astrology and the Seventeenth Century Mind. William Lilly and the Language of the Stars* (Manchester: Manchester University Press, 1995), 79.
39 Willsford, *Nature's Secrets*, 1–4, 137, 147, 150–2, 155–6. Bate had recommended vinegar, alcohol or any liquid that would not freeze for the making of weather glasses, 29.
40 Edward Topsell, *A History of Four Footed Beasts and Serpents* (William Jaggard, 1658); Browne, *Psuedodoxia epidemica*, Book III, Chapter 13, quoting Thomas Nicols, *Lapidary, Or, The History of Pretious Stones* (Cambridge University Press, 1652) Part II, Chap. XXXVI, 158–9.
41 British Library Add MS 54487, ff. 25–31.

42 Willsford, *Nature's Secrets*, PDF 5 and 71, 114–46; Morris Palmer Tilley, *A Dictionary of the Proverbs in England in the Sixteenth and Seventeenth Centuries: A Collection of the Proverbs Found in English Literature and the Dictionaries of the Period* (Ann Arbor: University of Michigan Press, 1950), 72, 103, 191, 403, 475–6, 513, 565 and 609 for vernacular weather omens.

43 Ozanam, *Recreations Mathematical*, 455–7; Heilbron, *Electricity in the Seventeenth and Eighteenth Centuries,* 28; Ephraim Chambers, *Cyclopedia: Or, an Universal Dictionary of Arts and Sciences*, 2 vols (Printed for James and John Knapton, et al., 1728), V2, 827.

44 Ozanam, *Recreations Mathematical*, 475; Jennifer Mori, 'Prognostic Birds and Vulgar Errors. Popular Naturalism in Early Modern England, c.1580-1790', in *Evidence in the Age of the New Sciences*, eds. Richard Raiswell and James T. Lancaster, International Archives of the History of Ideas, 225 (Cham: Springer, 2018), 269–92; Godfrey Smith, *The Laboratory; or, School of Arts* (C. Whittingham for H.D. Symonds, J. Wallis, Wynne and Scholey, and Vernor and Hoode 1799), 2 vols; Mary Fissell, *Patients, Power and the Poor in Eighteenth-Century Bristol* (Cambridge: Cambridge University Press, 1991); Roger Cooter, *The Cultural Meaning of Popular Science: Phrenology and the Organization of Consent in Nineteenth-Century Britain* (Cambridge: Cambridge University Press, 1984).

45 Anita McConnell and Philip Collins, 'Will the True Originator of the Storm Glass Please Own Up', *Ambix* 53, no. 1 (2006): 67–75.

46 BL Add MS 54487, 'Receipts of different concerns. With A Table at the End for finding any Receipt in ye Booke', c.1710, ff. 25–31; White, *Rich Cabinet*, PDF 18.

47 Bate, *Mysteries of Art and Nature*, 22, 32; Willsford, *Nature's Secrets*, 151; White, *Rich Cabinet*, PDF 20.

48 BL Add MS 54487, f. 31r; McConnell and Collins, 'True Originator of the Storm Glass', 67–8.

49 Yasuo Tanaka, Koichi Hagano, Kazishige Nagashima and Tomoyasu Kuno, 'Pattern Formation of Crystals in Storm Glass', *Journal of Crystal Growth* 310, no. 10 (2008): 2668–72, especially 2671; R. Fitzroy, *The Weather Book* (Longman: Roberts and Green, 1863), 439. Ethnographer Gerald Milnes was told by Appalachian quilt maker Dovie Lambert that she uses the cloud patterns in a bottle of American patent medicine on her windowsill to forecast the weather. She also said 'that a pint of moonshine with a piece of camphor gum dissolved in it will do the same thing'. *German Appalachian folklore. Signs, curs and witchery* (Knoxville: University of Tennessee Press, 2007), 76.

50 Antonio Perez-Ramos, *Francis Bacon's Idea of Science and the Maker's Knowledge Tradition* (Oxford: Oxford University Press, 1988), 48; Lissa Roberts, Simon Schaffer and Peter Dear, eds, *The Mindful Hand: Inquiry and Invention from the Late Renaissance to Early Industrialisation* (Amsterdam: Koninklijke Nederlandse

Akademie van Wetenschappen, 2007), 1–10; Wendy Wall, *Recipes for Thought. Knowledge and Taste in the Early Modern English Kitchen* (Philadelphia: University of Pennsylvania Press, 2016), 8–9.

51 Bate, *Mysteries of Art and Nature*, 39; Willsford, *Nature's Secrets*, 152; Ozanam, *Recreations Mathematical*, 431.

52 London Guildhall Library MS 06619, 'Late seventeenth-century clockmaker's workshop notebook, *c*.1690–1746', Vol. 1, Items 30c.-31, 50, 13.16.

53 A similar charm without prayers or angel can be found in David Rankine, ed., *The Grimoire of Arthur Gauntlet. A 17*th *Century London Cunning Man's Book of Charms, Conjurations and Prayers* (Avalonia, 2011), 54. This book dates from the 1620s or 30s. Stephen Wilson, *The Magical Universe. Everyday Ritual and Magic in Pre-Modern Europe* (Hambledon, 2000), xvii–xviii, 54–5, 66.

54 Reginald Scot, *The Discovery of Witchcraft* (Andrew Clark, 1665). See 153–5 for Latin and English charms against disease. Owen Davies, *Grimoires: A History of Magic Books* (Oxford: Oxford University Press, 2009), 69–71.

55 James Obelkevitch, *Religion and Rural Society: South Lindsey 1825-*1875 (Oxford: Clarendon Press, 1976), 259–63; Deborah Valenze, 'Prophecy and Popular Literature in Eighteenth-Century England', *Journal of Ecclesiastical History* 29, no. 1 (1978): 84, 88; Christopher Marsh, *Popular Religion in Sixteenth Century England. Holding Their Place* (Basingstoke: Macmillan, 1998), 147–53; Alison Shell, *Oral Culture and Catholicism in Early Modern England* (Cambridge: Cambridge University Press, 2007), 4, 55, 58–9.

56 Scot, *The Discoverie of Witchcraft* (Henry Denham for William Brome, 1584) Book VIII, Chapters I, XII–XXVII, 165; Ronald Hutton, *The Pagan Religions of the Ancient British Isles* (Oxford: Oxford University Press, 1991), 284, 289–92; Guildhall MS 06619, V1, Items 17A, 24–5; Rankine, *Grimoire of Arthur Gauntlet*, 35.

57 Bruno Latour, *Science in Action. How to Follow Scientists and Engineers Through Society* (Cambridge, MA: Harvard University Press, 1987), 182–3; Wall, *Recipes for Thought*, 31–46; Leong, *Recipes and Everyday Knowledge*, Chapter 1.

58 BL Add MS 54487, ff. 22, 33, 44, 51.

59 John T. Kelly, *Practical Astronomy During the Seventeenth-Century. Almanac Makers in America and England* (New York: Garland Publishing, 1991), 3–4; Henry C. King and John R. Millburn, *Geared to the Stars. The Evolution of Planetariums, Orreries and Astronomical Clocks* (Toronto and Buffalo: University of Toronto Press, 1978). The clockmaker would have done his celestial timekeeping with a quadrant and, possibly, an astrolabe.

60 Larry Stewart, 'Other Centres of Calculation, or, where the Royal Society didn't Count: Commerce, Coffee-Houses and Natural Philosophy in Early Modern London', *British Journal for the History of Science* 32, no. 2 (1999): 133–53; Guildhall MS 06619, V1, Items 10, 17, 24; Samuel Strangehopes, *A Book of Knowledge, in*

Three Parts (Charles Tyus, 1664), 112–28; Thomas Hill, *The schoole of skil containing two books: the first, of the sphere of heauen . . . The second, of the sphericall elements* (T. Judson for W. Jaggard, 1599).

61 Golinski, 'Barometers of Change: Meteorological Instruments as Machines of Enlightenment', in *The Sciences in Enlightenment Europe*, ed. Golinski, William Calrk and Simon Schaffer (Chicago: University of Chicago Press, 1999), 69–93.

62 Golinski, *British Weather*, 110, 122, 126–7; Guildhall MS 06619, V1, Item. 30C; John Patrick, *Rules and observations on the various rising and falling of the mercury to know the weather by the baroscope* (1692).

63 Henry Andrews, ed., *Vox stellarum: Or, a Loyal Almanack for the Year of Human Redemption* (Stationers' Company, 1789), 7.

64 Folger Shakespeare Library, MS V.a.391, 'Commonplace book of Thomas Jackson and Henry Pawson, 1683-4', no pagination or foliation; William Winstanley, *Poor Robin's book of knowledge shewing the effects of the planets, and other astronomical constellations. Excellent receipts for curing of most distempers incident to man. Useful observations in chirurgery and husbandry. With directions for ordering cattle, and medicines for the many diseases they are liable to* (R. Wild, 1688), 53–8.

65 Folger Library, MS M.a.59-60, 'Prose miscellany of William Seller, *c.* 1700–26, 2 vols', V2, 76, 1714; Ozanam, *Recreations Mathematical*, 476–8.

66 Ann Blair, *Too Much to Know: Managing Scholarly Information Before the Modern Age* (New Haven: Yale University Press, 2010); Mary Fissell, 'Imagining Vermin Early Modern England', *History Workshop Journal* 47, no. 1 (1999): 1–29. See, for example, London dentist Edward Fountaine's sixteen page *Melancholys bane: or, Choice, pleasant, and profitable recreations Gathered out of many most famous and industrious searchers of art and natures secrets* (1654) and J. M.'s 48 page *Sports and pastimes: or, Sport for the city, and pastime for the country; with a touch of hocus pocus, or leger-demain* (H. Brugis for John Clark, 1676).

67 White, *Rich Cabinet*, PDF 1; Burke, *Popular Culture*, 351–2.

68 Evernden, *Social Creation of Nature,* 30; Camporesi, *Anatomy*, 200 and *Magic Harvest*, 42; Jibu Mathew George, *The Ontology of Gods. An Account of Enchantment, Disenchantment and Re-enchantment* (Cham: Springer Nature, 2017), 98–100, 105.

7

Natural magic, experimentalism and tarantism in a Dutch Aristotelian professor

Manuel De Carli

7.1 Introduction

It is largely believed by historians of scientific thought that many practices, objects and theories from the Renaissance magic had been integrated into the natural and experimental philosophy that was emerging in the seventeenth century. We only need to think that such philosophy emphasized experimentation or the use of occult qualities and active principles to explain phenomena. In this context, many experiments or magical objects were used, transformed and employed, in order to discover new hypotheses on the laws of nature.[1]

In recent decades, several studies have highlighted the influence of Aristotelian reformist circles on the debate on occult qualities in the early modern period. Although there have been studies of specific magical objects, endowed with peculiar occult qualities, such as magnetism, planetary influences and remora,[2] little attention has been paid to the tarantula and to its inclusion in the context of the late seventeenth-century debate on the physics of qualities.[3]

The absence of specific studies on this subject is surprising not only because the tarantula – as other magical objects – was present in many records of occult qualities which in the seventeenth century filled the works of physicians, philosophers and natural magicians but also because of the presence of specific treatises about the 'occult' aspects of this magical object.[4] By reading much of this literature, it is clear that the tarantula's effects and its treatment were rightly ascribed to irregular and extraordinary phenomena, which require a more specific explanation than the regular facts of nature. This explains the tight connection with the occult qualities, a conceptual tool used by physicians, philosophers and natural magicians to justify extraordinary facts in a rational way. In addition, the tarantula, in comparison with other magical objects (like the remora, the magnet or the planetary influences), was considered to be the cause of a complex occult phenomenon, that is, the tarantism, which involved many aspects traditionally associated with occult causes: these are the extraordinary variety of the symptoms caused by spiders' poison, as well as the uncommon development of the disease which might occur periodically every summer; the fact that this disease spread only in a particular region in the south of Italy alongside its peculiar treatment seen through music and dance.[5]

An emblematic intervention on this subject, in which the tarantula and the occult qualities are presented as closely interrelated, was made in the *Tractatus physicus de tarantula*[6] (Leiden, 1668) by Wolferd Senguerd (1646–1724),[7] son and student of the neo-Aristotelian Arnold Senguerd (1610–67),[8] as well as Doctor of Philosophy and then professor of peripatetic philosophy at the University of Leiden. This work was preceded, few months before, by the discussion of the *Disputatio philosophica inauguralis de tarantula*[9] (Leiden, 1667), which was written in order to obtain the title of doctor. In both these works, the author shows how the different aspects involved in the poisoning caused by the tarantula, traditionally attributed to occult causes, could instead be explained with alternative solutions. This is particularly significant since it presented, for the first time in a systematic way, all the occult aspects implicated by the tarantism. The interest in this topic increased, and the study of the tarantula and its occult qualities was also carried out later in the author's life, in particular during the years of his experimental activity supervising the *Theatrum physicum* of Leiden, characterized by the record of *matters of fact*.[10] In 1715, indeed, he published a third intervention on the subject, the *Disquisitio de tarantula*, adding it to the *Rationis atque experientiae connubium*,[11] a manual that wanted to offer a report of his private courses of pneumatic as well as the instructions to the experimental use of the air pump to specialist readers.

Starting from Wolferd Senguerd's reflection on the tarantula, this chapter aims to illustrate the modus operandi of an Aristotelian professor of the second seventeenth century in explaining the occult causes of the marvellous effects handed down by the tradition of natural magic. More specifically, this study will show how Wolferd's experimental attitude towards the occult develops already in the years of his Aristotelian formation under the aegis of his father Arnold. Also explored in this chapter is the contribution of his subsequent encounter with English experimental philosophy and his work as an experimenter in the *Theatrum physicum* of Leiden, with particular regard to his pneumatic experiments. From this perspective, the various solutions identified by Senguerd regarding tarantism are emblematic of the commitment of the Dutch scientific circles of the second half of the seventeenth century to experimentally reveal the most occult aspects of nature.

7.2 The tarantula and the occult qualities

Wolferd's attention to the Apulian tarantula, to the effects of its bite and to the choreutic musical therapy was part of his wider interest in the occult qualities, which was one of the main themes of the physical debate during the sixteenth and eighteenth centuries.

In the peripatetic glossary, which was still used in the seventeenth century, the term 'occult' was placed in opposition to 'manifest' to indicate the qualities that are unknowable to the reason and the intellect and cannot be attributed to the mixture of elementary qualities (hot, cold, wet and dry). Traditional examples of the occult qualities were the attractive virtue of the magnet, the planetary influences, the properties of some substances to cure specific diseases (such as rhubarb that is a remedy for cholera) or the properties that some poisons have to cause extraordinary effects, such as the paralysing power of the electric ray and the power of the remora to stop ships, and also the ability of the wolf's gaze to silence people and the lethal properties of the basilisk.[12]

In the first part of the Modern age, thanks to the rapid growth of fauna and flora – due to the flourishing of the observational natural history – and to the development of new chemical remedies and the general progress of knowledge in chemistry, there was a proliferation of the occult qualities. The peripatetic reformers, being them physicians, philosophers or natural magicians, followed two main approaches. The first approach focussed more on the reality of the occult qualities, concentrating on the empirical undeniability of their effects. The second approach aimed to suggest alternative means of natural causality which, although insensitive, seemed to be comprehensible. It was possible, for example, to invoke the emission of subtle spirits or the effusion of small and invisible particles. Both these approaches had a great influence on the empirical research on nature in the first part of the modern age.

As far as the first approach is concerned, especially in the Anglo-Saxon context, the natural philosophers focussed more on empirical ratification. The scholastic distinction between manifest and occult qualities was not used anymore by the Baconian method of collecting and systematizing empirical facts within the 'tables of instances'. The so-called 'experimental philosophy' as it was developed by Bacon's English disciples allowed one to study those physical phenomena which were apparently inexplicable, provided that their effects could be demonstrated through experimental methods.

As regards the second approach, it is important to underline that the Aristotelians' aim to include the occult qualities in natural philosophy and to explain them through an insensible but physical way was not so different from the purpose of Descartes and other disciples of mechanical philosophy, who aimed to explain the occult qualities by means of the collision and interlocking among insensible particles of matter. Besides, it should be noted that the scholastic distinction between 'occult' and 'manifest' was not so important for mechanical philosophy, since all the explanations could ultimately lead to the movement and interaction among insensible particles. At the same time, there was the spreading of the idea that the manifest qualities could also be explained through the methods of mechanical philosophy, as it happened for the occult qualities. This tendency became very widespread in the rest of Europe.[13]

The work done by the young Senguerd aimed to identify some alternative physical explanations for the occult qualities. This project, as much as the previous *Disputatio*, symbolized the second approach to the occult qualities just mentioned. Both in the *Disputatio* and in the *Tractatus*, the author uses an explanatory model based on mechanics and particles, which called upon the fermentative procedures of Iatrochemistry as well as the manifest qualities of the Aristotelian-Galenic tradition, which were deduced from the natural history of the tarantula.

This eclectic solution, seen also as a compromise in a certain way, was identifiable in Senguerd's general discourse upon the occult qualities. In the *Disputatio philosophica inagurualis de tarantula*, he openly admitted that carrying out a research *de occultis qualitatibus* was a difficult and an unpopular challenge (*arduam et invidiosam*).[14] This was demonstrated by the various disputes upon this subject, philosophers had. He did not question the existence of the occult qualities.[15] However, resorting to a lexicon that was widely spread among the *novatores* – we need to think, for example, about the renowned intervention of Walter Charleton *Occult qualities made manifest*[16] – he observed that for many authors the occult qualities are just an asylum of ignorance (*ignorantiae asylum*). The authors who invoked the presence of an occult quality were indeed unable to give a real explanation of the phenomenon and preferred to persist in ignorance rather than demonstrate the occult qualities. According to Wolferd, as a consequence 'many things are considered occult qualities, even though they are actually manifest'.[17] It is worth mentioning the various, marvellous and terrible (*varii, mirabiles et horrendi*) effects of the tarantula's bite. Many authors, indeed, believed they are occult. Senguerd, however, intended to demonstrate how they could be explained without resorting to the occult qualities.[18] Wolferd's strategy aims, therefore, to recognize the existence of these qualities, but it denies that they could explain the tarantula's bite.

In the *Tractatus physicus de tarantula*, the theoretical discourse upon the occult qualities becomes more explicit and radical. He claimed that nothing occult exists in nature; therefore, everything is knowable. According to this historic perspective, he believed that there are not qualities which are intrinsically occult, but, on the contrary, occult qualities are so defined because they have not been explained yet. The philosopher's task is to clarify these qualities.[19]

As rightly revealed by Gerhard Wiesenfeldt, Senguerd's purpose is to identify a compromise solution among the scholastics' attempts to keep, on the one hand, a rigid version of the concept of occult qualities and, on the other hand, the anti-Aristotelian objections. In this sense, the concept of occult quality is connected to the limits of the human mind – in a sceptical perspective which was common in the works of many *novatores*. These limits, however, can only be overcome over the long term, in a historic perspective, by means of the contribution of more men and more research disciplines.

Such results are identifiable since the work's frontispiece:

> The *Tractatus physicus de tarantula* in which, besides its description, there is an explanation, with natural reasons and illustrations, of the effects of the tarantula's poison, which *so far* had been attributed to the occult qualities.[20]

The Latin adverb originally used *hactenus* (so far) – which seems to recall the famous *incipit* of Gassendi's discussion *de qualitatis vocatis occultis*[21] – is not just a captivating editorial choice. It states the 'historic' perspective employed by Wolferd in this work. This perspective is present, after all, *in nuce* in the considerations of his father Arnold. It is not by chance that, in the third edition of the *Introductio ad physicam* – a very familiar text to Wolferd – after asserting that the individual occult qualities come from an occult disposition of the bodies' matter, which can depend on either the altering primary qualities or small particles of matter, Arnold invited the physicists to commit themselves in order to make the occult qualities manifest, as long as that was possible (*ut, quantum fieri potest, occulta fiant manifesta*).[22]

Wolferd considered the tarantula responsible for a pathological phenomenon that implies many aspects, which were traditionally explained through different occult causes (the poison, music, the instruments and the place). Some of these aspects were considered *fabulosi* (unreal); therefore they had been rejected, while others had been explained and made manifest by means of alternative solutions to the occult qualities.

The starting point of Senguerd's reasoning in his studies *de tarantula* is represented by the reconstruction of the natural history of this pathological phenomenon and of the animal responsible for it. In line with the Baconian ideology, natural history is for Senguerd the foundation of the philosophical work of unveiling the marvellous phenomena of nature.[23] It is within natural history that he found those elements that, once critically analysed, appear to be determining in the process of clarification of the 'occult' aspects implied by this poisoning. His reconstruction is not based upon a direct observation of the tarantula or the tarantulated; Senguerd, instead, from his sources deduced a substantial amount of data which were functional for the reconstruction of the phenomenon's natural history. It is not by chance that the first parts of the *Disputatio philosophica inauguralis de tarantula* and of the *Tractatus phyisicus de tarantula* are dedicated to the reconstruction of the spider's natural history as well as the pathology it can cause with its poison. In this regard, Senguerd refers to the works of Ulisse Aldrovandi, Philipp Kammermeister, Pliny, Aelianus and above all the *Magnes, sive de arte magnetica* (1641, 1643 and 1654) by Athanaius Kircher. From the *Magnes*, Senguerd deduced a series of information about the tarantula, its places and its victims.

After offering a detailed reconstruction of this phenomenon in all its different aspects, Senguerd started to examine those aspects traditionally attributed to occult causes.

In this way, he mentioned fermentative processes and mechanical actions in order to explain how the tarantula's poison – although exiguous – could provoke such various and marvellous symptoms. In the *Disputatio philosophica inauguralis de tarantula*, after demonstrating through the natural history that the tarantula attacks by means of the mouth (and not by a sting), Senguerd clarifies that it releases a substance, similar to saliva, that contained particles of poison. It is, therefore, a substance that can ferment. The particles of poison spread through the body and slowly affect the nerves. Overheated by the summer Apulian sun, the poison excites the nervous spirits and the tarantula's victim starts to dance. This explanatory pattern shows a corpuscular approach deriving from a Cartesian-inspired chemistry.

The influence of the Cartesian thought in Senguerd's considerations is evident. Even in later works, he supposed that all natural phenomena must be explained through moving particles of matter. Moreover, the concept of fermentation plays a central role in his research, including the one carried out in the years of his maturity. This tendency to combine corpuscular and chemical theories was widespread among Dutch chemists and physicians in the second half of the seventeenth century. Among the main supporters of this tendency, it is worth remembering Franciscus Del e Böe Sylvius,[24] professor of medicine at the University of Leiden during the same year of Senguerd's doctorate.[25] Although Sylvius and his disciples did not accept in toto the Cartesian doctrine, they believed in a physiological mechanism similar to the Cartesian one. In the said mechanism, however, the chemical reactions provided the energy necessary to activate several processes.[26] This lesson had a great influence on Senguerd's proposal, in which the fermentative process activates the consecutive mechanical effects that cause the tarantulated to dance.

If in the *Disputatio philosophica inauguralis de tarantula* Senguerd illustrated the ways of inducing the dancing spasms, attributing the actions performed by the tarantulated to a lesion of the *phantasia*, in the *Tractatus physicus de tarantula*, Senguerd's aim is more ambitious, demonstrating the ways through which the poison causes its particular and variable effects. These effects are deduced from his reconstruction of the aforementioned pathological phenomenon's natural history, influenced by the teachings of Kircher and Pietro Andrea Mattioli's *Commentarii* to Dioscorides.[27] Senguerd intended to illustrate the production of the following effects recorded by the tradition: burning fevers, cachexia, bad skin tone, physical immobility, desire to dance, sleepiness, insomnia and various movements. As regards to this new and more ambitious purpose, it is also worth mentioning the changes and the detailed studies that characterized this new work.

In the *Tractatus physicus de tarantula*, Senguerd explained that the poisoning particles can be found within a substance that, besides being humid, is very viscous. In compliance with the glossary of the Aristotelian-Galenic tradition, even the *viscositas* is a secondary and tangible quality.[28] Senguerd deduced such information from the animal's natural history thus observing that spiders abound with a viscous humidity, as can be seen from their ability to weave their webs.[29] Humidity – which in the previous work was, indeed, necessary to grant the fermentative process – is now functional to demonstrate further physiological failures in those bitten by the tarantula.

Therefore, Senguerd observed that the poison, acting on the nervous spirits and on the heart, causes agitation, spasms and fevers. In addition, an excessive heat in the heart can corrupt the bile in the nearby blood vessels. Moreover, the poison's viscosity obstructs the pores and immobilizes the spirits from the nerves, causing an excessive torpidity in those who have been bitten.[30]

Tracing back this chain of physiological actions, it is then possible to explain how the toxin is expelled, without postulating the presence of occult qualities in music, as Daniel Sennert did, or in the musical instruments, as Kammermeister did. According to Senguerd's reasoning, when the sound of musical instruments in the air reaches the ears, it pushes the victims to dance. Through this kind of agitation, the blood starts to overheat, the pores dilate and the poison rarefies, lessens and disappears. At the same time the sweat increases and the poison is expelled through the dilated pores.[31]

Through this mechanical system of actions and reactions, it is possible to offer a mechanical explanation of the terrible effects of the tarantula's poison and its remedies (music and dance), without postulating the existence of some occult qualities. The qualities acknowledged to the poison are manifest, also according to the principles and the glossary of the peripatetic philosophy. They are hot, humid and viscous. Unsurprisingly, in the Aristotelian-Galenic tradition, heat is a primary quality, while humidity and viscosity are secondary qualities. Moreover, all the consecutive processes triggered by the poison are 'manifest' and can be entirely recreated through the mechanical collision of corpuscles. The same can be said for the mechanistic explanation of sound, completely based on the mechanical motion of the air that affects the body spirits. Thanks to this complex structure of mechanistic explanations, fermentative processes and manifest qualities of the Aristotelian-Galenic tradition, everything is knowable. It is useless, therefore, to postulate the existence of the *occultae qualitates* in the poison and in its remedies.

7.3 Occult and experimentalism. The tarantula at the *Theatrum physicum* in Leiden

In 1675, the *Theatrum physicum* was established in Leiden on the impulse of Burchard de Volder. After this date, Senguerd completely devoted himself to prepare the experimental lectures, with particular emphasis on pneumatic studies. In 1705 – after de Volder retired – Wolferd took the direction of the *Theatrum physicum*.[32] The years of Wolferd's maturity were characterized by a deep orientation towards the experimental study of facts, the *matters of fact*.[33]

In connection with this important event of his career, it is also possible to explain the new approach that characterized his reasoning about an old issue, such as the poisoning caused by tarantula. Senguerd, indeed, reflected again upon this poisoning also in his late *Disquisitio de tarantula* (1715). The work is attached to the *Rationis atque experientiae connubium*, a manual aimed to offer a report of his private courses of pneumatics only for specialist readers, including the instructions on the experimental use of the air pump.

The *Disquisitio de tarantula* contains many differences in comparison with his earlier works on tarantula. First of all, we need to highlight how the work is not expressly presented as a study on the occult qualities. In comparison with half a century before, the discussion about this issue was not the main focus of academic interests; besides, the occult qualities – interpreted as 'occult active principles' – had been absorbed within the experimental philosophy.[34]

The *Disquisitio de tarantula* is an example of this complex and varied change of approach towards the concept of occult. Indeed, although the work is no more presented as a dissertation about the occult qualities, the author debates the pathological phenomenon caused by the tarantula with the same intentions of his two previous treatises. Also in this work, he aimed to explain the several occult aspects involved in this phenomenon. In the *Disquisitio de tarantula*, however, the discussion does not have the assertiveness that was present in his previous works, thus acquiring a more experimental approach. While in his earlier works the author had the urgency to find alternative explanations to those based on scholastic occult qualities – with the necessity to make explicit all the mechanisms involved in the production of extraordinary phenomena – in this new work Wolferd's proposal is often more hypothetical. He clearly observed that 'in the big things, it is sufficient to establish even something'. For this reason, his aim is presenting his 'conjecture' about the effects of tarantism (*nostram de eo conjecturam*).[35]

This hypothetical and conjectural approach towards the study of the occult aspects of the pathological phenomenon is affected by the renovated experimental interests that grew as Senguerd grew older himself. However, it is important to highlight that, in the years that preceded this event, Senguerd was adjusting his position on the occult. This is evident in Wolferd's studies about another phenomenon linked to the occult qualities, which shows several analogies with tarantism – canine rabies. Senguerd, indeed, was the author of three *disputationes De rabie canum*, which were discussed in Leiden in December 1674. During that year, he was a lector at the Faculty of Philosophy and Liberal Arts, while the next year he was an associate professor of peripatetic philosophy. Georgius van Ophoven was the *respondens* of the three *disputationes*.[36]

In the premise of the *disputatio De rabie canum prior*, he observed that some of these qualities are occult in many ways. Some of them are particularly occult that it is really hard to know anything about; others have both occult and manifest aspects. Regarding these mixed qualities, their effects are known, as well as some of their operating mechanisms, their causes and their origins. According to Wolferd, the existence of such qualities is demonstrable through some experiments (*aliis experimentis*) and through the effects of the rabid dog's bite. In Senguerd's early studies *de tarantula*, spiders' venomousness was a matter of fact, resulting from the animal's natural history. It is a spider that is naturally provided with a venom that causes the poisoning. As far as rabies is concerned, instead, examinations should be made about the reasons why it afflicts some animals – especially dogs – making them poisonous. However, he proposed some natural hypotheses after considering its effects. According to Senguerd, the cause could be linked to food rather than the external air.

The following mechanisms triggered by these possible external causes can entirely be investigated, as well as all the consequent effects of the saliva, once it has been transmitted to man.[37] To be more specific, these phenomena will be manifested following the same explicative patterns used for the study about the tarantula, which were based on the mechanic motion of the particles of matter and on fermentative processes.[38]

In light of these considerations, it is possible to observe how the study about rabies led Senguerd to a redefinition of his concept of occult. Unlike the research about the tarantula, the investigation about the rabid dog does not allow the complete annihilation of the disease's occult aspects. Some of them can only be approached by means of hypotheses. There is no guarantee that, while studying the occult qualities, all the aspects of the phenomenon can be made manifest, as happened in the case of tarantism. For this reason, Senguerd had to recognize the existence of several gradations of occult. This guaranteed to his successors the possibility of clarifying these phenomena, in a historical perspective. In this regard, we need to notice that, within the experimental philosophy of the time, there was the tendency to recognize the impossibility of identifying definite causal explanations of various natural phenomena. Despite the ignorance about the causes, the experimental method could, therefore, describe the variety of phenomena that happen in nature. Senguerd's considerations about the rabid dog, which are present in the *disputationes*, seem to confirm this general tendency.

These reflections can also be found in the *Philosophia naturalis* (1680), a work devoid of explicit references to the sources, in which there is the analysis of some fundamental concepts of physics, as well as the description of specific experiments carried out during the lectures. In this work, Wolferd claimed that there is no distinction between manifest and occult qualities. There are, on the contrary, some qualities that, until a certain historical moment, had not been unveiled, because of the limits of the human mind.[39] Repeating the same reasoning in the second edition of the *Philosophia naturalis* (1685), Senguerd reaffirmed his position, stating that nothing can be considered completely manifest or occult.[40] The nature of the intellect guarantees a margin for the occult. This margin does not invalidate the assumptions of the natural research. Such limits can be overcome, in a historical perspective, with the contribution of more men.

These thoughts are reflected in the *Disquisitio de tarantula*. Although the work is no more explicitly presented as a treatise about the occult qualities, it is clear how the author analysed the pathological phenomenon caused by the tarantula with the same purposes of the two earlier works, that is explaining the phenomenon in all its extraordinary aspects. The explicative patterns used, however, are different in some ways.

When studying the problems related to music and dance, Senguerd sourced the information from his experimental research upon elasticity; it is not by chance, indeed, that he chose to republish the *Disquisitio de tarantula* and the *Rationis atque experientiae connubium* jointly. The latter contained some principles that can be used by the author to clarify some occult aspects of the disease.

To be more precise, the interpretation of the treatment with sounds and dance in response to the poisoning caused by the tarantula took benefit from a massive use of the concept of elastic force, which was the basic principle of Senguerd's research on pneumatics during his more mature years. The research upon air physical-chemical properties, and in particular upon elasticity, had become very popular thanks to Robert Boyle's work and also to his experiments with the air pump, which became a model of scientific practice not only in England but also in several European countries.[41] Besides, the foundation of the *Theatrum physicum* in Leiden had found a point of reference in the activity of Boyle and of the experimenters of the Royal Society. Both de Volder and Senguerd – who both possessed an air pump – based their experimental lectures on the experiments described by Boyle in the *New Experiments physico-mechanicall*.[42]

Within the experimental context of the University of Leiden, the issue of air's elasticity was widely debated. This is confirmed, indeed, by the various *exercitia* concerning elastic force that were discussed under Senguerd's presidency.

Moreover, the issue is also discussed in Wolferd's main works. In the *Rationis atque experientiae connubium*, Wolferd, after explaining the ways of fabricating and using the pneumatic pump, demonstrated – in an experimental way – the existence of air's elastic force and his modes of action. While providing a theoretical frame to experiments, Senguerd clarified that the term 'elastic' means an inner force of the bodies, which is contractive and expansive. In other words, we are talking about the effort of some bodies that do not resist to the motion of other bodies and at the same time they react, pushing away and striving to reach a different state, place, position and shape.[43] In order to be elastic and to exercise its force, a body has four requirements: appropriate configuration, rigidity or coherence of its parts, preternatural state and external cause that gives an impulse and stimulates elasticity.[44]

This is a specific property of the air, and for this reason it is part of Senguerd's experimental interests. However, he insisted on demonstrating how this force also belongs to other bodies. In this regard, Wolferd mentioned the example of the strings of musical instruments such as the lyre, the guitar, the *fidicula*, the barbitos and the harp.[45] Moreover, according to Senguerd, the human body is made up of various parts that can exercise their function only through the elastic force. This is the case, for example, of the veins, the arteries and the vessels that – expanded by the fluid that runs within them – contract on the basis of the elastic force, accelerating the motion of the transfused substance and provoking an impulse.[46] In his opinion, the nerves (like the strings) contorted or extended, once they are stimulated by the external air, want a circular motion.

In light of these considerations, it is possible to affirm that tarantism – which brought into play the pneumatic study of sound's mechanisms of propagation as well as the analysis of its effects upon the human body – confirmed the validity of his experimental knowledge in the field of elasticity. The acknowledgement of the elastic force was efficient not only to explain the ways of sound's physical propagation but also to explain some physiological phenomena that regard some parts of the body provided with such force.[47]

In the *Disquisitio de tarantula*, he specified that sound 'consists of a vibration or a tremulous motion of the air'. Such motion, in particular, is associated by Senguerd to the inflection of air's twigs and to the rejection caused by the collision between two bodies and air's elastic force.[48]

In order to clarify the mechanisms of propagation of sound in connection with the characteristics of airborne particles and their elasticity, it is advisable to report what Senguerd wrote in the *Philosophia naturalis* (1685). In this work, indeed, while discussing the nature of the sound and its transmission, Senguerd explained that air is a 'very suitable' subject able to transmit the tremulous motion of which sound is made. In his opinion, air particles are branchy, more rigid and have the capability of elasticity. Thanks to these properties, when the air particles are powered towards some resistant body, first they are inflected – because of their twigs – then they are reflected, because of their rigidity and their elastic force.[49] The latter has a fundamental role in the transmission of the sound. According to Senguerd, the repulsion of airborne particles requires the dilation of its branches, which at first is inflected after the collision with a body. In order to have a dilation, there must be an effort to dilate, which corresponds to the elastic force.[50] In the *Rationis atque experientiae connubium*, Senguerd clearly established that the production, propagation, transmission and reduction of sound are all effects of air's elasticity.[51]

In light of these principles, in the *Disquisitio de tarantula*, he observed that when the voice or the musical instruments communicate a special tremulous and oscillating motion to the air, they stimulate, with the same agitation, the nerves, the hearing organs and the nerves fibrils suitable to the touch which are disseminated through the body. The spirits on the nerves are tickled and provoke pleasant or unpleasant perceptions in the brain. Since there is a strong connection between sensor nerves and motion nerves, the perceptions appreciated by those bitten are followed by the irritation of the spirits. In this way, the spirits transmit a movement to the motion nerves and the limbs connected to them; this movement is at first weak but then becomes more and more accelerated under the impulse of music. For this reason, Wolferd explained, the tarantulated start moving and burst into dancing.[52] At the foundation of Senguerd's analysis, there is the impact of sounds upon sensorial nerves. The tight connection between these and the motion nerves can explain the stimulus to dance and, more in general, all the involuntary movements triggered in the body. The nerves and their natural elastic force, therefore, guarantee the efficacy of the iatrophysics of sounds.[53]

Within this point of view, it is possible to explain why music and dance can cure the poisoned. Dance gives movement to all the body, both to the solid and the liquid parts. Besides, it facilitates processes like the melting, the subtilization, the secretion and the expulsion of the substances. In order to better explain such a process, Senguerd took the example of the tubule, inside which there is a viscous, brown and heterogeneous fluid. The tubule is surrounded by fibres provided with elastic force; therefore, it has an oscillating and vibratory motion. In light of this configuration, Senguerd believes that the fluid directed towards the tubule – due to a compression caused by an oscillating motion – will melt, secrete and expel the particles, and if so it may crash against traversable pores.[54]

In accordance with what is said in the *Rationis atque experientiae connubium*, Senguerd claimed that the nerves, the muscles and all the tools used to perform the motions in our body, as well as the various vessels that carry the fluid – as demonstrated by the arteries impulse – are provided with elastic force.[55] At the same time, he explained that these elements are moved in every part by an oscillating and vibratory motion.

While the musician stimulates the fibrils to move and the tarantulated is overwhelmed by dance (with a movement of nerves, muscles and all the body), the fluid vessels are hit alternately and then compressed. From the impulse and the compression, there is the dissolution of the particles of blood, spirits and the fluids which before had been clotted by the venom. In this way, the initial efficacy of coagulation is eliminated; the poison's corrosive particles are decomposed and the sharp ones are smoothed. When the oscillating motion alternately causes the contraction and dilation of the vessels that transport the fluids, there is also the shrinkage and expansion of the pores. By means of this escape route, the attenuated particles, filled with an accelerating motion, can be expelled through the sweat. In this way, 'the tarantism poisonous seeds' can be expelled from the body and the tarantulated can recover. This is true at least until the following year, when the same weather may cause the resurgence of the disease.[56]

Rereading the processes of sound's propagation and the poisoned's physiopathology with the knowledge of the concept of elasticity, Senguerd can efficiently explain some of the occult aspects of the phenomenon, by means of a principle which is distinctive of many bodies and that can be experimentally studied by scholars.

7.4 Conclusions

Senguerd's research studies about the tarantula are part of an experimental approach towards the study of occult phenomena. Within this approach, it is possible to distinguish two phases. Initially, the interest in the tarantula came from his father's Aristotelian and empirical teachings. Influenced by Bacon,[57] Arnold invited his students to explain experimentally the occult qualities, resorting also to the instruments of natural history. Starting from these premises, the explanation of the tarantism's occult qualities elaborated by Wolferd reached a more radical position. He clearly based his research about the tarantula upon the Baconian methodology of natural history. Basing his studies of the tarantula on experience and on the comparison with the main sources of natural history (in particular Kircher), Wolferd located himself in the same field of research preconized by Bacon. This approach was not unnoticed within the Royal Society, as demonstrated by the positive review written by Oldenburg.

Moreover, Senguerd used a model that combined both chemical explanations and Cartesian-inspired mechanical operations. These attempts showed a tendency which was widespread in the contemporary experimental environments, that is, conciliating the Cartesian natural philosophy explicative patterns and the Baconian methodology, as can be seen, for example, from the research carried out in the botanical field.[58]

Wolferd's empirical sensitivity towards the occult phenomena is clear in his choice to base the explanation of physio-pathological processes on fermentation – these processes are triggered by the tarantula and rabid dog's saliva and were once explained by means of the occult qualities. This choice expresses a widespread approach within the Dutch medical and philosophical environments of the time, which aimed to develop a new chemical-mechanical physiology based on observation and experience. According to Sylvius – who was influenced by the Aristotelian teachings[59] – it is possible to acquire new knowledge in the natural field only by combining reason and experience.

In the second part of Senguerd's life, his experimental approach towards the study of the tarantula became more marked, also because of the clearer English experimental philosophy's influences and his increasing work as experimenter in the *Theatrum physicum*. It is true that this major event had a great influence on his conceptualization of tarantism; however, it is also evident that it was gradual and that it had been preceded by a reorganization of the Aristotelian discussion about the occult qualities. This redefinition can be found in some *disputationes* about canine rabies, which were discussed before he started to work as experimenter in the *Theatrum physicum*. In these writings, the author – in contrast to what he said in his earlier studies upon the tarantula – recognized that some occult aspects of the disease can be clarified, but only through hypotheses. If, in the studies about tarantism, the occult – interpreted as the knowledge ne plus ultra – had been rejected, in the studies about rabies the occult is recognized as a starting point of the experimental research. Afterwards, Senguerd admitted that the existence of the occult is guaranteed by the limits of the human mind. However, these limits can be overcome, in a historical perspective, through the gradual contribution of more scientists and more disciplines. In this way, Senguerd, in the *Disquisitio de tarantula*, re-examined the magical object of tarantula in a new light, using an experimental and hypothetico-deductive methodology. In this work, the new acknowledgements about elasticity, which were fundamental in research conducted in his later years, were helped by the use of the air pump and allowed the author to refine his analysis, introducing a middle ground between the sound produced by the musical instruments and the behaviour of nerves and vessels in the human body. The poisoning caused by the tarantula, with its intrinsic complexity, can test the solidity of the explicative patterns of the tradition, together with his experimental acquisitions. Such an extraordinary phenomenon – with its various mysterious aspects that involve the body machine and the physical power of sounds – allows one to successfully demonstrate, to his readers, the validity of his research upon elasticity, a principle that can also be investigated through experimentation.

Notes

1   See John Henry, 'The Fragmentation of Renaissance Occultism and the Decline of Magic', *History of Science* 46, no. 1 (2008): 1–48; Brian Copenhaver, *Magic in Western Culture From Antiquity to the Enlightenment* (New York: Cambridge University Press, 2015); Doina-Cristina Rusu 'Magic in the Seventeenth Century', in *Encyclopedia of Early Modern Philosophy and the Sciences*, eds Dana Jalobeanu and Charles T. Wolfe. https://doi.org/10.1007/978-3-319-20791-9_604-12020.

2   See Brian Copenhaver, 'A Tale of Two Fishes: Magical Objects in Natural History from Antiquity Through the Scientific Revolution', *Journal of the History of Ideas* 52, no. 3 (1991): 373–98; Silvia Parigi, *Spiriti, effluvi, attrazioni. La fisica 'curiosa' dal Rinascimento al secolo dei Lumi* (Naples: Istituto Italiano per gli Studi Filosofici, 2011); Donato Verardi, *La scienza e i segreti della natura a Napoli nel Rinascimento. La magia naturale di Giovan Battista Della Porta* (Florence: Firenze University Press, 2018).

3   See Manuel De Carli, 'Tracing Senguerd's Footprints: Sciences and Tarantism at Leiden University (1667–1715)', in *Scientiae in the History of Medicine*, eds Fabrizio Baldassarri and Fabio Zambieri (Rome-Bristol: 'L'Erma' Di Bretschneider, 2021), 289–311.

4   See, for example, Georg Caspar Kirchmajer, *De aranea, inprimis vero de tarantulis*, publice disputabit Andreas Flachs (Wittebergae: typis Johannis Borckardi, 1660); Wolferd Senguerd, *Disputatio philosophica inauguralis de tarantula* (Leiden: apud Viduam & Haeredes Joannis Elsevirii, 1667); Senguerd, *Tractatus physicus de tarantula* (Leiden: apud Gaasbeeckios, 1668); Christoph-Andreas Schöngast, *Enkurek Persarum Morsumque Tarantulae*, respondente Andrea Peterman

(Lipsiae: Literis Christiani Michaelis 1668); Johannes Valentinus Hübner, *Dissertatio inauguralis de tarantismo* (Argentorati: Typis Johannis Wilhelmi Tidemanni, 1674); Christian Friedrich Braun, *Disputatio physica de tarantula*, sub praesidio M. Johannis Mulleri (Wittebergae: Literis Christiani Schrödteri 1676); Hermann Grube, *De ictu tarantulae, & vi musices in ejus curatione, conjecturae physico-medicae* (Francofurti: Ex Bibliopolio Hafniensi, Danielis Paulli, 1679); Bernhardus Albinus, *Dissertatio Inauguralis De Tarantismo*, publico examini submittit Nicolaus Benjamin Noël de Pivier (Francofurti: Typis Christoph. Andr. Zeitleri 1691).

5 See Manuel De Carli, *Le tarentisme et les qualités occultes en Hollande aux XVIIᵉ et XVIIIᵉ siècles : l'oeuvre de Wolferd Sengeurd (1646-1724). Tarantismo e qualità occulte in Olanda nei secoli XVII–XVIII: l'opera di Wolferd Sengeurd (1646-1724)* (Ph.D. thesis, Université de Tours-Università degli studi Roma Tre, Tours, 2019); Manuel De Carli, 'Wolferd Sengeurd, le qualità occulte e i meravigliosi effetti della tarantola', in *Meravigliosi ragni danzanti. Interpretazioni del tarantismo nel Seicento*, ed. Manuel De Carli (Calimera: Kurumuny, 2020), 149–81.

6 See Sengeurd, *Tractatus physicus de tarantula*.

7 On Wolferd Sengeurd, see Edward G. Ruestow, *Physics at Seventeenth and Eighteenth-Century Leiden. Philosophy and the New Science in the University* (The Hague: Nijhoff, 1973); Gerhard Wiesenfeldt, *Leerer Raum in Minervas Haus. Experimentelle Naturlehre an der Universität Leiden, 1675-1715* (Berlin, Diepholz, Amsterdam: Verlag für Geschichte der Naturwissenschaften und der Technik – Royal Netherlands Academy of Arts and Sciences, 2002); Wiesenfeldt, 'Sengeurd, Wolferd (1646–1724)', in *The dictionary of Seventeenth and Eighteenth-Century Dutch philosophers*, eds Wiep van Bunge, Henri Krop, Bart Leeuwenburgh, Paul Schuurman, Han van Ruler, and Michiel Wielema, 2 vols (Bristol: Thoemmes Press, 2003), vol. 2, 911–13; De Carli, *Tarantismo e qualità occulte in Olanda nei secoli XVII-XVIII*.

8 On Arnold Sengeurd, see Paul Dibon, *La philosophie néerlandaise au siècle d'or. Tome I. L'enseignement philosophique dans les universités à l'époque précartésienne (1575–1650)* (Amsterdam: Elsevier Publishing Company, 1954); Dirk van Miert, *Humanism in an Age of Science: The Amsterdam Athenaeum in the Golden Age, 1632–1704* (Leiden and Boston: Brill, 2009); Wiesenfeldt 'Sengeurd, Arnold (1610–1667)', in *The dictionary of Seventeenth and Eighteenth-Century Dutch philosophers*, 909–11.

9 See Sengeurd, *Disputatio philosophica inauguralis de tarantula*.

10 See Wiesenfeldt, *Leerer Raum in Minervas Haus*, 169.

11 See Sengeurd, 'Disquisitio de tarantula', in Sengeurd, *Rationis atque experientiae connubium* (Rotterdam: apud Bernardum Bos, 1715), 277–328.

12 See Keith Hutchison, 'What Happened to Occult Qualities in the Scientific Revolution?', *Isis* 73 (1982): 233–53; Copenhaver, 'Scholastic Philosophy and

Renaissance Magic in the *De vita* of Marsilio Ficino', *Renaissance Quarterly* 37 (1984): 523–54; Ron Millen, 'The Manifestation of Occult Qualities in the Scientific Revolution', in *Religion, Science and Worldview: Essays in Honour of Richard S. Westfall*, eds Margaret J. Osler and Paul L. Farber (Cambridge: Cambridge University Press, 1985), 185–216; William Eamon, *Science and the Secrets of Nature: Books of Secrets in Medieval and Early Modern Culture* (Princeton: Princeton University, 1994); Henry, *The Scientific Revolution and the Origins of Modern Science*, 2nd edn (New York: Palgrave, 2002 [1997]); Franco Giudice, 'Isaac Newton e la tradizione dei principi attivi nella filosofia naturale inglese del XVII secolo', in *Scienza e teologia fra Seicento e Ottocento. Studi in memoria di Maurizio Mamiani*, eds Chiara Giuntini and Brunello Lotti (Florence: Olschki, 2006), 39–55; Verardi, *La scienza e i segreti della natura a Napoli nel Rinascimento*; De Carli, *Tarantismo e qualità occulte in Olanda nei secoli XVII-XVIII*; Nicolas Weill-Parot, 'Secretus et occultus: lexique et modalité de l'occultation dans la science médiévale (Albert le Grand, Roger Bacon, Henri de Langenstein)', *Arcana Naturae. Revue d'histoire des sciences secrètes* 1 (2020): 1–20.

13 See Henry, *The Scientific Revolution and the Origins of Modern Science*, 64–9.
14 See Senguerd, *Disputatio philosophica inauguralis de tarantula*, A2r.
15 See Senguerd, *Disputatio philosophica inauguralis de tarantula*, C1v.
16 See Walter Charleton, *Physiologia epicuro-gassendo-charletoniana* (London: T. Newcomb, 1654), 341–82.
17 Senguerd, *Disputatio philosophica inauguralis de tarantula*, A2r.
18 Senguerd, *Disputatio philosophica inauguralis de tarantula*, A2r.
19 Senguerd, *Tractatus physicus de tarantula*, 10–11.
20 Senguerd, *Tractatus physicus de tarantula*, 4.
21 Pierre Gassendi, *Animadversiones in decimum librum Diogenis Laertii* (Lyons: apud Guillelmum Barbier, 1649), 355–6.
22 Arnold Senguerd, *Introductionis ad physicam libri sex. Editio tertia prioribus auctior* (Amstelaedami: apud Joannem a Ravestein, 1666), 83.
23 About the correlation between natural history and marvellous phenomena in Francis Bacon, see Lorraine Daston and Katharine Park, *Wonders and the Orders of Nature 1150–1750* (New York: Zone Books, 1998), 220–31. An example of good reception, in Baconian contexts, of the reconstruction of the tarantula's natural history carried out in the *Tractatus physicus de tarantula* – which represents an extended version of the reconstruction made in the first *disputatio* – is Henry Oldenburg's review about the *Philosophical Transactions*. See Henry Oldenburg, 'An Account of: W. Sengwerdius P. D. de Tarantula', *Philosophical Transactions 1669* III (1668): 660–62.
24 See Antonio Clericuzio, 'La chimica della vita: fermenti e fermentazione nella iatrochimica del Seicento', *Medicina nei Secoli. Arte e Scienza. Journal of History*

of Medicine 15 (2003): 227–45, especially 232–3. See also Allen G. Debus, *Chemistry and Medical Debate: van Helmont to Boerhaave* (Canton: Science History Publications, 2001), 57–64; Evan R. Ragland, 'Chymistry and Taste in the Seventeenth Century: Franciscus Dele Boë Sylvius as a Chymical Physician between Galenism and Cartesianism', *Ambix* 59 (2012): 1–21; Ragland 'Mechanism, the Senses, and Reason: Franciscus Sylvius and Leiden Debates Over Anatomical Knowledge After Harvey and Descartes', in *Early Modern Medicine and Natural Philosophy*, eds Peter Distelzweig, Benjamin Goldberg and Evan R. Ragland (Dordrecht: Springer, 2016), 173–205.

25 See Philipp C. Molhuysen, *Bronnen tot de Geschiedenis der Leidsche Universiteit*, 7 vols ('s-Gravenhage: Martinus Nijhoff, 1913–24), vol. 3 (1918), 210*–2*.

26 See Harold J. Cook, 'The New Philosophy in the Low Countries', in *The Scientific Revolution in National Context*, eds Roy Porter and Mikuláš Teich (Cambridge: Cambridge University Press, 1992), 115–49, especially 126.

27 See Senguerd, *Tractatus physicus de tarantula*, 22–3, 36–44. See also Pietro Andrea Mattioli, *Commentarii in libros sex Pedacii Dioscoridis anazarbei, de medica materia* (Venetijs: in officina Erasmiana, apud Vincentium Valgrisium, 1554), 199; and Athanasius Kircher, *Magnes sive de magnetica arte libri tres* (Romae: sumptibus Blasii Diversini et Zenobii Masotti, 1654 [1641]), 587–8.

28 See Giuseppe Bezza, 'Il *Lessico* di Gerolamo Vitali', in Bezza, *Scripta minora*, eds Emanuele Ciampi and Ornella Pompeo Faracovi (Lugano: Agorà&co. 2016 [2003]), 347–4, especially 365.

29 See Senguerd, *Tractatus physicus de tarantula*, 38. See also Kircher, *Magnes*, 600.

30 See Senguerd, *Tractatus physicus de tarantula*, 40–2. On mechanism in early modern medicine and philosophy, see Antonio Clericuzio, 'Le forme e i moti della materia. Trasformazioni del meccanicismo del Seicento', in *Il libro della natura. Scienze e filosofia da Copernico a Darwin*, ed. Paolo Pecere, 2 vols (Rome: Carocci editore, 2015), vol. 1, 67–107; Fabio Zampieri, *Il metodo anatomo-clinico tra meccanicismo ed empirismo. Marcello Malpighi, Antonio Maria Valsalva, Giovanni Battista Morgagni* (Rome-Bristol: L'Erma di Bretschneider, 2016) and Domenico Bertoloni Meli, *Mechanism. A Visual, Lexical, and Conceptual History* (Pittsburgh: University of Pittsburgh Press, 2019).

31 See Senguerd, *Tractatus physicus de tarantula*, 51.

32 About this event and, more in general, about the first years of the *Theatrum physicum* in Leiden, see Hand Hooijmaijers and Ad Maas, 'Enterpreneurs in experiments: the Leiden Cabinet oh Physics and the motives of its founders (1675–1742)', in *Cabinets of Experimental Philosophy in Eighteenth-Century Europe*, eds Jim Bennett and Sofia Talas (Leiden and Boston: Brill, 2013), 27–47.

33 About the experimental production of *matters of fact* in Wolferd's time, with particular reference to the work of one of his main sources, such as Robert Boyle,

see Steven Shapin and Simon Schaffer, *Leviathan and the Air-Pump. Hobbes, Boyle and the Experimental Life* (Princeton: Princeton University Press, 1985) See also Wiesenfeldt, *The Virtues of New Philosophies or How the Leiden Philosophical Faculty Survived the Crisis of 1676*. Paper presented at the nineteenth International Congress of Historical Sciences, Oslo, Sweden, 2000: http://www.oslo2000.uio.no/AIO/AIO16/group%203/Wiesenfeldt.pdf.

34 About this point, see Hutchison, 'What Happened to Occult Qualities in the Scientific Revolution?', as well as about the distinction between the occult qualities of the Scholastic philosophy (such as specific, real and causal qualities, used to explain some particular features) and the 'occult active principles' (principles that have a real explicative power, whose existence is experimentally confirmed and can be verified by anyone).

35 See Senguerd, 'Disquisitio de tarantula', 295.

36 See Senguerd, *Disputationum physicarum selectarum decima quae est De rabie canum prior*, publicae, ac placidae disquisitioni subjicit Georgius ab Ophoven (Leiden: Apud Viduam et Heredes Johannis Elsevirii, 1674); Senguerd, *Disputationum physicarum selectarum decima quae est De rabie canum altera*, publicae, ac placidae disquisitioni subjicit Georgius ab Ophoven (Leiden: Apud Viduam et Heredes Johannis Elsevirii, 1674); Senguerd, *Disputationum physicarum selectarum decima quae est De rabie canum posterior*, publicae, ac placidae disquisitioni subjicit Georgius ab Ophoven (Leiden: Apud Viduam et Heredes Johannis Elsevirii, 1674).

37 The study about the transmission of the disease to man and the explanation of its various aspects are discussed in the *Disputatio de rabie altera* and in the *Disputatio de rabie posterior*.

38 As the tarantula's venom, also the rabid dog's saliva is – for Senguerd – a substance particularly suitable for fermentation. It is, indeed, made up of both viscous, firm and coherent particles, and volatile, thin and spirituous particles. See Senguerd, *Disputationum physicarum selectarum decima quae est De rabie canum posterior*, A2r.

39 See Senguerd, *Philosophia naturalis, quatuor partibus. Primarias corporum species, affectiones, vicissitudines, et differentias exhibens* (Leiden: apud Danielem à Gaasbeek, 1680), 78–80.

40 See Senguerd, *Philosophia naturalis, quatuor partibus primarias corporum species affectiones, differentias, productiones mutationes et interitus exhibens. Editio secunda, priore auctior* (Leiden: apud Danielem a Gaesbeeck, 1685), 107.

41 About Boyle's pneumatic research, with particular reference to elasticity, see Shapin-Shaffer, *Leviathan and the Air-Pump*.

42 After a trip to England, in the summer of 1674, during which he met Newton in Cambridge and maybe also Boyle in London, de Volder pushed the curators in

order to found experimental lectures, like the foreign academies. About this, see Wiesenfeldt, *The virtues of New Philosophies or How the Leiden Philosophical Faculty Survived the Crisis of 1676*.

43 See Senguerd, *Rationis atque experientiae connubium*, 23.
44 See Senguerd, *Rationis atque experientiae connubium*, 41.
45 See Senguerd, *Rationis atque experientiae connubium*, 23.
46 See Senguerd, *Rationis atque experientiae connubium*, 23.
47 See Senguerd, *Rationis atque experientiae connubium*, 23–4.
48 See Senguerd, 'Disquisitio de tarantula', 309.
49 See Senguerd, *Philosophia naturalis, quatuor partibus primarias corporum species affectiones, differentias, productiones mutationes et interitus exhibens. Editio secunda, priore auctior*, 135.
50 See Senguerd, *Philosophia naturalis*, 135.
51 See Senguerd, *Rationis atque experientiae connubium*, 101.
52 See Senguerd, 'Disquisitio de tarantula', 311–14.
53 About the connection between music and nerves in the first decades of the eighteenth century, see *Music and the Nerves, 1700–1900*, ed. James Kennaway (New York: Palgrave Macmillan, 2014).
54 See Senguerd, 'Disquisitio de tarantula', 315.
55 See 'Disquisitio de tarantula', 315–16.
56 See 'Disquisitio de tarantula', 316–17.
57 See Dibon, *La philosophie néerlandaise au siècle d'or*, 206; van Miert, *Humanism in an Age of Science*, 266, 306.
58 See Fabrizio Baldassarri, 'Descartes and the Dutch: Botanical Experimentation in the Early Modern Period', *Perspectives on Science* 28, no. 6 (2020): 647–83.
59 See Ragland, 'Mechanism, the senses, and reason: Franciscus Sylvius and Leiden debates over anatomical knowledge after Harvey and Descartes', 200–3. See also Dimitri Levitin, 'Early Modern Experimental Philosophy: A Non-Anglocentric Overview', in *Experiment, Speculation and Religion in Early Modern Philosophy*, eds Alberto Vanzo and Peter R. Anstey (New York and London: Routledge, 2019), 229–91, especially 242–3.

8

The domestication of spirit power in a German handbook on natural magic

Michael Pickering

8.1 Introduction

Sometime between 1700 and 1706, a recent graduate of medicine at the University of Erfurt made his way to the Duchy of Braunschweig-Wolfenbüttel in Lower Saxony. Although it is unclear precisely when Johann Nikolaus Martius arrived in Braunschweig, by 1706 he had been appointed to the Vikarie of the Holy Ghost by Duke Anton Ulrich[1] and already by 1705 he was referring to himself as a 'Braunschweig physician' in the second edition of his text on the medical uses of natural magic.[2] From this, it seems reasonably safe to assume he made the move from Erfurt quite soon after concluding his studies there. While relatively little is known about Martius, it appears that he may have operated within a Pietist network stretching from Lower Saxony to Halle.[3] Further to this, Martius' immediate network in Braunschweig included one Georg Sievers, Secretary of the Ducal Library,[4] and by 1729 he had been appointed one of the personal physicians (*Leibmedici*) to Duke August Wilhelm.[5] Notwithstanding a potentially long and successful career at court, Martius may well have been consigned to historical oblivion had it not been for his one publication: *Unterricht von der Magia Naturali* (1717, 1st German ed.), a text that began life as his medical dissertation, *De magia naturalia eiusque usu medico ad magica curandam* (1700). The book appeared in three Latin editions followed by five German editions; after which it would, in 1779, undergo something of a 'sanitizing' transformation at the hands of one Johann Christian Wiegleb, apothecary in Langensalza. While there is little evidence that this text garnered much critical attention, various contemporary authors made passing reference to it, including the encyclopaedist Zedler, confirming that it was widely known.[6]

The significance of Martius' text on the therapeutic uses of sympathetic magic is to be found, in part, in its systematic presentation of the theory, terminology and practices associated with natural magic in the healing arts. Indeed, the text itself carries a title denoting its function as a technical manual: *Unterricht*, as with the verb '*unterrichten*', refers to the act of instructing, informing and educating and was an addition to the Latin title that merely referred to the medical uses of natural magic. By 1717, the text was therefore being promoted not simply as an academic rumination on the uses of magical power in medicine but as an instructional text detailing precisely how one was to conceive of, classify and direct natural magical processes towards medical ends. As a *technical* manual, the *Unterricht* presented magic as systematized, accessible knowledge in a way that differed in degree not only from that well-known text, *Magia naturalis*, by Giambattista Della Porta, but also significantly from the eponymous text of Wolfgang Hildebrandt. Indeed, Martius' aim in writing the *Unterricht* was to provide a 'useful' and 'usable' set of guidelines that could be readily understood and applied by anyone.[7] In one sense, this applied focus connects the *Unterricht* to the plethora of early modern pharmaceutical texts (*Arzneibücher*) directed at the 'common man'. In another sense, however, the technical nature of Martius' text sets it apart from pharmaceutical texts of this genre, many of which were chiefly compendia of recipes rather than technical manuals per se. It is this relationship between magic and technology – as systematized knowledge serving an applied function – that is chiefly of interest here.

Indeed, the relationship between magic and technology is a curious one. At first glance, one is reminded of that class of magic referred to variously as 'artificial magic' or 'mathematical magic': a category of magic concerned with the creation and operation of technical wonders such as talking statues and mechanical flying animals.[8] Thought of narrowly in this context, the question concerning the relationship between 'technology' and 'magic' has the capacity to orient itself towards the fantastic but thoroughly mechanical causes and manifest effects of machines.[9] This is, of course, only if one assumes an indelible nexus between machines and technology;[10] a connection that was, at best, vaguely delineated in the eighteenth century. Indeed, in its purest expression, 'technology' referred to the systematic exposition of discipline-specific terminology (*Kunstwörter-Lehre*).[11] At once relational, *technologia* stood on the threshold of things-as-they-are and the representation of this complex, sometimes unclear, often messy reality. As 'words of the craft', *technologia* afforded the ability to not only translate experience into knowledge – to describe, define, circumscribe and 'capture' the relations between subject and world – but to articulate, organize and structure experience itself in the first instance. In a slightly later permutation, *technologia* began to take on one of its modern guises as systematized knowledge (technology) designed for practical application.

The *Unterricht* readily lends itself to an incorporation of both conceptions: as *technologia* – an explication and explanation of the words of the craft (in this instance, the terms applied to explain different types of transplantation and the corresponding action at a distance necessary for sympathetic magic); and as technology – systematized, applied knowledge. While this conceptual framework is not one that Martius himself overtly articulated and applied, I suggest that it serves as a useful means of conceptualizing the central aim of his work, which was to indicate the dual regenerative capacity of nature: as a source of medical remedies serving the needs of the fallible, fallen body; and, importantly, as a fundamental impulse towards spiritual regeneration. In utilizing the construction technology/*technologia*, we are readily able to probe this multifaceted undertaking in the *Unterricht*. As technology/*technologia*, the text attempts to articulate, concretize and structure the existence and workings of spirit in nature, and this it does through the deployment of analogue visualizations and terminological constructions which, taken together, 'package-up' and communicate this knowledge for the eminently practical purpose of self-healing. Indeed, the technology/*technologia* of magic contained in the *Unterricht* reveals an attempt to represent that which by its nature eschews easy representation: the workings of spirit power not only *in* nature but *as* nature; and, through this, the numinous source of all such power. Indeed, Martius' approach is not a passive reflection on the powers of spirit but rather, as I argue, an attempt to 'domesticate'[12] them: to reveal spirit; to render it knowable, controllable and manipulable; to systematize (and through this, to make readily applicable) its power for the benefit of fallen humans in a post-Lapsarian world; and through this, to articulate a regenerationist conception of the relationship between nature, the divine and the self.

8.2 Magic as technology/*technologia*

In order to understand how Martius systematizes spirit power, and indeed, what this means in the context of natural magic, it is helpful to briefly consider what he means by spirit, magic and nature, and their tight interrelation. Martius explains his understanding of nature through the prism of matter-spirit theory. For Martius, matter (and by extension, outer nature) is ultimately a manifestation of spirit (inner nature). While never maintaining an overt pantheism, Martius nonetheless draws strongly upon the matter-spirit theory of Christian Thomasius, the Halle professor of jurisprudence, to articulate his understanding of spirit. In his later-recanted pneumatology, *Versuch vom Wesen des Geistes* (1699), Thomasius conceives of matter as deriving its substance from an inner spirit essence in nature,[13] which, in turn, draws its being and potency directly from God. This inner nature is, if not twofold, nonetheless multilayered: an active spirit (*anima mundi*) that is itself an emanation of the divine spirit.[14]

Although I will at present refrain from a full discussion of Martius' understanding of spirit operations and the processes of natural magic, it is important at this juncture to indicate that there is in no sense an ontological distinction between matter and spirit in Martius' cosmology. Indeed, the distinction is organizational in nature: matter is visible and immediately tangible, while spirit is not; however, there is no sense that matter does not derive from spirit, as Martius' discussion shows. This conception of spirit appears to align Martius' views, superficially, with those of the organicist school at Halle, initiated by the physician Georg Ernst Stahl. According to the organicist approach – which, as Johanna Geyer-Kordesch has demonstrated, was intrinsically linked to Pietism[15] – soul and body worked together in a neo-Aristotelian conception of the *systema influxus physici*: that is, the will of the soul caused movement within the body, and external stimuli worked on and through the body to be cognized and felt within the soul. The terms 'matter' and 'spirit' were organizational designations for things that worked within and upon each other to produce life.[16] In the organicist model, mental states were understood to have a significant impact on physical well-being, and vice versa, giving rise to the *cultura animi* tradition.[17] What is significant here is that, while Martius' understanding of spirit may seem to align well with the organicist model, I suggest that Martius' conception most likely aligns far more with Thomasius' model in which the soul is tripartite in nature and a determination of the universal world spirit. Knowing how fraught the question of the influence of the soul on the body was[18] – and how heterodox the Thomasian model was – could explain Martius' hesitancy to bring the soul into the discussion on spirit. As I will discuss further on, Martius likely did not draw a distinction between the soul and natural spirit – the source of magical power.

Martius' understanding of vital nature (if not strictly *vitalist* nature in the later mid-eighteenth-century sense of the term) relies upon a distinction between matter and spirit in which spirit is perpetually at work, active and effective. The foundation of natural magic, then, is the movement of spirit, according to

Martius.[19] A key distinction emerges between non-directed spirit interaction (*actio naturalis*) and that which is the result of human control and manipulation (*actio animalis*).[20] For Martius, the key to performing natural magic is an understanding of spirit power and the application of this knowledge to bring about effects beneficial to human well-being through *actio animalis*. Natural magic is, in essence, the manipulation of spirit power by means of material objects and substances to bring about tangible effects on matter.

As I have argued elsewhere, Martius presents natural magic as having two chief aims: the primary aim being to heal oneself or another; and the secondary, to provide a reflection on the hidden, divine essence beyond nature as a means of bringing about spiritual regeneration.[21] The primary aim is not only explicitly stated in the *Unterricht* but can also be gleaned from Martius' position as a 'practical physician' (*practicus*). In the early eighteenth century, a practical physician would visit patients in person and dispense substances normally administered by an apothecary.[22] Such a position was by its very nature an active role, and the medicus retained one foot in the academic realm, and one in the quotidian, interpersonal context of health and healing. The secondary aim, as I have argued, reveals itself indirectly through Martius' inclusion of several key ideas associated with, inter alia, Paracelsus, Jakob Böhme and the early Johann Arndt, as well as Thomasius: that the secondary goal of natural magic is to probe the inner core of nature through its outer signatures and manifestations (a sort of 'praxis pietatis') as a means of cultivating a divine wisdom akin to that of Solomon.[23] Such knowledge served not to exalt the intellect of the practising subject but to lay a path towards spiritual regeneration and deification; and through this, the attainment of *magia divina* – the ability to command nature through the will alone.

The consideration of Martius' treatment of natural magic as a form of technology/*technologia* – as a systematizing approach incorporating words of the craft to articulate and structure spirit power – helps to emphasize the overriding impulse in his text to render the knowledge of and ability to perform magic eminently do-able for the ordinary person. I suggest that one can think of systematization as the presentation of knowledge as a set of interrelated and interdependent parts, rendered readily comprehensible and applicable through a thorough understanding of theory, coupled with a series of graduated steps or processes. The construction of technology as a form of systematized knowledge appears, for example, in later eighteenth-century texts, such as Johann Beckmann's *Anleitung zur Technologie* (1777). Indeed, Beckmann defines technology – in contrast to the face-to-face, workshop experience of the apprentice learning the craft from the master – as a science communicated through 'rigorous instruction, in systematic order' based upon 'true principles and reliable experience'.[24] Further on, Beckmann reiterates this emphasis on the clarifying and ordering feature of technology when he states that it should serve to 'completely, clearly and in an orderly manner explain the processes, outcomes and principles' of a craft.[25]

This later eighteenth-century understanding of technology incorporates within itself an earlier understanding of the term.[26] In the late seventeenth and early eighteenth century, *technologia* referred to the systematic exposition of *Kunstwörter*: while denoting invented words or neologisms today, in an early modern context *Kunstwörter* were quite literally 'words of the craft', designed to encapsulate and truncate complex discipline-specific ideas and their relations to one another.[27] An early eighteenth-century *technologia* could appear as something of a glossary of terms, with their respective meanings embedded in the context of their shared discipline area.[28] This sort of systematization of discipline-specific terminology – listing, defining and contextualizing it – served in part to define particular fields of knowledge and to demarcate them from other others. In a general sense, the importance of the genre and concept of *technologia* was to be found in its representational and relational aspects. As Christian Thomasius stated in his *Einleitung zu der Vernufft-Lehre* (1719), a *technologia* relevant to philosophy in its broadest conception as a general area of inquiry does not represent the 'knowledge of the essence of things', from which truth derives, but rather 'the concepts and abstractions' that we construct to represent *our understanding* of the essential nature of things.[29] As we will see later, Martius presents us with an array of analytical constructions by which he articulates the powers of spirit and, through this, the operations of natural magic.

8.3 Conceptualizing and visualizing spirit operations

The *Unterricht* is divided into five chapters: Martius begins with the relevant background to the term 'magic' in chapter one, along with a taxonomy of magic; chapter two considers the theoretical basis of natural magic, with an emphasis on what spirit is and how it operates; chapter three details the praxis of natural magic – the use of words, characters and processes of sympathetic magic known as transplantation; chapter four provides an array of remedies for common ailments; and chapter five concludes the text with a discussion of how one is to cure 'magical illnesses'.

The background and taxonomy presented in chapter one is useful as it begins the process of articulating what constitutes magic – and the practising magician – and it attempts to represent natural magic as both a licit and legitimate form of knowledge. A *magus*, according to Martius, is a person experienced in both divine and natural things and who, through the 'artificial conjoining of physical and mathematical things performs awesome wonders, observes, with time, the divine powers, and who instructs others in these secrets'.[30] This initial revelation serves to position Martius himself – instructing others in the manipulation of the powers of nature – as magician. The key distinction between what constitutes magic and what does not, then, is whether the art being performed draws upon the hidden powers of nature (*natürliche Kräffte*)[31] and delves into the divine mysteries or not. Martius is very clear to distinguish mechanical wonders, which he refers to as 'artificial or mathematical magic' from natural magic, the latter of which relies upon 'natural powers', while machines do not.[32] Although Martius does not define natural magic at this point, he further distinguishes between natural magic and diabolic magic (whether this is directly through the intervention of the devil or in fact harmful natural magic instructed by the devil); which, in turn, leads Martius to a distinction between licit and illicit magic.[33] Martius develops this distinction through a rehabilitation of Heinrich Cornelius Agrippa von Nettesheim's reputation (Martius insists that Agrippa was in no sense associated with diabolic magic) and he depicts scholars such as Albertus Magnus, Trithemius, Ficino, Cardano, Paracelsus and Robert Fludd as 'pious and diligent investigators of nature'.[34] This eclectic uptake of scholars includes those from the medieval scholastic tradition, such as the aforementioned Albertus Magnus, as well as Thomas Aquinas and Roger Bacon, and also draws upon the authority of Aristotle, citing his *Historia animalium* on the generation of insects.[35] Indeed, the inclusion of scholars from a variety of traditions serves the core function of the chapter, which is to open the way for a discussion of natural magic as both legal and legitimate. To further buttress this point, Martius sidesteps any in-depth consideration of other forms of magic, such as geomancy, necromancy and theurgy, consigning them to no more than a brief, dismissive mention.[36] Kabbalah is considered insofar as it is, in its widest sense according to Martius, little different to natural magic in that it 'explains the powers of created, natural and heavenly things, and clarifies the secrets of Holy Scripture with philosophical principles'.[37]

Having opened up the way for a discussion of natural magic, Martius then proceeds to define it and to discuss its theoretical underpinnings in chapter two. *Magia naturalis* is, according to Martius, 'none other than the secret natural philosophy of the ancient sages, through which they performed great wonders'.[38] This does not clearly define what natural magic is, and it isn't until further on in the chapter that Martius states its foundation: the interaction of spirits.[39] Beginning his explanation of what spirit is and how it operates, Martius states that utilizing the hylomorphic occult qualities of the scholastics would not be satisfactory, as these do not provide definite, concrete foundations upon which to explain manifest phenomena.[40] In order to best describe the workings of hidden, spirit properties in nature, Martius states that he will turn to a corpuscular-mechanist understanding of sub-visible matter. In this system that Martius (by his own admission) borrows from Kenelm Digby, spirit can be thought of as fine, sub-visible particles that float within light. While light, itself a 'spiritous, fluid substance',[41] does not cause the movement of particles, it is nonetheless the medium through which and by which particles move,[42] and it takes with it particles of substances that it touches.

It is vitally important to understand Martius' utilization of a corpuscular theory of matter to explain what spirit is and its ability to effect change on material bodies as primarily an analytical tool or framework. By this I mean that Martius in no sense maintains that spirit *actually* comprises fine, sub-visible particles floating aloft on rays of light and air, as we will see further on; rather, this is chiefly a useful way of conceptualizing and concretizing it.[43] As part of rendering spirit operations readily comprehensible, Martius visualizes that which readily evades easy definition – the essence and properties of spirit – as sub-visible particles, which he then likens to macro-dimensional, real-world analogues. Martius' emphasis on visualizing the hidden properties of nature parallels the challenge to scholastic occult qualities in the seventeenth and eighteenth centuries. As Keith Hutchison has argued, proponents of the new science were not opposed to occult qualities on account of their occult (i.e. hidden) status per se, but rather because of the scholastic emphasis on the unintelligible nature of the hidden properties of natural bodies and the hylomorphic view that these occult *qualitates* constituted the forms of such bodies.[44] In the context of early eighteenth-century German metaphysics, there was the growing awareness that the distinction between manifest and occult properties – that the former were accessible directly via the senses, whereas the latter were known only through their effects – was false and that no properties could ever be considered truly manifest.[45] One can understand Martius' visualization of sub-visible particles and their operations as, in part, a refutation of scholastic *scientia* with its emphasis on the visible and manifest; and his reluctance to give up occult properties in toto as evidence of the obvious fact that his investigation deals precisely with those properties of nature that are, by definition, known only through their effects. As he states further on in the text, one will never truly be able to show the manifest causes of natural magic, as these hinge upon the (hidden) 'powers of natural bodies'; and then in the footnote below the body text, he goes so far as to say that – having established the existence of a phenomenon – if one cannot show a manifest cause, then one should rather accept this fact than 'completely deny the wonderful powers of nature'.

To address the question of how sub-visible particles could exist in great enough abundance to bring about sympathetic effects, Martius invokes infinite divisibility as a property of natural bodies: that, conceptually, any natural body is composed of parts (which distinguishes it from simple substances) and that therefore there should theoretically be no limits on the divisibility of such an object.[46] Although at a large-scale level, we notice gross divisions, at a sub-visible level such particulate matter splits off of natural bodies all the time. This is how we smell things, such as fine Spanish leather, according to Martius.[47] The appearance of corpuscles is further conceived of in terms of geometrical structure: just as a crystal of common salt has eight corners at its intersection, and a snowflake has six, so too can one think of all sub-visible particles – including those responsible for disease and healing – as likewise possessing certain shapes, as well as sizes and weights; and it is this particular similarity and mutual affinity (*eine absonderliche Gleichheit*) between certain particles that accounts for their mutual attraction to one another.[48]

Conceptualizing and visualizing spirit operations in this way – as the exchange of particulate matter between various natural bodies – greatly helps to establish a conceptual framework in which sympathetic cures might be expected to function. Indeed, geometry is key to thinking about why some herbs and roots work for the treatment of some ailments and not others: the pores of a particular root used to treat an illness might be three-cornered, while the dimensions of the disease particle might be round or four-cornered.[49] Successful treatment is therefore not only a matter of compatibility between the nature of the particles concerned but also the pores of the patient and the substance being utilized in treatment:

> This difference in the pores is also the cause of why bad effluvia that have been brought into a [healing substance] cannot always go back to the sick body from whence they came; and is also why transplantation cannot successfully be carried out using thick [natural] bodies, stones and metals. For the pores [of a healing substance] cannot be extended in such a way that they take on the

effluvia of this or that illness if they are not so constituted to have between them a similarity and mutual affinity.[50]

Gleichheit is conceptually very important for the corpuscular analytical tool which Martius applies to the operations of spirit and, through this, sympathetic medicine. However, it eventually proves to be the undoing of the very framework it is ostensibly designed to support. While none of this is in any sense troubling for Martius, it does yet again emphasize the journey on which Martius takes his reader towards a grounded and conceptually concrete understanding of occult operations in nature. In rendering the fundamentally *invisible* and – by its very nature – immaterial substance of spirit 'seeable' and tangible through the invocation of the *sub-visible* and material, Martius presents a view of magic as occult but not unintelligible, hidden but nonetheless readily comprehensible. Tensions emerge with the question of how it is that particles attract one another and move in particular, rather than general and random ways. Martius attempts to demonstrate that particles do adhere to like particles when he uses the example of the Welt-Kugel:[51] no matter how many times one shakes it, the various liquids and particles inside eventually return to a heterogeneous state,[52] similar to the separation one sees with water and oil. Martius takes this as proof that particles attract and adhere to like particles, which in turn suggests a deep mutual affinity or *Gleichheit*. Such a principle can also be seen in the case of witchcraft:

> one may not doubt that the spirits of a person have the power to move about outside of the body and to conjoin with other things . . . as the matter has been revealed in the case of witchcraft; that through the enchanted items, the sorcery can be turned back on the witch.[53]

Beyond these examples, however, Martius directs the reader to Christian Thomasius' *Versuch vom Wesen des Geistes*.[54]

Although it is true to say that Martius draws upon a wide array of sources in crafting his text, the backbone of his explanation of the nature of spirit is Thomasius' pneumatology. Martius states very clearly, after his discussion of the corpuscular framework, that one should not think of the foregoing remarks in materialist terms and that all those 'corpuscules, atoms and particles endowed with a certain form' are in fact a 'composite' of matter and spirit, a feature common to all natural bodies.[55] This pivot is entirely necessary, as it becomes impossible to explain the directed movement necessary for sympathy unless one turns to an inherent power of movement in matter attributed to a materialist dynamism ('although most do not know what this power is', as Martius states) or to a spirit model in which matter is vitalized and moved by a spirit of nature created by

God. Martius, in this footnote, sides firmly with the spirit model, stating that it is manifest that 'matter can neither exist nor be moved without spirit'.[56] It is at this point that Martius begins to paraphrase Thomasius in asserting the necessity of spirit: that matter does not possess its own inherent power of movement; that matter is passive and extended, but that for it to be extended, something must have extended it in the first instance; that form is nobler than matter; that a power of movement must itself be a substance; that for such power of movement to be accorded the status of *accidentia* is absurd, given that this would make *accidentia* nobler than substance. Following on: 'Movement cannot happen if all space is filled with matter, as movement requires space, and space is not a vacuum; therefore, it must by necessity be full of a spirit substance.'[57]

Turning to *Versuch vom Wesen des Geistes*, we note that not only is Martius drawing heavily from Thomasius but also Thomasius constructs a system in which matter is brought forth from spirit:

> I maintain that in all corporeal stuff there is a spirit, and that consequently no corporeal thing can exist without a spirit; a spirit, however, can well exist without a corporeal form . . . what is purely passive cannot exist in and of itself, rather it requires something active to bring it forth from nothing and make it into something.[58]

The conceptual fulcrum holding Thomasius' – and by extension, Martius' – spirit model together, and indeed, that which allows for the existence of sympathetic attraction, is an all-pervasive spirit of nature, commonly known as *anima mundi*.[59] In Thomasius' system, this substance is twofold, comprising a 'warming' aspect and a 'cooling' aspect, and both derive from God, the 'uppermost spirit'.[60] It is through this and by way of this spirit of nature that material things, endowed with spirit, can exert hidden influences upon one another.[61] Although Thomasius is somewhat vague on the exact operations of sympathy and its opposite, antipathy, stating that they refer to the 'love' or 'hate' that one thing feels for another,[62] it is easy to extrapolate from his system how these would work: if all matter is brought forth from spirit and that spirit forms the matrix in which all natural operations occur, then it is the relationship between different states ('warm/light' and 'cold/air') of spirit – manifested in material things that are, in essence, emanations of spirit – that forms the basis of sympathetic attraction and antipathetic repulsion. The 'warm' spirit is the 'spirit of light' (*Licht-Geist*), the 'cold' spirit is the 'spirit of air' (*Lufft-Geist*), and matter is the 'fruit of their union'.[63] Although speculative at this juncture, it would not be too much of a stretch of the imagination to think that this could have provided the inspiration for Martius to include 'light' and 'air'[64] as the mediating substances through which particles move. Indeed, Martius even goes so far at the outset of the *Unterricht* to state that one might think in terms of this universal spirit, *anima mundi*, as the connecting, binding influence on all things in nature, articulating, also, that he is aware of how 'abhorrent' the matter is to many and recommending that the 'reader desirous of truth' read Thomasius' 'lovely little book'.[65]

The process of theorization calls spirit into being – defining it and explaining its nature while presenting it in tangible terms. Indeed, the corpuscular framework that Martius adopts as an analytical tool primes the reader for conceiving of spirit action at a distance in terms far more readily accessible and comprehensible than the Thomasian framework. Continuing this process of concretization, the application of *technologia* – technical terminology – not only explains how to 'do magic' but also structures expectations of its effects. This invocation requires words, but not in a ceremonial or theurgic sense.[66] Rather, as words of the craft, the *technologia* of transplantation absorbs procedural information and, through this, forms a conceptual 'code' for how to think about – and a prescriptive framework for how to harness and apply – spirit power. Each term is active in that it explains the necessary action of the practising subject, and the substance used in all operations is mumia, that is, extract of the patient's own spirit.

As Martius explains, the process of transplantation is one in which a person's illness is transferred, or transplanted, into another object to bring about a healing process.[67] Transplanting the 'illness' is in this sense code for transplanting an aspect of the individual's spirit, or mumia, into the object of choice. The term 'mumia' has a complex history: in one sense, it could refer to a powder made from Egyptian mummies used as a general and highly valued panacea; in another sense, it referred to any number of preparations made from a distillate of macerated fresh human body parts; and in the broadly Paracelsian sense it referred to the vital spirit essence within the human body (and it was, through the preparation of human flesh, that such essence could be extracted and used as a general panacea).[68] Martius adopts this latter definition of the term and provides a method for how to prepare mumia from human blood:

> take healthy blood that has been let in springtime... let it stand until a watery substance forms on the top, and then pour this off; dry the coagulated blood in the shade and then baste it with [some of] the water you removed earlier, and let it dry once more. Repeat this until all the water has been absorbed... and then you can use it.[69]

With this powerful 'mumia-magnet' in hand, the practitioner is ready to perform magic. The forms of transplantation that Martius enumerates and defines all emphasize the active nature of the process: they indicate to the subject what he or she is to do with the mumia, and the corpuscular framework sketched earlier – not only the overarching theory of spirit but also the geometrical visualization of the operation of transplantation – buttresses these processes. Indeed, in rendering spirit sub-visible, it becomes possible to readily visualize the corresponding operations of spirit via transplantation. Martius presents six core varieties of transplantation, and in keeping with what one would expect to find in an early modern *technologia* presents the technical terms along with a description of each: 'insemination' (*das Einsäen*) – mumia is placed in earth containing the seeds of a healing plant and the earth has the water used to wash the infected part of the patient's body poured on it; 'implantation' (*das Einpflantzen*) – the same as 'insemination', except that in addition to the seeds of a healing plant, the root is also added; 'imposition' (*Einsetzung*) – mumia is placed inside a healing plant, root or tree; 'irroration' (*Befeuchtung*) – the mumia (in the form of wet excrement) is smeared on the healing plant or herb; 'inescation' (*Anetzung*) – in the 'most common and sure way', mumia is fed to an animal; 'adproximation' (*Annäherung*) – the healing plant (or animal) is applied directly to the body of the patient so as to draw the illness to it.[70] In Chapter 4, Martius explains that there are numerous remedies from a variety of well-known authors that all utilize the general principle of transplantation. For the treatment of general ailments, one option is to make a mumia magnet by pouring some of the patient's blood into an empty eggshell, sealing the shell and placing it beneath a brooding hen to coagulate; when this is ready, feed part of the blood egg to an animal (alternatively one could smear breadcrumbs soaked in the patient's urine onto a tree for birds to eat). Against fever, the patient's finger and toenails could be clipped and bound to a crab that is then to be thrown back into the water. Against ailments of the head, one can create a mumia magnet from mucous and either bury it in rich earth sown with sage, verbena and petunia (or poppy seed for 'hot cases') or place it inside a walnut tree.[71] Crucially, Martius structures expectations when he states that the practitioner should keep trying and not give up hope if cures don't work the first time, 'for a medicus, above all one who does not understand the fundament of natural magic well, can readily err in the process'.[72]

The terms pertaining to transplantation are all drawn from a text on sympathetic medicine by the seventeenth-century Scottish physician William Maxwell.[73] In opening pages, Maxwell states that a key driving impulse behind his work is to demonstrate the operation of the spirit outside of the body[74] – a means of better understanding the hidden properties of nature, we are ultimately led to conclude,[75] not unlike Martius' intentions in the *Unterricht*. When confronting the question of how 'magnetic' cures of this kind work, a corpuscular framework is incredibly useful to think with; however, it conceals a far more complex and fluid reality, as Martius eventually admits. In Maxwell, spirit is the means by which and the medium through which the soul (the 'pure spirit') directs its will outside of its body.[76] In Martius, the question of the soul is not addressed directly, and this is likely because of an underlying unwillingness to overtly state what spiritual regeneration means.[77] Indeed, in Martius' text on natural magic, the knowledge of spirit power and how to direct it to various ends is largely a matter of faith, in both a colloquial and spiritual sense: belief that one has observed the great web of nature in sufficient detail and depth to garner some sense of its inner workings, and belief that one has ascertained at least part of the divine plan as to the relationship between the natural order and the capabilities of post-Lapsarian humanity.[78] It is unsurprising, therefore, that Martius presents his readers with a system of fizzing, floating and bouncing sub-visible particles. The alternative (as he eventually lets his readers know) is something far more complex and ultimately harder to grasp: that the familiar distinctions between different orders of being (the world of matter, the realm of spirits) are artificial at best – a mere construction of convenience belying a deeper truth: that the world itself was brought forth *from* spirit, exists *as* an emanation of spirit, and that it is to spirit that one should aspire to return.

8.4 Conclusions

As I hope to have shown, Martius' handbook on natural magic ostensibly seeks to demonstrate how one is to harness spirit power for the healing of oneself or another. Although Martius does not at any point refer to his text as a 'technology' I have suggested that we might read it through the roughly contemporary lenses of *technologia* and technology-as-systematized-knowledge as a means of better understanding its inner dynamic. I have argued that when considered in this manner, the text presents a concretization of spirit power that acts as a conceptual fulcrum for a consideration of how sympathetic magic works. Such an approach structures how the practitioner-subject is to engage with the unseen, including how spirit can be understood to manifest its effects on matter. Thought of in this way, the text becomes more than just a rumination on natural magic or a how-to guide for the novice magus (or *medicus*) – although of course this latter factor is fundamentally important. When considered as technology, the text can be seen to deploy an organizing schema as a means of capturing and subordinating the inner powers of nature. As Heidegger suggests, the essence of technology is not its emphasis on machines or the modus of control. It is, rather, the instantiation of a relationship of dominance towards, and exploitation of, the hidden properties of nature; the perpetual capturing of its bounty;[79] and as I suggest, its domestication.

Although such a dynamic might suggest the kernel of a deeply 'modern' sensibility embedded in Martius' approach to magic – a sideways glance ahead down the thorny path of modernity – I would like to situate this domesticating impulse chiefly within the ambit of early modern spirituality. As I have argued elsewhere, Martius presents two main objectives in his text, one primary and the other secondary and latent: the primary objective, as we have already seen, is to present a means of self-healing for the individual in need of a certain remedy; the secondary is to articulate (albeit in deliberately understated terms) the possibility of spiritual renewal – and through this, the performance *magia divina*, a far higher-order class of magic to *magia naturalis*. Indeed, the connecting thread between the key thinkers that Martius draws upon in expressing his conception of spirit, natural sympathies and celestial influence – Christian Thomasius, Jakob Böhme and Johann Arndt – is that of spiritual regeneration. For it is through such a transfiguration that one reunites the individual will with the divine will and so becomes like God, capable of performing wonders in the manner of the Old Testament prophets.[80] In a highly important section concerning the power of the stars to affect people, Martius states:

> all sublunary bodies and all humans are subject to the influence and control of celestial bodies, except for those Christians who possess a true and living faith, in whom the power of the Holy Spirit has broken and choked off celestial influence, such that they shall no longer be known as the children of Saturn, Mars, Venus etc., but rather as the children of God, as the blessed Arndt has shown from Scripture.[81]

The fantasy of subordinating the forces of nature to the individual will – a return to Eden and the pre-Lapsarian state of grace – provides the 'thick description', to coin a Geertzian phrase, for understanding Martius' emphasis on controlling spirit power: not merely to capture spirit temporarily, nor to tame it in an individuated and singular sense, but to tame it permanently and universally. Such a fantasy outlines the necessity of overcoming one's own inner 'Thier-Geist' through rebirth and, in turn, allowing the inner divine spark to emerge, grow and dominate.[82] It is this broader context that informs Martius' attempt to explain, structure and ultimately control a power that defies ready articulation. In one sense then, Martius' technology of the unseen represents the domestication of spirit; in another, perhaps a technology of the self.

Acknowledgement

I would like to acknowledge and thank the Herzog August Bibliothek Wolfenbüttel for funding to undertake much of the research for this chapter.

Notes

1. Appointment of Martius to the Vikarie of the Heiliger Geist (21 March 1706), Niedersächsisches Landesarchiv (NLA), 2 Alt, Nr. 9054, fol. 26. All translations, unless otherwise stated, are my own.
2. *Joh. Nicol. Martii, Med. D. Et Practici Brunopol. Dissertatio De Magia Naturali Ejusqve Usu Medico Ad Magice & Magica Curandum . . .* (Erfurt: Ehrt, 1705).
3. While still in need of further development, there is some evidence to suggest that Martius may have been in contact with August Hermann Francke (all entries have been found via Kalliope Verbundkatalog): Letter from Johann Nikolaus Mertz [i.e. Martius] to August Herman Francke [?] (9 April 1714), Hauptarchiv, Franckesche Stiftung, AFSt/H C 799:61; and that he was in any case mentioned to Francke in third-party correspondence: Letter from Johann Heinrich Köpper to August Hermann Francke (12 October 1714), Hauptarchiv, Franckesche Stiftung, AFSt/H C 362:4; and was in contact with Francke's son, Gotthilf August Francke: Letter from Johann Nikolaus Mertz to Gotthilf August Francke (s.d.), Missionsarchiv – Indienabteilung, Franckesche Stiftung, AFSt/M 3 H 2:30.
4. Georg Sievers, Letter of Resignation and Recommendation (16 December 1705), NLA, 2 Alt, Nr. 9054, fols. 21–2.
5. Duke August Wilhelm, Appointment of Martius to the Position of *Leibmedicus* (20 March 1729), NLA, 3 Alt, Nr. 603, microfiche.
6. Johann Georg Walch, *Philosophisches Lexicon* (Ledipzig: Gleditsch, 1726), 108; Georg Wilhelm Wegner, *Schau-Platz Vieler Ungereimten Meynungen und Erzehlungen* (Berlin and Leipzig: Haude, 1735–6), 2:658. Johann Heinrich Zedler, *Grosses vollständiges Universal Lexicon aller Wissenschafften und Künste* (Leipzig and Halle, 1732–54), 19, especially 299–300; Christian Friedrich Daniel, *Beyträge zur medicinischen Gelehrsamkeit* (Halle: Renger, 1749), 4–5.

7   Martius emphasizes this in the preface to the *Unterricht*, stating that any initial qualms that one may hold would very soon dissipate at the realization of the usefulness of the knowledge contained in the text. He also reiterates this at the end of the book, implying strongly that one should apply the knowledge contained within it: Johann Nikolaus Martius, *Unterricht von der Magia Naturali Und derselben Medicinische Gebrauch auf Magische Weise, wie auch bezauberte Dinge zu curiren* ... (Frankfurt: Nicolai, 1717), 128.
8   Zedler, *Lexicon*, 19, especially 299–300. These terms stem from earlier usage by Gaspar Schott and Athanasius Kircher. Anthony Grafton, *Magic and Technology in Early Modern Europe* (Washington: Smithsonian Institution Libraries, 2005), 11. Publication based on the Dibner Library Lecture given 15 October 2002.
9   On the absorption of mechanical wonders into the ambit of magic, see: Grafton, *Magic and Technology*, esp. 35 ff. For background on the relationship between mechanics and nature more generally, especially the breaking down of the dichotomy between nature and art in the context of early modern mechanics, see: Natacha Fabbri, '*Deus Mechanicus* and *Machinae Mundi* in the Early Modern Period', *Historia Philosophica* 9 (2011): 75–112. For an insightful analysis of the place of Hermetic currents in cultivating the notion of *deus mechanicus*, see especially 93 ff.
10 If one is to speak of a nexus between machines and technology, we must be prepared to relinquish, or at least significantly modify our modern understanding of the relationship between technical instruments and 'utility', as Koen Vermeir demonstrates in a fascinating article on the relationship between certain technical instruments of Athanasius Kircher, his metaphysics and the Jesuit context in which he worked. Koen Vermeir, 'Athanasius Kircher's Magical Instruments: An Essay on Science, Religion and Applied Metaphysics (1602–1680)', *Studies in History and Philosophy of Science* 38 (2007): 363–400.
11 Zedler, *Lexicon*, 42, especially 508–9; Walch, *Lexicon*, 2514–15.
12 I take my usage of this term from Ghassan Hage. In his probing analysis of nationalism and multiculturalism in modern Australia, Hage develops the idea of 'domestication' to explain the subordination of non-White, ethnic 'others' by a dominant White majority. Drawing from the nineteenth-century French naturalist, Geoffroy de St Hilaire, Hage adopts the conceptual framework of 'captive', 'tame' and 'domesticated' animals: 'captive' animals are subordinated through caging and would run wild without such physical restraints; 'tame' animals no longer require caging to subordinate them as they 'have internalised their state of captivity', although this is on an individual rather than a species level, and caging nonetheless still helps to control their movement; while domesticated animals are those who 'are subjugated as a self-reproducing community of tame animals'. Ghassan Hage, *White Nation: Fantasies of White Supremacy in a Multicultural Society* (Annandale: Pluto

Press, 1998), 114–15. Hage utilizes this term – including the related term of 'caging' – to articulate strategies of institutional coercion and order-making in which the 'national will' is imposed on (in order to domesticate) the ethnic immigrant 'other'. I adopt this framework for thinking about the control of spirit power. As I suggest, Martius suggests more than simply capturing and, consequently, 'taming' spirit; he articulates, albeit in understated form, the importance of the wholescale subordination of natural spirit by the spiritually regenerated, deified spirit of a Christian.

13 Christian Thomasius, *Versuch vom Wesen des Geistes Oder Grund-Lehren, So wohl zur natürlichen Wissenschafft als der Sitten-Lehre: In welchen gezeiget wird, dass Licht un Lufft ein geistiges Wesen sey, und alle Cörper aus Materie und Geist bestehen, auch in der gantzen Natur eine anziehende Krafft, in dem Menschen aber ein zweyfacher guter und böster Geist sey* . . . (Halle: Salfelden, 1699), 35–6. As Thomas Ahnert notes, Thomasius later recanted these ideas under pressure from the Halle Faculty of Theology as well as external detractors. Thomas Ahnert, 'Enthusiasm and Enlightenment: Faith and Philosophy in the Thought of Christian Thomasius', *Modern Intellectual History* 2, no. 2 (2005): 155–6; 164–88.

14 Thomasius, *Versuch*, 72–3.

15 Johanna Geyer-Kordsch, *Pietismus, Medizin und Aufklärung in Preußen im 18. Jahrhundert: Das Leben und Werk George Ernst Stahls* (Tübingen: Max Niemeyer Verlag, 2000), 78–9.

16 Johanna Geyer-Kordesch, 'Georg Ernst Stahl's Radical Pietist Medicine and Its Influence on the German Enlightenment', in *The Medical Enlightenment of the Eighteenth Century*, eds Andrew Cunningham and Roger French (Cambridge: Cambridge University Press, 1990), 67–87.

17 Andreas Rydberg, *Inner Experience: An Analysis of Scientific Experience in Early Modern Germany*, Uppsala Studies in the History of Ideas 48 (Uppsala: Acta Universitatis Upsaliensis, 2017), 159.

18 The Leibniz-Stahl controversy pertained, inter alia, to the fraught discussions over the relationship between body and soul, and this debate about whether the soul did or did not interact with the body continued in the conflict between Christian Wolff, a discipline of Leibniz and proponent of the *systema harmoniae praestabilitae* and Andreas Rüdiger, a proponent of the *systema influxus physici*. Wolff, arguing from within a causal-deterministic framework, maintained that the ability of the soul to bring about changes in the body would ultimately constitute an *ex nihilo* event, i.e. one through which the will of the soul would bring about movement in the body (thus creating a force that had not previously existed). Wolff implied that such actions were reserved for God alone. Christian Wolff, *Vernünfftige Gedanken von Gott, der Welt und der Seele des Menschen* . . . (Halle: Renger, 1751), 473–4. It should be noted that this comment was an addition to the

first edition, published in 1719, quite probably a response to criticism levelled by various scholars. Rüdiger, on the other hand – in the preface to his commentary on Wolff's treatise – argued for a rehabilitation of the Aristotelian conception of the soul as 'an immaterial power that is in matter'. Andreas Rüdiger, *Herr Christian Wolffens... Meinung von dem Wesen der Seele und eines Geistes überhaupt: Und D. Andreas Rüdigers... Gegen-Meinung* (Leipzig: Heinsius, 1727) [15]. Stating that the scholastics had completely mangled the Aristotelian definition of the soul, Rüdiger maintained that Aristotle had argued *in the abstract* for the immateriality of the soul, but that in a concrete sense he in no way suggested that it was immaterial, but was rather an incorporeal substance, according to Rüdiger. The scholastics had then conflated immateriality with incorporeality, and thus began the notion of the soul as immaterial juxtaposed to the material body. Rüdgier, *Herr Christian Wolffens... Meinung von dem Wesen der Seele* [16]. This neo-Aristotelian concept would be highly important for the Stahlian organicist model of the body-soul relationship and one that contrasted strongly with the model that Martius adopted.

19 Martius, *Unterricht*, 54–5.
20 Martius, *Unterricht*, 55, note GG.
21 Michael Pickering, 'Succour for a Fallen World: Magic and the Powers of Spirit in Johann Nikolaus Martius's *Unterricht von der Magia Naturali* (1717)', *Cromohs* 22 (2019): 42–60.
22 Paul Jacob Marperger, *Curieuses und Reales Natur- Kunst- Berg- Gewerck- und Handlungs-Lexicon* (Leipzig: Gleditsch, 1731), 1581; Johann Peter Eberhard, *Onomatologia medica completa oder Medicinisches Lexicon das alle Benennungen und Kunstwörter welche der Arzneywissenschaft und Apoteckerkunst eigen sind, deutlich und vollständig erkläret* (Ulm, Frankfurt and Leipzig: Stettin, 1772), 974.
23 Pickering, 'Succour for a Fallen World', 58.
24 Johann Beckmann, *Anleitung zur Technologie, oder zur Kentniß der Handwerke, Fabriken und Manufacturen, vornehmlich derer, die mit der Landwirthschaft, Polizey und Cameralwissenschaft in nächster Verbindung stehn* [sic] ... (Göttingen: Vandenhoeck, 1777), XV.
25 Beckmann, *Anleitung*, XVI.
26 Indeed, Beckmann not only includes within his discussion of technology the importance of clear 'technical terminology' (xii) but also works methodically through the definitions of key terms associated with manufacturing and industry as a means of developing a technology of the field.
27 Thomasius, in line with later definitions found in Zedler and Walch, defines *Kunstwörter* as referring to those terms particular to a given discipline area, including terminology associated with philosophy in a general sense. One should, Thomasius cautions, not consider such terms to themselves be constitutive of truth.

Christian Thomasius, *Einleitung zu der Vernunfft-Lehre* (Halle: Salfelds, 1719), chp. 4, sec.1–3.

28 For an example of the application of the term to music, see: Nicolaus Gengenbach, *Musica Nova, Newe Singekunst . . . Und begreifft in sich drey Theil . . . 3. Technologicam, Wie die nothwendigsten Lateinsichen, Griechischen uund jetzo ublichen italienischen Termini Musici zu verstehen . . .* (Leipzig: Rehefelds & Grosse, 1626).

29 Thomasius, *Einleitung*, chp. 4, sec. 4.

30 Martius, *Unterricht*, 4.

31 Martius, *Unterricht*, 6.

32 Martius, *Unterricht*, 6. Such a distinction is, however, somewhat curious given Martius' emphasis on how mathematics is part of the magician's remit.

33 Martius, *Unterricht*, 10–16.

34 Martius, *Unterricht*, 17–21.

35 Martius, *Unterricht*, 12, note (n).

36 Martius, *Unterricht*, 24–5: 'Geomancy has an extensive theory, which – because it is not based on certain natural principles – I will pass over in silence'; 'What one should believe about geomancy and theurgy is easy to see'.

37 Martius, *Unterricht*, 22.

38 Martius, *Unterricht*, 29. Martius is, in note (a) on the same page, quick to add that such wonders are only apparent wonders, not miracles outright, which, he states, are of godly provenance alone.

39 Martius, *Unterricht*, 54.

40 Martius, *Unterricht*, 36. Although, in note (h) he also states that one should not discard occult qualities in toto.

41 Martius, *Unterricht*, 39, note (l).

42 In addition to air, which also moves particles. Martius, *Unterricht*, 41.

43 Martius even goes so far as to suggest that he wanted to show how spirit operations could be explained through 'mechanical laws' so that the Cartesians could not dismiss his ideas as mere 'superstition'. Martius, *Unterricht*, 51–2. However, as we note earlier, this was likely just rhetorical bluster given that Martius was ultimately unable to explain spirit motion without recourse to the monist system of Thomasius' pneumatology; which, in turn, reduced any (from a dualist perspective) fundamental ontological difference between spirit and matter to an organizational distinction.

44 Keith Hutchison, 'What Happened to Occult Qualities in the Scientific Revolution?', *Isis* 73, no. 2 (1982): 233–53.

45 Zedler, *Lexicon*, 47, especially 188.

46 Martius, *Unterricht*, 43–4; also notes (q) and (r). To emphasize this point, Martius states that 'even if a body is indeed utterly tiny, it can nonetheless – through divine

power – be divided infinitely even if our intellect cannot grasp such infinite division as well as the infinite number [of parts]'. This statement further helps to bolster the corpuscular-mechanist construction that Martius develops, as we find a similar emphasis on the disaggregated yet imperceptibly and incomprehensibly small scale of matter in the works of other mechanist philosophers, such as Christian Wolff. See: Wolff, *Vernünfftige Gedancken von Gott, der Welt und der Seele des Menschen, auch allen Dingen überhaupt, den Liebhabern der Wahrheit mitgetheilt* (Halle: Renger, 1720), 375.

47 Martius, *Unterricht*, 44.
48 Martius, *Unterricht*, 46–8.
49 Martius, *Unterricht*, 48, note (z).
50 Martius, *Unterricht*, 48, note (z).
51 Effectively something like a snow-globe.
52 Martius, *Unterricht*, 47, note (y).
53 Martius, *Unterricht*, 57.
54 Martius, *Unterricht*, 46.
55 Martius, *Unterricht*, 53.
56 Martius, *Unterricht*, 52–3, note (dd).
57 Martius, *Unterricht*, 54.
58 Thomasius, *Versuch*, 35–6.
59 For an overview of the origins of this concept, see: Daniel P. Walker, *Spiritual and Demonic Magic: From Ficino to Campanella* (Leiden: Brill, 1958), 13. As Walker notes, Ficino interposed a *spiritus mundi* between the *anima mundi* and *corpus mundi* (12–13); however, one tends not to see this distinction in the early eighteenth-century German context, in which the two concepts are conflated and referred to as the *Weltgeist*. Walch provides a contemporary definition of this term: 'A spiritual entity . . . that extends itself throughout all of nature, and is the principle, or the effective cause of everything; and as the soul operates in our body, it happens that this spirit operates likewise in all bodies in the whole of nature'. Walch, *Philosophisches Lexicon*, 2885.
60 Thomasius, *Versuch*, 72. That Thomasius understands the uppermost spirit to be God: *Versuch*, 69.
61 Thomasius, *Versuch*, 151.
62 Thomasius, *Versuch*, 151.
63 Thomasius, *Versuch*, 73.
64 See notes 41 and 42.
65 Martius, *Unterricht*, 38.
66 Indeed, Martius largely dismisses the efficacy of words and written characters. Martius, *Unterricht*, 71–7.
67 Martius, *Unterricht*, 77. The concept of transplantation hinged upon the idea that either changes *in*, or the properties *of* the object or animal into which the

patient's spirit was transplanted healed the spirit of the patient; and through the natural affinity of the transplanted spirit to the spirit in the patient's body, healed the patient. Transplantation appeared across learned and non-learned medical and pharmaceutical texts, see, for example: Michael Ernst Ettmüller, *Disputatio medica corpus humanum sympatheticum* (Leipzig: Georg, 1701), 36–8; Anonymous, *Curiese, Neue, seltene, leichte, wohlfeile, gewisse, bewehrte, nuetzliche, noethige, ergoetzliche und Verwunderungs-wuerdige Haus-Apothec* (Frankfurt: Knochens, 1699), 121, 123–46 (for a list of remedies based on transplantation).

68 For an overview of meanings associated with the term 'mumia', see: Karl Dannenfeldt, 'Egyptian Mumia: The Sixteenth-Century Experience and Debate', *The Sixteenth-Century Journal* 16, no. 2 (1985): 163–80. For a roughly contemporary overview of the term, as well as several remedies based upon mumia, see: Johann Schöder, *D. Johann Schröders trefflich-versehene Medicin-Chymische Apotheke, Oder: Höchstkostbarer Arzeney-Schatz* (Nuremberg: Hoffmann, 1686), 1301–5. For an indication of how the term could be deployed in a broadly Paracelsian sense, ie. to refer to extract of life essence, see for instance: Andreas Tenzel, *Medicinisch-philosophisch- und sympathetische Schrifften* (Leipzig: Strauss, 1725), 12–13. Admittedly this is a much later reprint of his work.

69 Martius, *Unterricht*, 78. Martius also includes a recipe for making mumia from human faeces (78–9).

70 Martius, *Unterricht*, 80–2. That such remedies were widely known can be seen, for instance, in the use of *adproximation* (although not labelled as this) in an anonymously authored, handwritten seventeenth-century book of remedies from the court of Rohrau in Lower Austria: Arzneibuch [seventeenth century], Österreichisches Staatsarchiv, Allgemeines Verwaltungsarchiv, Familienarchiv, Harrach, HS, 402 [no pagination]. For a cure for bubonic plague, the recipe requires that a live pigeon be sliced in half, with one half placed directly on the patient's buboe.

71 Martius, *Unterricht*, 87–9.

72 Martius, *Unterricht*, 87.

73 Guillelmo Maxvello [William Maxwell], *Drey Bücher der Magnetischen Artzney-Kunst, Worinen so wohl die Theorie also Practic, wie auch viel Neues, Wunderbares, und höcht Nützliches erhalten* ... (Frankfurt: Zieger, 1687), 167–81.

74 Maxwell, *Drey Bücher*, 4–7 (for an overview of the postulates to be discussed in chapter two).

75 Maxwell, *Drey Bücher*, 239–69. In this section, Maxwell presents various postulates (he terms these particular points 'aphorisims') concerning the existence of the 'world soul', the formation of bodies from spirit and the importance of spirit as an intermediate entity between the corporeal and the 'pure' spirit of the individual soul and, by extension, the world soul.

76 Maxwell, *Drey Bücher*, 4–7.
77 Going by the Thomasian schema, suggested throughout Martius' text, one notes a tripartite anthropology predicated on a division between body, soul (comprising the natural spirit, which is in turn responsible for the animal, carnal urges in humans) and spirit (a spark of the divine essence). The struggle to overcome the base tendencies of the individuated, animalistic will is only made possible through an awakening to the existence of the inner divine spark and the growing of this influence. Thomasius, *Versuch*, 188–90. To state this emanationist position openly would be overtly heterodox and risk arousing the suspicion of the orthodox Lutheran establishment.
78 The question of how one is to garner such knowledge of the hidden workings of innermost nature pertains most directly to a knowledge of signatures, which is, for Martius, only painstakingly acquired through diligent study and divine inspiration. Martius, *Unterricht*, 68. See also: Pickering, 'Succor for a Fallen World', 54–6.
79 Martin Heidegger, *The Question Concerning Technology and Other Essays*, trans. William Lovitt (New York: Harper & Row, 1977), especially 14–16.
80 Pickering, 'Succor for a Fallen World'.
81 Martius, *Unterricht*, 61–3.
82 Such a narrative of overcoming the baser self, often represented as bound to the 'astral' or 'syderial' or 'animal' spirit – the latter admittedly not in the medical sense of the term – is widespread in early modern esoteric texts. See, inter alia: Jean Baptiste van Helmont, *Aufgang der Artzney-Kunst* (Nuremberg: Endter, 1683), 1030–1, especially 1034. J. B. van Helmont here refers to the 'slumber' of the inner divine powers of the soul. A similar emphasis is seen in Arndt's letter to Erasmus Wolfart on how the chief consequence of the Fall was the 'animal nature' buried within Adam 'breaking out' and ruling over the self. Johann Arndt, *Das Grosse Geheimniß der Menschwerdung des ewigen Worts. In einem Sendschreiben an seinen guten Freund Erasmum Wolfartum . . . erkläret und verfasset* in *Theologia Mystica; Oder Geheime Krafft-Theologia der Alten*, ed. Christian Hoburg (Amsterdam: Bektius, 1700), 4–6. Arndt maintains that spiritual rebirth will bring about a triumph over this animal nature, restoring the individual to the pre-Lapsarian condition (20–1). One sees similar themes a later radical Pietist context, for example: Konrad Dippel, *Weg-Weiser Zum Liecht und Recht in Der äussern Natur. Oder Entdecktes Geheimnüß, Des Segens, und des Fluchs in denen natürlichen Cörpern* (s.l: s.n, 1704), 37–59. Paracelsus' notion of the pre-Lapsarian 'illiastric' nature of Adam being, after the Fall, dominated by his syderial, baser 'cagastric' nature is in some respects the progenitor of the narrative: Paracelsus, *Opera: Bücher und Schriften, Darinnen die Magischen und Astrologischen Bücher, sampt ihren Anhängen und Stücken, auch von dem Philosophischen Stein handlende Tractatus, begriffen*, ed Johannes Huser (Strassburg: Zetzner, 1616), 2, especially 521–2.

Index

Academia Secretorum Naturae (Academy of Secrets)   90
Achillini, Alessandro   65–7, 70, 77
Adelard of Bath   17
Aelianus   176
Agricola, Georgius   85
Agrippa, Heinrich Cornelius   4, 9, 39, 49, 53–5, 70, 72, 78 n.36, 88, 89, 199
Alain de Lille   34n
Albertus Magnus   9, 41, 65, 67–9, 76 n.23, 149, 199
Albertus Magnus, Ps.-, *Secreta Alberti*   44, 46
  Opusculo de alchimia   68
Albinus, Bernhardus   187
alchemy   2, 40, 47, 65, 67, 68, 70, 71, 73, 74 n.5, 110, 113, 118, 124, 141 n.49, 151. *See also* natural magic; occult sciences
Aldrovandi, Ulisse   176
Aleotti, Giovanni Battista   121
Alexis of Piedmont   149
Alfonso X of Castile   45
Alí, Abenragel   66
angels   18, 19, 39, 41, 45, 51, 84, 88, 158, 169n. *See also* demons; intelligences
Antonini, Daniello   118–20
Appier, Jean Hanzelet   149–51, 153, 157
Aquinas, Thomas   9, 26, 28, 40, 199
Arab science   10, 16–18, 44, 65, 125
Archimedes   90, 92, 98, 99
Archytas   99
Aristotle   1–3, 5, 6, 9, 10, 15–17, 21, 24, 25, 28, 44, 56, 61, 62, 65–71, 73, 76, 77, 92, 96–8, 120, 121, 147, 148, 155, 199, 211 n.18
  De anima   2, 17, 24, 25
  De Caelo et Mundo   17
  De somno et vigilia   17
  Historia animalium   199
  Metaphysica   2, 15, 17
  Meteorologica   67, 147
  Organon   2

Physica   2
Aristotle, Ps.-, *Astronomia*   80 n.53
  Astrologia   80 n.53
  De lapidibus   68
  De plantis   68
  De regiminibus coelestibus   69, 80 n.53
  De viginti octo mansionibus Lunae   70, 80 n.53
  Hermetica   18, 65
  Liber Novem Judicum   69
  Mechanica   98, 100
  Mors animae   69, 70, 72, 73, 80 n.62
  Secretum secretorum   4, 5, 40, 61, 64–9, 72, 73, 76 n.22, 77 n.26, 79 n.47, 80 n.62, 81 n.68
  Theologia Aristotelis   65
Arnau de Vilanova   58
Arndt, Johann   197, 207
astrology   2, 40, 44, 63–7, 69–71, 74 n.5, 78 n.43, 80 n.53, 86, 90, 154, 155, 161, 162. *See also* Aristotle, Ps.-; Peter of Abano; *Picatrix*; Pomponazzi, Pietro; Ptolemy; Ptolemy, Ps.-; Scot, Michael; Storella, Francesco; Willsford, Thomas
  and alchemy   2, 70
  and Aristotelianism   44, 64, 65
  and chiromancy   67
  and divination   86
  and magic   2, 63–5, 70, 74 n.5, 78 n.43, 86, 90, 154, 162
  and medicine   64, 66, 67
  and occult sciences   64, 74 n.5
  and physiogmomy   67, 90
  and religion   64, 162
astronomy   40, 41, 148, 160, 161. *See also* Ptolemy; Wing, Vincent
Augustine   21, 40
Augustine, Ps.-   49
authority, principle of   1, 2, 5, 41, 43, 44, 69, 199
Averroes   54, 66, 70, 72
Avicenna   17, 18, 44, 49

Index

Bachot, Ambroise 100
Bacilieri, Tiberio 70
Bacon, Francis 29, 48, 109, 112, 134, 145, 148, 174, 184, 185. *See also* Baconism
Bacon, Roger 9, 15, 19, 21, 24, 25, 29, 41, 76, 99, 149, 185, 199. *See also* secrets
Baconism 101
  and tarantism 173, 176, 188 n.23
Balduino, Girolamo 5, 63
Bartolomeo da Messina 77
Bate, John 151–3, 157, 158, 163
Beckmann, Johann 197, 198
Berengar of Tours 28
Bernard of Clairvaux 56
Bertoloni Meli, Domenico 111, 122, 124, 125, 134
Besson, Jacques 96, 100
Biancani, Giuseppe 120
Bible 199. *See also* Holy Scripture
Biringuccio, Vannoccio 98
Blavatsky, Helena 88
Böckler, Georg Andreas 100
Bodin, Jean 70, 72, 86
Böhme, Jakob 197, 207
Boillot, Joseph 100
Bonatti, Guido 70
Bonaventure 37 n.60
Bono, Pietro 67
Borrelli, Arianna 7
Boteler, Edward 155
Boureau, Alain 25
Boyle, Robert 150, 181, 190
Brahe, Tycho 161
Branca, Giovanni 98, 100
Braun, Christian Friedrich 187
Browne, Thomas 147
Bruegel the Elder 21, 22
Bruno, Giordano 4, 61, 68, 71, 72
Burke, Peter 151
Burnett, Charles 1

Cabeo, Niccolò 120, 143
Calvin 29
Campanella, Tommaso 29
Camporesi, Piero 147, 160
Cardano, Girolamo 29, 70, 199
Cartesianism 163, 176, 177, 185. *See also* Bacon, Francis; Descartes, René; Sylvius, Franciscus de Le Böe; Senguerd, Wolferd
  and Aristotelian meteorology 163
  and Baconism 185
  and popular magic 163
  and tarantism 176, 177, 185
Catharism 3, 17, 19
Champier, Symphorien 50
Chang, Hasok 147
Charleton, Walter 174
chiromancy 2, 66, 67, 74 n.5, 77 n.26
  See also occult science
Clarke, Arthur C. 105
Cock, Hieronymus 22
Cocles, Bartolomeus della Rocca 65–7
Copernicus 161
Corbin, Henry 18
Crisciani, Chiara 67
Cusanus 53. *See also* Nicholas of Cusa

dance 172, 176–8, 181, 183, 184. *See also* music; tarantism
Daniel of Morley 19
Daston, Lorraine 148
Debus, Allen 110
De Carli, Manuel 8
Dee, Arthur 46
Dee, John 46
Della Porta, Giambattista 5–7, 29, 42, 62, 63, 68, 70, 71, 89–91, 98, 100, 106, 108, 111, 112, 119, 120, 125, 130, 132–5, 143 n.73 145, 152, 194. *See also* Academia Secretorum Naturae; natural magic
Del Rio, Martin 39, 40, 48–51. *See also* Jesuits
demonology 3, 5, 19, 21, 25–9, 89, 91
demons 1, 3, 5, 18–21, 24, 26–8, 70, 85, 86, 88, 132. *See also* demonology, goëtia; necromancy; occult sciences
  and black magic 1, 5, 20, 88, 109, 132
  and demonology 5, 21, 27–9
  and illusionism 20, 21, 24, 26, 28, 29
  and natural magic 3, 5, 20
  and popular magic 86
  and venefical magic 70
  and witchcraft 85
Descartes, René 109, 144 n.91 174. *See also* Cartesianism
Digby, Kenelm 200

Dioscorides 177
divination 7, 40, 86, 148, 150. *See also* astrology; occult sciences
Dove, Heinrich 131
Draper, Clement 47
Drebbel, Anna 113
Drebbel, Cornelis 7, 106–8, 111–35, 136, 144 n.91

Eamon, William 5, 6, 42, 108–10, 151, 153
empiricism 147, 148, 154, 184, 185
  and magic 5, 7, 10, 63, 64, 67, 76 n.22, 86, 134, 145, 160
Errard, Jean 100
van Etten, Hendrick 149
Ettmüller, Michael Ernst 214 n.67
Euclid 98
experimental philosophy 9, 171–3, 179, 180
experiments 3, 42, 43, 112, 119–21, 126, 129, 131, 135, 149–51, 156, 160, 172, 180–2
  experiments books 4, 25
  and magic 4, 6, 42, 46, 47, 55, 64, 89, 90, 100, 112, 119, 135, 160, 171

Falloppia, Gabriele 62
Fara, Patricia 150
Fausto, Vittore 98
Fernel, Jean 52
Ficino, Marsilio 50, 61, 72, 88, 199
Flachs, Andreas 186
Flint, Valerie 83
Fludd, Robert 122, 145, 152–4, 157, 163, 199
Fontana, Domenico 94, 95
Francke, August Hermann 208 n.3
Francke, Gotthilf August 208 n.3
Fraser, John 51
Frederick II 44

Galen of Pergamon 72
Galilei, Galileo 98, 118–22, 126, 143 n.75, 144 n.91, 145
Galluzzi, Paolo 96
Gassendi, Pierre 175
Gengenbach, Nicolaus 212n
Genua, Marcantonio de' Passeri 62
Geyer-Kordesch, Johanna 196
Goad, John 155, 156

goëtia 1. *See also* demons; necromancy
Golinski, Jan 147, 148
Goltzius, Hendrik 113
Goltzius, Sophia 113
Goulding, Robert 25
Grafton, Anthony 6, 92
Grollier de Servière, Gaspard 100
Grube, Hermann 187
Gundisalvi, Domingo 19

Hage, Ghassan 209 n.12
Håkansson, Håkan 47
Hall, Trevor 151, 153
Hartmann, Johann 121
al-Haytham, Ibn 24
Heeffer, Albrecht 149
Heidegger, Martin 207
van Helmont, Johann 52, 215 n.82
Henri III 96
Henry Frederick, Prince of Wales 113, 117
Hermes Trismegistus 67, 68, 76, 88, 95
Hero of Alexandria 92, 98, 119, 121
Hickman, Bartholomew 46
Hiesserle von Chodaw, Heinrich 115–17
Hildebrandt, Wolfgang 194
Hill, Thomas 151, 161, 162
Holy Scripture 199. *See also* Bible
Hooke, Robert 100
Hübner, Johannes Valentinus 187
Hugh of St Victor 19
Hutchison, Keith 200
hylomorphism 18, 68, 200

illusionism 3, 15, 19–22, 24–9, 44, 83, 114, 149–51. *See also* demons; natural magic; William of Auvergne
Institoris, Heinrich 26
Intelligences 18, 24. *See also* angels
Isidore of Seville 20

Jackson, Thomas 162
Jalobeanu, Dana 112
James I 113–16, 123, 128
Jesuits 3, 13 n.11, 39, 87, 104 n.48, 120, 209 n.10
John of Salisbury 15
John of Seville 19

Kammermeister, Philipp 176, 178
Keller, Alex 96

Keller, Vera   128–31, 133, 134
Kelley, Edward   46
Kepler, Johannes   87, 88, 161
al-Kindī, Abū Yūsuf Yaʿqūb ibn Isḥāq   52
Kircher, Athanaius   176, 177, 185, 209 n.10
Kirchmajer, Georg Caspar   186
Klaassen, Frank   43
Köpper, Johann Heinrich   208 n.3
Kraye, Jill   1
Kuffler, Abraham   113

Lanfranc   28
Láng, Benedek   68
Latour, Bruno   160
Lazardzig, Jan   109, 110, 135
von Leibniz, Gottfried Wilhelm   210 n.18
Leong, Elaine   160
Leurechon, Jean   104
Libavius, Andreas   121
Long, Pamela   95
Longo, Giovan Bernardino   63
Lynn, Michael   150

McVaugh, Michael   42
Maimonides   41
Malinowski, Bronislaw   148
Malthus, Francis   149
Marcello, Cristoforo   65
Marrone, Steven P.   17
Martius, Johann Nikolaus   9, 10, 193–208, 213 n.46
marvels   5, 20, 22, 45, 46, 53, 87, 91, 97, 98, 108–10. See also wonders
   marvellous   7, 8, 20, 62, 68, 69, 73, 81 n.68., 83, 89, 90, 92, 97–9, 109, 110, 132, 172, 174, 176
mathematical magic   6, 9, 99, 110, 194, 199. See also Della Porta, Giambattista; Martius, Johann Nikolaus; mathematics; mechanics; Wilkins, John; wonders
mathematics   6, 89, 96, 98–100, 107, 108, 110, 120, 127, 129, 132, 134–6, 150, 151, 155, 160–2, 194, 199, 212 n.32
Mattioli, Pietro Andrea   177
Maxwell-Stuart, Peter G.   3, 4
Maxwell, William   205, 206
mechanics   6, 96, 98, 99, 109–12, 118, 130–5, 144 n.91, 155, 174, 209 n.10. See also mathematics

medicine   13 n.11, 45, 67, 72, 154, 168 n.49, 177, 193, 194, 202, 205
Mertz, Johann Nikolaus   208 n.3
Mesue, Giovanni   66
Meteorology   7, 8, 107, 111, 120, 126, 129, 131–3, 143 n.75, 147–9, 154, 160, 161, 163
Moffett, Thomas   47
Moles, Bartolomeo   65
Monti, Panfilo   62
Mori, Jennifer   7, 8
von Müller, Johannes   187
music   52, 172, 175, 178, 180, 183. See also dance; tarantism
   musical instruments   106, 113, 178, 182, 183, 186
   musical therapy   173

natural magic   2, 3, 5–10, 15, 17, 18, 20, 40, 44, 47, 61–5, 68–70, 72, 73, 79 n.52, 81 n.68, 83, 87–91, 98–100, 106, 107, 109–12, 119, 130, 132, 134, 149, 156, 160, 162, 172, 193–201, 205, 206. See also alchemy; illusionism; occult qualities; occult sciences; venefical magic
   and alchemy   2, 68, 70, 71, 73, 74 n.5
   and Aristotelianism   5, 8, 15, 17, 18, 20, 61–5, 68, 70, 73, 79 n.52, 81 n.68, 160, 162
   and astrology   2, 63–5, 70, 74 n.5, 78 n.43, 90, 154, 162
   and demonic magic   5, 18, 20, 44, 61, 62, 64, 70, 83, 88, 89, 91, 109, 132, 199
   and experiments   5–8, 61, 62, 83, 88–91, 100, 106, 107, 111, 112, 119, 130, 132, 160, 172
   and illusionism   3, 15, 17, 18, 20, 44, 83, 90
   and Kabbalah   199
   and medicine   72, 193–201, 205, 206
   and popular science   149, 156, 160, 162
   and technology   7, 8, 99, 100, 106, 107, 109–11, 119, 130, 132, 134, 197, 199, 206
   and venefical magic   62, 71, 72, 80 n.58, 81 n.63, 156
   and witchcraft   5, 56n., 62, 70–2, 81 n.68, 87, 89, 91

natural philosophy   1, 3–5, 7, 10, 15, 17, 18, 25, 77 n.26., 84, 87, 89–91, 108, 111, 112, 114, 118, 119, 121, 122, 124, 125, 128, 130, 131, 135, 148, 174, 185
necromancy   1, 65, 69–73, 80 n.62, 89, 199. *See also* demons; *goëtia*; occult sciences
Newton, Isaac   99, 190
Nicholas of Cusa   53. *See also* Cusanus
Nifo, Agostino   65
Noël de Pivier, Nicolaus Benjamin   187

occult qualities   3, 5, 9, 68, 69, 83, 87, 99, 100, 171–6, 178–81, 184, 185, 190 n.34, 200
occult sciences   2, 61, 64, 74 n.5., 123
Oldenburg, Henry   185
van Ophoven, Giorgius   179
Oresme, Nicole   15, 16, 29, 51
Oughtred, William   104
Ozanam, Jacques   149, 150, 157, 158, 162

Pacioli, Luca   29
Paracelsus   56, 57, 127, 197, 199, 215 n.82
Paré, Ambroise   52, 53
Patrick, John   161
Pereira, Gómez   50
Perez-Ramos, Antonio   158
Peterman, Andrea   186
Peter of Abano   65–7, 70
Peter of Corbeil   16
Peter of Nemour   16
Peter Peregrinus of Maricourt   24
Philip of Tripoli   65
physiognomy, physiognomics   2, 44, 65–7, 77 n.30, 90. *See also* occult sciences
Picatrix   64
Piccolomini, Alessandro   98
Pickering, Michael   9, 10
Pico della Mirandola, Gianfrancesco   65, 67, 70
Pico della Mirandola, Giovanni   61, 65, 70–2
Plat, Hugh   151
Plato, Platonism   1, 15, 18
Pliny   43, 147, 162, 176
Plotinus   65

poison   40, 62, 70, 71, 87, 172, 175–8. *See also* tarantism; venefical magic; *veneficium*
Pomponazzi, Pietro   6, 61–4, 70
popular magic   86, 91, 163
popular science   2, 149–60
Porphyry   65
Porzio, Simone   62
Ptolemy   64, 161
Ptolemy, Ps.-   64, 67

Rabelais, François   29
Ramelli, Agostino   96, 100
al-Rāzī, Abū Bakr   78
Rioult, Thibaut   3
Royal Society of London   100, 112, 150, 155, 181
Rüdiger, Andreas   210 n.18, 211 n.18
Rudolf II   113
Rusu, Doina-Cristina   112

Sagredo, Giovanfrancesco   120
Saint-Hilaire, Étienne Geoffroy   209 n.12
saints   84
Santorio, Santorio   120
Saul, Barnabas   46
Savonarola, Michele   66
Schmitt, Charles B.   1, 69
Schöngast, Christoph-Andreas   186
Schott, Gaspar   209 n.8
Scot, Michael   77
Scot, Reginald   29, 158
secrets   24, 25, 40, 44, 45, 47, 48, 91, 107, 108, 119, 123, 129, 149, 162, 199. *See also* experiments; marvels; natural magic; wonders
   books of   4, 25, 40, 48, 58 n.34, 149, 151, 154, 156
   of materials   98
   of nature   90, 98, 106, 110, 123, 128, 132, 134, 149, 153, 155
Seller, William   162
Senguerd, Arnold   172, 175, 184
Senguerd, Wolferd   8, 9, 172, 173, 175–85
Sennert, Daniel   178
Shapin, Steven   100
Sievers, Georg   193
Silvestris, Bernard   43
Smith, Pamela   134
Solomon   197

Sperling, Johan 87
Sprenger, Jacob 26
Stafford, Barbara 150, 155
Stahl, Georg Ernst 196, 210 n.15
Stimmer, Tobias 93
Storella, Francesco 4–6, 61–73, 77
Storella, Giovanni 62, 66, 68
Strangehopes, Samuel 161
Strato of Lampsacus 97
Streete, Thomas 161
Suhrawardī 18
Sylvius, Franciscus de Le Böe 177, 185
Szőnyi, György 46

tarantism 8, 9, 172–86. *See also* baconism; cartesianism; occult qualities; Senguerd, Wolferd
Telesio, Bernardino 125, 143 n.73
Teske, Roland J. 16
theurgy 1, 199, 204, 212 n.36. *See also* demons
Thomas, Keith 157
Thomasius, Christian 196–8, 202–4, 207, 211 n.27., 215 n.77
Thomas of Chobham 15
Tollemache, Catherine 46
Tomitano, Bernardino 62
Trevor-Roper, Hugh 26
Trithemius, Johannes 47, 199
Tymme, Thomas 122

Valleriani, Matteo 121
Van Dyck, Maarten 136
venefical magic 5, 62, 70–2, 81 n.63, 156. *See also* natural magic; necromancy; poison; *veneficium*
  and Aristotelianism 5, 62, 70, 71, 73
  and natural magic 62, 71, 72, 80 n.58, 81 n.63, 156
  and necromancy 70, 71, 73
  and witchcraft 5, 71, 81 n.68
veneficium 5, 69, 71–3, 80 n.58, 81 n.63. *See also* demons; poison; venefical magic; witchcraft
Verardi, Donato 5
Vermeir, Koen 136
virtuosi 100
de Volder, Burchard 178, 181, 190

Walch, Johann Georg 208 n.6, 211 n.27, 213 n.59
Weber, Max 100
Whiston, William 161
White, John 150, 151, 153–5, 157, 163
Wiegleb, Johann Christian 193
Wier, John 71
Wiesenfeldt, Gerhard 175
Wilhelm, August 193
Wilkins, John 99, 109–11, 135
William of Auvergne 3, 15–22, 25, 26, 28, 44, 89
William of Conches 17
Willsford, Thomas 154–8, 162, 163
Wing, Vincent 161
witchcraft 5, 6, 19, 25–7, 29, 54, 56 n.10, 62, 70–3, 81 n.68, 85–7, 91, 158, 202. *See also* demonology; demons; popular magic; venefical magic; *veneficium*
Wolff, Christian 210 n.18, 213 n.46
wonders 6, 10, 19–21, 44, 47, 48, 89–91, 99–101, 105, 107, 109, 110, 128, 134, 194, 199, 200, 207, 209 n.9, 212 n.38. *See also* marvels; secrets
sense of wonder 10, 45, 89, 91, 97, 105, 107, 134

Zedler, Johann Heinrich 193, 211 n.27
Zeising, Heinrich 100

www.ingramcontent.com/pod-product-compliance
Lightning Source LLC
Chambersburg PA
CBHW071834300426
44116CB00009B/1535